THE MALDIVE ISLANDS

XLIII.—1881

THE
MALDIVE ISLANDS

AN ACCOUNT OF
THE PHYSICAL FEATURES, CLIMATE, HISTORY, INHABITANTS, PRODUCTIONS, AND TRADE.

BY

H. C. P. BELL, ESQ.
Ceylon Civil Service

Ordered by His Excellency the Governor.

GYAN

Published by

Gyan Publishing House
5, Ansari Road
Daryaganj, New Delhi-110002
Phone: 011-47034999, 9811692060
E-mail: books@gyanbooks.com

Distribution Network
gyanbooks.com
India, USA, Canada, UK, Australia, France

ISBN : 978-81-212-3743-7 (PB)
First Published, 1883

2nd Impression 2020

Printed at: Gyan Press, Delhi.

THE

MALDIVE ISLANDS:

AN ACCOUNT OF

THE PHYSICAL FEATURES, CLIMATE, HISTORY, INHABITANTS, PRODUCTIONS, AND TRADE.

BY H. C. P. BELL, ESQ.,
Ceylon Civil Service.

Ordered by His Excellency the Governor to be Printed.

Colombo:
FRANK LUKER, ACTING GOVERNMENT PRINTER, CEYLON.

1883.

CONTENTS.

Maps and Diagram.

THE

MÁLDIVE ISLANDS.

INTRODUCTION.

THE MÁLDIVES. INTRODUCTION.

It is attempted in the present Memoir to do some justice to a people little known and less regarded.

Probably but very few persons have more than a hazy notion that the Máldive group lies somewhere in Eastern seas, or would be able to fix its position at all approximately. The worse than ignorance occasionally displayed even by would-be instructors is astounding. As late as 1811 a standard treatise on Geography* gravely asserted that these Islands were "governed by a chief called Atoll," and were inhabited by "some Mahometans"!

The notices regarding the Máldive Islands are so few and far between, so dispersed up and down scarce works, mostly travels, difficult of reference, that it is hoped an effort to collect and bring into one focus the scattered rays of information on the subject may serve some useful purpose.

Authorities.

The whole of the authorities on the Máldives may be almost counted on the fingers. The chief are :—

1. Ibn Batúta (A.D. 1343–4).
2. François Pyrard de Laval (A.D. 1602-1607).
3. The Government Surveyors of the Indian Navy—Captain Moresby, and Lieutenants Christopher, Powell, and Young (A.D. 1834–1836).

Ibn Batúta.

1. Of Ibn Batúta's Travels an English translation was made by Dr. S. Lee in 1829, but the manuscript copies used were abridged, and the old traveller was not fairly dealt with.† Within the last ten years, however, an excellent edition in four octavo volumes of the Arabic text, with translation at foot, has been issued through the *Societé Asiatique* by M. M. Defrémery and Sanguinetti.‡

François Pyrard.

2. Pyrard, the French adventurer, who spent five years of captivity on the group, has left the fullest account of the Islands extant. Unfortunately, copies of his *Voyage aux Indes Orientales* are extremely rare, and portions only have been translated into English.§

---

* Pinkerton's Modern Geography, Vol. I., p. 757.

† Travels of Ibn Batúta, printed for the Oriental Translation Committee, London, 1829.

‡ From this French edition Mr. Albert Gray has just completed an English translation of Ibn Batúta's visit to the Máldives and Ceylon, which will shortly be published in the Ceylon A. S. Journal. "The first detailed account of his (Ibn Batúta's) book was published in Europe only in 1808 [Kosegarten and Apetz] Moura in 1845 issued at Lisbon an incomplete translation in Portuguese of a copy obtained at Fez at the end of last century. The abridgment translated by Lee was brought from the East by Burckhardt. It was not till the French conquest of Algeria that the best and completest texts were obtained. Five are in the Imperial Library at Paris, only two of which are perfect. From these M. M. Defrémery and Sanguinetti made their translation [Paris, 1874–9] for the *Societé Asiatique*; and it is from their version that the present account has been extracted."—From Mr. Gray's Introduction.

§ "This is one of the exactest pieces of Travels, and the most diverting, hitherto made publick. M. Pirard the Traveller furnished the materials, which were digested and methodized by several very able men in France. Many who have travelled after him mension much of what he does, and yet he has some curiosities which others have not touched upon." *(Journ. des Scav.*, Vol. 7, p. 85.)—Introduction to a Collection of Voyages and Travels, London, 1704, Vol. I., p. lxxxi. "His adventures, and his evident honesty in their narration, created so warm an interest in the publication of his book, that it went through no less than four editions in the 17th century," viz., 1611, 1615-6, 1619, 1679.—Gray, in J. R. A. S., Vol. X., N.S., 1878, p. 175. A translation of Pyrard has been undertaken for the Hakluyt Society.

The Colombo Museum, and Ceylon Asiatic Society's Libraries are without a copy of Pyrard's Travels —a want much to be regretted. A private copy (4th edition, 1679, 4to) came to hand only after this Report had gone to press, too late to be turned to full account.

THE MÁLDIVES.

INTRODUCTION.

Christopher and Young.

3. At the time of the survey of the Atols in 1834, permission was obtained from the Sultan for Lieutenants Christopher and Young to remain at Málé (Sultan's Island), in order to acquire some knowledge of the "productions and resources, the language, disposition, customs, &c., of the inhabitants." After struggling some time against the fever, which shortly attacked them, they were forced to quit. During their stay, however, they kept a journal from which a Memoir was subsequently compiled, containing such information as they were able to collect. It was published in the Bombay Geographical Society's Transactions,* and, though more than forty years have since elapsed, continues to be the most modern report in any detail of the Islands. Wanting only in systematic arrangement, it may unhesitatingly be accepted as reliable, so far as it goes, and as generally applicable to the present condition of the Máldivians.

Ceylon's Chief Dependency.

It cannot but be a matter of surprise that a political connection with the English Government in Ceylon, extending over eighty years, has tended to throw little or no light either on the internal administration of the Islands or on the habits of the people.

Whilst the Indian Government has from time to time—and of late years regularly—called for reports on the smaller and far less important Northern cluster, the Lakkadives—action which has borne fruit in the marked general improvement of those Islands, the Government of this Colony has omitted—may be from mistaken delicacy—to take more than an annual passing notice of its dependency, except upon occasions when the "enlightened humanity" of the Máldive ruler and his subjects towards persons shipwrecked on their Atols has necessitated special acknowledgment.

Several causes may have combined, in greater or less degree, to bring about this result—the isolation and insignificance of the group—the rare opportunities of contact and intercourse with the Islanders—their own timid and suspicious nature—and, perhaps above all, official uncertainty concerning the exact status of the Máldive Sultan as respects this Government.

In the interest of a race constitutionally peaceful, by no means wanting, according to their lights, in commercial activity and intelligence, nor averse to beneficial innovations, if introduced with tact and discrimination, it is not unreasonable to express the hope that this apathy on the part of the protecting Government may now at length give place to real and permanent concern for the welfare of its hitherto neglected dependency. For the Máldivians a closer connection with Ceylon is "a consummation devoutly to be wished," and, it may safely be predicted, would not be without advantage to this Colony itself.†

Contents of Memoir.

Much of the following pages, especially in Sections I., II., III., and V., has been taken of set purpose—often *verbatim*—from accounts, (wherever considered reliable,) which have already been given to the world, but methodized, corrected as far as possible where necessary, and brought up to date.

On all that concerns their character, pursuits, and life in general, a marked unanimity prevails between the few reliable biographers the Máldivians have hitherto found. This consensus naturally follows from the close conservatism these Islanders have preserved for centuries. No account, therefore, of the state of things existing at present on the Atols can lay claim to accuracy without being at the same time in great part a *réchauffé* of past observations.

The scanty sum total of knowledge on record regarding these Islands will be held sufficient excuse for the insertion of minor details, which would otherwise be out of place in an *opuscule* of this kind.

Sections IV., VII., and VIII.—viz., those on History, Trade, and Weights and Measures—will, it is believed, be found to contain considerable matter entirely new.

---

* Trans. Bombay Geo. Soc., 1836-8 (reprint 1844), pp. 54-86.

† See Mr. Albert Gray's concluding remarks in his article on the Máldives (J. R. A. S., Vol. X., Art. VIII., N. S., 1878, p. 209) :—"Measures should be taken by the Ceylon Government without delay to render more intimate the connection with its dependency, and overcoming the jealousy of the Maldive ruler, if any still exists, to extend to his subjects some of the benefits of Ceylon civilization."

The greater part of the early Portuguese period in the Historical section has been worked in from notes kindly furnished by Mr. Gray, whose recent interesting Article in the Royal Asiatic Society's Journal has further been freely drawn on.*

The Records (Dutch and English) of the Colonial Office, Colombo, have yielded a store of information bearing on the history of the Islands from the middle of the 17th century, cropping up where least expected, but not unearthed without some difficulty.

The accompanying Maps and Diagram have been prepared in the Surveyor-General's Office, Colombo.

Finally, it should not be forgotten that the materials available in Ceylon for the compilation of this Report have been somewhat limited, and that further investigation is more than likely to show that many statements require modification.

---

* Mr. Gray's MS. translation of the French editors' *Voyages d' Ibn Batoutah*, received very recently, has also, by courteous permission, been occasionally utilized in revising the proof-sheets. The writer desires at the same time to express his obligation to Major A. Ewing and L. J. E G. Tate, C.C.S., for suggestions in the rendering of the old French correspondence quoted—to Messrs. W. Ferguson, F.L.S., and A. Haly, in helping to identify botanical and mollusc specimens— to A. C. Dixon, B. Sc., for an analysis of Máldive coins—and lastly to the learned scholars Subhúti Unnánsé, Dhammálóka Unnánsé, and Mudaliyár B. Guṇasékara, Government Translator, for their valuable aid in elucidating the Sanskṛit portion of the Máldive Sultan's letter.

*ERRATA.**

Page 4, lines 2, 16, *for* 'Mr. Darvin' *read* 'Mr. Darwin.'
5, „ 17, 19, *for* 'isles' *read* 'des isles.'
12, „ 20, *for* 'breach' *read* 'beach.'
20, „ 13, *delete* '(1790 ?).'
25, „ 14, *for* 'Chibâb eddîn' *read* 'Chihâb eddîn.'
27, note ‡‡, *for* 'Insarte' *read* 'Jusarte.'
28, „ ‖, *for* 'Muhammadism' *read* 'Muhammadanism.'
31, „ ††, *for* 'T. A. Rumpf' *read* I. A. Rumpf.'
33, „ ‡, *for* 'escades' *read* 'escadres.'
34, last line, '*' *should be* '††.'
34, note ¶, *delete* 'Ghâzí.'
35, five lines from bottom, *for* 'account' *read* 'accounts.'
36, line 6, *for* 'the matter' *read* 'the dispute.'
37, last line and margin, *for* 'St. Clare' *read* 'St. Clair.'
38, note ‖, *for* 'Note (15)' *read* 'Note (11).'
42, six lines from bottom, *for* 'honneurl' *read* 'lhonneur.'
four „ *for* 'Jεy' *read* 'Icy.'
43, line 6, *for* 'Mattele' *read* 'Mattelo.'
53, „ 16, *for* '175' *read* '182.'
58, 60, 61, 62, 63, 64, notes, *for* 'Harris, Vol. II.' *read* 'Harris, Vol. I.'
61, line 38, *for* 'candouittes' *read* '*candou*.'
64, *for* '* Note (11),' '‡ Note (10)' *read* '* Note (10),' '‡ Note (11).'
71, line 12, *for* '[A D. 1435 *circa*] *read* '[? 600, *i. e.*, A.D. 1235 *circa*]'
78, „ 13, *for* '*Fâmeldâry*, "Receiver-General of Revenue,"' *read* '*Fámeldáry*, "Chief of the Treasury."'
84, „ 13, *for* 'mastification' *read* 'mastication.'
85, „ 10, *for* '*Eudyamys*' *read* '*Eudynamis*.'
99, „ 33, *for* '*Achtbear*' *read* '*Achtbaer*.'
100, „ 23, *for* '(about £14)' *read* '(about £246).'
100, „ 27, *for* '*seclusive*' *read* '*seclusie*'; *for* '*ander*' *read* '*andere*.'
104, note §, *for* 'Princep's' *read* 'Prinsep's.'
108, lines 12, 13, *place* '*' *after* '*horses*,' *and delete* '†' *after* 'later.'
108, in Tonnage table, *insert* '§' *after* '4,145.'
118, line 16, *place* '100 = 25' *directly under* '4 = *Boḍu lári*.'
133, in List of Wrecks *insert* '†' *after* '1862' *and* '1868.'

* Errors in the transliteration of native words are not included.

THE

MÁLDIVE ISLANDS.

I.—PHYSICAL FEATURES.*

THE MÁLDIVES.

PHYSICAL FEATURES.

Atols.

THE MA'LDIVE ISLANDS† extend in the Indian Ocean from lat. 7° 6′ N. to lat. 0° 42′ S., and between long. 72° 33′ and 73° 44′ E., a space 470 miles in length N. and S., and 70 miles E. and W. They are grouped together in clusters called *Atols (M. Atoḷu)*,‡ of which there are more than twenty in all, though ordinarily divided into *thirteen* groups, to which number they have been confined for centuries by the Máldivians themselves for political purposes.

At the N. and S. extremities of the chain the Atols lie singly: in the centre they lie in double rows, with an intervening space of from 10 to 25 miles. Ihavandiffuḷu, the most Northern Atol, is distant about 350 miles from Cape Comorin, the nearest point of Hindústán, and Mále Atol (central) about 400 miles from the nearest port of Ceylon.

Reefs.

Barrier reefs encircle the Southern Atols, fortifying them admirably against the violence of the waves and the severe storms which not unfrequently visit these Islands; but North of lat. 3° 30′ N. none of the Atols are thus protected, except in a few detached parts. These reefs are in many places just awash; in others, they form long stretches of sand less than eight feet above sea level, and are either circular or oblong. The descent on the sea-face of islands and reefs is very abrupt, no soundings having been obtained at 200 fathoms close outside; but the rock does not appear to curve inwards below the surface so as to lessen the base.

Passages.

Each of the enclosing reefs contains *openings* or *gateways*§ *(M. kaḍu)* which constitute convenient passages for vessels and boats. They are very deep and used by Máldive boats in passing from one Atol to another; some will admit the largest ships. Within the Atols the sea is free from storms, and safe anchorage is found in 20 or 30 fathoms very smooth water with bottom of coral and sand.

Channels.

The *channels*‖ which divide the Atols are in some cases deep and safe, but others are intricate and only fit for steamers, as the currents run strong through them to East or West, according to the season.

By day, all the channels, and some of the openings, amongst the islands and reefs, may be traversed without anxiety, as all the coral dangers are visible at some distance from the masthead, owing to the clearness of the water and the intense whiteness of the coral.

By night, ships prefer to pass only through the four larger channels between the Atols; these are :—

1. The KARDIVA, or FIVE-DEGREE CHANNEL *(Kaharidú Kaḍu)*, between Fádiffoḷu, Máḷosmaḍulu, and Goidú (Horsburgh) Atols, on the N.W., and Mále and Ari Atols, on the S.E., 24 miles in breadth and 67 in length. *Kaharidú* (Kardiva Island) lies athwart the way in mid-channel.

2. The VÉIMANDU', or KOḶUMAḌULU CHANNEL *(Véimandú Kaḍu)*, between Koḷumaḍulu and Haddummatí Atols, 15 miles in breadth.

3. The ONE-AND-A-HALF-DEGREE CHANNEL, 50 miles broad, between Haddummatí and Huvadú (Suvádiva) Atols, the widest and safest of all the channels, usually traversed by homeward bound steamers during the S.W. monsoon.

---

* Summarised chiefly from Taylor's Sailing Directory, 1874, Part I., pp. 567, 569, and Encyclopædia (Horsburgh, Owen, and Moresby, in R. Geo. Soc. J., Vols. II. & V.)

† Note (1). ‡ Note (2). § Note (3). ‖ Note (4).

THE MÁLDIVES.

PHYSICAL FEATURES.

South of the Equator :—

4. The EQUATORIAL CHANNEL, between Huvadú (Suvádiva) and Aḍḍú Atols, 46 miles in breadth, but having the island *Mulaku* lying a little S.E. of its centre.

" No general description will do for the *currents** in the many channels that exist amongst this chain of islands, and as yet there are but few recorded observations, and these are for only a very small portion of the year. Regular *tides* also occur throughout the group, and a tide may be mistaken for a current. As a general rule the currents set Eastward from June to September : then Southerly along the West side of the Islands till December, in the end of which month they commence setting Westward strong through the Kardiva and other channels below that to the Equator (but only extending to Aḍḍú Atol from mid-January to mid-February), and they run in that direction till April. In May they are variable and uncertain till the S.W. monsoon is established.

" The Equatorial Channel currents are very strong ; for half the year they set Westward, and for the other half Eastward, according to the monsoon, but are subject to checks from variable winds."†

Islands.

The *islands* ‡ are generally situated along the enclosing coral reefs, the central part of the Atols containing comparatively few. They are usually circular, or oval, in shape, and all are small, not many exceeding a mile in length and breadth. Many are mere narrow strips 50 to 100 yards wide, enclosing a lower tract filled with broken coral rock, and dry at spring tides. In such places there is sometimes a considerable depth of water forming perfect lagoons. The islands are in general not more than 5 or 6 feet above the level of the sea, so that until near approach the cocoanut trees on them appear to be growing out of the water.

Among the natives an idea is prevalent that the islands gradually waste away and decrease in number by the constant action of the surf.§ In some the fringing cocoanuts stand in the water, whilst in others the submerged black soil of the islands is discernible at low water, some yards from the beach. It is, however, acknowledged that reefs have risen from the water, and barren sandbanks become habitable wooded islands.‖

Geological structure.

A glance at a map of the Indian Ocean will suffice to induce the conviction, that the Lakkadive, Máldive, and Chagos groups, belong to the same submerged mountain range on which the coral polypi have constructed their reefs extending from lat. 12° 24′ N. to lat. 7° 39′ S., a distance N. and S. of 1,200 miles. The madrepore reefs and islands of this long chain crop up here and there with unequal intervening spaces of ocean, but possessing a similar character as to their geological formation throughout.

The substructure of the Máldive group appears to be generally as follows. On the surface sand mixed with vegetable matter, forming a dark-coloured light soil, which covers two or three feet of pure sand. Below this there is a soft sandstone, resembling particles of beach sand indurated. This sandstone is about two feet thick, when it softens again to sand, in which fresh water is found.

Water.

Nearly all the inhabited islands possess *fresh water*, a remarkable fact mentioned as early as the 6th century by Cosmas, and confirmed thirteen centuries later by an analysis of some of the water itself.¶

Vegetation.

Most islands are covered by a thick, in parts impenetrable, jungle, among which are to be found all the ordinary shrubs and plants common to the seaboard of Ceylon :—screwpines (*M. Karhikeyo, S.* Veṭakeyiyá, වැටකෙයියා, *Pandanus Odoratissimus*, L.), and cocoanuts (*M. Kárhi-ru, S.* Pol-gaha, පොල්ගහ, *Cocos Nucifera*, L.) tower thickly over all ; the bamboo (*M. Uni, S.* Una, උන, *Bambusa Vulgaris*, Wendl.) is rare. On some islands there are many fine large trees, such as the banyan (*M. Nika-gas, S.* Nuga-gaha, නුගගහ, *Ficus Indica*, L.), the bread fruit (*M. Bambakeyo-gas, S.* Del-gaha, දෙල්ගහ *Artocarpus incisa*, L.), and the *kaḍú* (*M.*)

* Note (5).

† Taylor's Sailing Directory, Part I., p. 656.

‡ Note (6).

§ Note (7).

‖ Trans. Bombay Geo. Soc. 1836-8 (reprint 1844), pp. 56, 105.

¶ Note (8).

NOTES.

(1)

Máldive Islands.

MÁLDIVE ISLANDS.—Various derivations of the appellation have been favoured by different writers :—

1. From *mal* and *diva* (dwípa) "the thousand islands." (Barros ; Pinkerton, Vol. VII. p. 182 ; Bennett, p. 351.)
2. From *maha laala diva.* (Pridham, Vol. II. p. 605.)
3. *(a) Malaya-dwípa :* "from the mountain of *Maloya.*" (Sir W. Jones, Vol. III. p. 173.)

   (b) "The *Maldives* may have been the *dives* or islands of *Malĕ*, whilst *Malabár* was the continent or mainland of *Malĕ* [*Mala,* "mountain," Mal.]." (Caldwell, Comparative Dravidian Grammar, p. 27-8.)
4. From *Mál*é, the name of the chief (Sultan's) island, and *diva* (dwípa) "island."

The last is undoubtedly the correct explanation, as Ibn Batuta stated five and a half centuries ago. He calls them collectively *Dhibat-al-mahál*, and the principal island *Mahál* "the province after which all the islands are called." *Mahál* naturally contracts into *mál*, as in Tamil. Pyrard (p. 89) too is clear on this point :—"L'isle principale, comme j'ay dit, s'appelle *Malé, qui donne le nom à tout le reste des autres :* car le mot de *Dives* signifie un nombre de petites isles amassées." Elsewhere (p. 63) : "Ce royaume en leur langage, s'appelle *Malé-ragué*, Royaume de Malé, et des autres peuples de l'Inde il s'appelle *Malé-divar*, et les peuples *dives.*"

The name *Málediva*—probably assumed after the Arab ascendancy—may mean either *(a)* 'the wealthy island' (Arabic, *mál*, 'riches' or 'wealth') owing to its pre-eminence in the group ; or more naturally *(b)* 'the palace island,' *Mahaldiva* (Hind. *mahal* 'palace').

To this day the Islanders appear to use no general name for themselves, or for the whole Archipelago, but distinguish between the several Atols and their inhabitants, as *Tiladummati*, *Gaufaru, Huvadú*, and speak of the Sultan's Island alone as *Málé*, or less frequently *Málediva.* By the natives of Ceylon, Máldivians are commonly called *Gundara kárayo—i. e.,* 'the gundara (boat) men'—and the Islands *Máladiva* or *Máladiv dúpat.*

It is interesting to find the name 'Islanders' (*Divi*) under which they figure in the account of the embassy to the Emperor Julian (A. D. 363) surviving in the annual letters of the Máldive Sultans of the last century at least. In these the Sultan's dominion is always distinguished as *Divehi rájjé* *—*i. e.,* 'the Island Kingdom,' and his subjects as *Divehi mihun*†—*i. e.,* 'the Islanders.' The old Máldive character bears the name *Dives* or *Divehi akuru* ‡—*i. e.,* 'the Island letters.'

(2)

Atols.

ATOLS.—"The coral formations and reefs of Ceylon belong to what are called 'rising' or stationary reefs, in contradistinction to atolls, or 'sinking reefs,' to which the Maldives and Laccadives belong......According to Mr. Darwin's theory, which is generally accepted as correct, the singular circular form of the Maldive Islands, in common with most 'atolls,' is owing to the gradual sinking of the bed on which the madrepore originally raised their coral superstructure. Thus, the Maldive Islands indicate or mark the peaks of a long chain of mountains which have gradually sunk beneath the ocean. Viewed in this light, there must have existed formerly where those islands now are, a large tract of land, the shores of which, from their proximity to Ceylon, would have been very near it, if not actually joined............'The coral-forming polypi begin to build in water at a moderate depth, and while they are yet at work the bottom of the sea subsides gradually, so that the foundation of their edifice is carried downwards at the same time that they are raising the superstructure ; if, therefore, the rate of subsidence be not too rapid, the growing coral will continue to build up to the surface, the mass always gaining in height above its original base, but remaining in other respects in the same position. Not so with the island : each inch lost is irreclaimably gone ; as it sinks, the water gains foot by foot, till in many cases the highest peak of

---

* ދިވެހި ރާއްޖެ † ދިވެހި މީހުން ‡ ދިވެހި އަކުރު

THE MÁLDIVES.

PHYSICAL FEATURES.

Notes.

the original island disappears. What was before land then becomes a lagoon. (Lyell on Coral Reefs, ii, 602, quoting Mr. Darvin.)'

"A singularity in the formation of the Maldive atolls consists in their being made up not of one continuous circular reef, but of a ring of small coral islets sometimes more than one hundred in number, each of which is a ring-shaped strip of coral surrounding a lagoon of salt water, nearly every ring having an opening in it, and the same occurs in the principal atolls, which enables vessels to sail into them. The lagoons vary from 15 to 49 fathoms in depth......the openings in them are attributed to the passage outward of this sediment during a reflux of the sea......Many of the minor atolls are 3, and some 5 miles in diameter. The larger atolls of the Maldives appear to have been broken up into smaller ones by currents sweeping across them and making a passage. The channel dividing the Madow Atoll [Máḷosmaḍulu Atol] is attributed to this cause." (Ceylon by an Officer, Ceylon Rifles, 1876, Vol. I. p. 70-2.)

"Aussi on diroit à voir le dedans d'un de ces Atollons, que toutes ces petites isles et la mer qui est entre-deux n'est qu'une basse continuée, ou que ce n'eust esté anciennement qu'une seule isle, coupée et divisée depuis en plusieurs." (Pyrard, p. 72.)

"Mr. Darvin considers it not improbable that the first formation of the Maldive Archipelago was due to a barrier reef of nearly the same dimensions as the long narrow island of New Caledonia. The greater part of the inhabited atolls is formed of breccia; they are all higher on the windward side, where the broadest and most habitable portion lies." (Ceylon, by an Officer, Ceylon Rifles, Vol. I. p. 72.)

"The aspect of these annular reefs is very striking, in their more or less concentric rings of different colours. First, there is the central portion of the lagoon, an exquisite chrysophrase green—a colour that 'never was on sea or land' save only in gems and these coral atolls; then a broad zone of the same, dotted and freckled with olive green; then the reef itself, a deep olive brown, interspersed with little patches of dark green, and everywhere frosted with the snowy curls of the breakers; then a narrower or wider belt of bright apple-green, and beyond the deep purple of the open sea." (A. Hume, in "Stray Feathers," Vol. IV. p. 429.)

(3)

Openings.

OPENINGS OR GATEWAYS.—Pyrard (p. 76-77) notices as "very remarkable" that the Atols have each *two* of these entrances on either side, thus allowing ingress and egress to vessels at all times. Some are fairly broad, others very narrow, ranging from about 200 paces to 30 or even less. "Aux deux costez de chacune de ces entrées par tous les Atollons, il y a deux isles, une de chacun costé. Vous direz que ce seroit pour garder l'entrée, *comme de fait il seroit fort aisé, si on vouloit avec du canon, d'empescher les navires d'y entrer.*"

(4)

Channels.

CHANNELS.—Laval (p. 74-78), omitting the *Véimandú* and *One-and-a-half Degree Channel*, enumerates as the four channels *(Candou)* "which are much broader than the rest, and easily navigable by the largest vessels":—

1. That through the *Malos madou* [Máḷos maḍulu] Atol—"at the entrance of which we were wrecked"—probably the *Moresby Channel (M. Dekunu kaḍu).*
2. The *Caridou* [Kaharidú] Channel.
3. The *Addou* [Ariyadú] Channel.
4. The *Souadou* [Equatorial] Channel, "which is directly below the Equator—the broadest of all, more than twenty leagues across."

(5)

Currents.

CURRENTS.—"Le plus grand inconvenient, ce sont les courants *Oyvarou* [*M. oyivaru*], lesquels courent tantost à l'Est, tantost à l'Oüest, entre les canaux des isles, et en divers endroits de la mer, six mois d'un costé. six mois de l'autre: non pas si certainement six mois d'un costé et d'autre, mais quelquefois plus, quelquefois moins. C'est ce qui les trompe et les fait perdre d'ordinaire...... principalement les courants y portent les navires malgré eux, quand les calmes ou les vents contraires les surprennent et qu' ils ne peuvent bien s'aider de leurs voiles, pour se tirer des courants." (Pyrard, p. 75, 77.)

(6)

Islands.

ISLANDS.—Their number has been variously stated. The two Muhammadan travellers of the 9th century make it 1,900; Ibn Batuta says "about 2,000." (Gray, J. R. A. S. Vol. X. Art. 8, p. 196, Note 4.) "The number" [of Indian islands], writes Marco Polo, "is quite incredible. I have heard indeed from mariners and eminent pilots of these countries, and have seen in the writings of those who have navigated the Indian seas, that they amount to no fewer than 12,700.

including the uninhabited with the inhabited islands." And Linchoten (cap. XIII. p. 16): "*Quidam harum insularum numerum ad* 11,000 *ferunt, sed non est certa ratio. Innumerabiles enim sunt.*" (Marsden's Marco Polo, p. 717.) Captain Owen believed the total number was three or four times 12,000 (J. R. G. S. Vol II. p. 84); whilst Captain Hamilton sneers at them as "a parcel of islands that cannot be counted." (Pinkerton, Vol. VIII. p. 389.) According to Pyrard, the Máldive Sultan claimed to rule 12,000 islands. "This," as Col. Yule observes, "is probably the origin of the proverbial number." (Marco Polo, Vol. II. p. 358.)

No one had better means of ascertaining the approximate number than Pyrard, who thus disposes of the difficulty (p. 71-2):—"Au dedans de chacum de ces enclos [*atollons*], sont les isles tant grandes que petites, en nombre presque infiny. Ceux du pays me disoient qu'il y en avoit jusques à douze mille. *J'estime quant à moy, qu'il n'y a pas apparence d'y en avoir tant, et qu'ils disent douze mille, pour designer un nombre incroyable, et qui ne se peut compter.* Bien est il vray qu'il y en a une infinité de petites, qui ne sont *quasi* que des mottes de sable toutes inhabitées. Davantage le Roy des Maldives met ce nombre en ses titres, car il s'appelloit *Sultan Ibrahim dolos assa ral tera atholon*, c'est à dire *Ibrahim Sultan Roy de treize provinces et de douze mil isles.*"

(7)

Islands wasting.

ISLANDS WASTING.—"Quoy qu'il en soit, les courants et les grandes marées diminuent tous les jours ce nombre [isles], comme les habitans m'ont appris, qui disoient mesme qu'aussi à proportion le nombre du peuple diminuë, et qu'il n'y en a pas tant qu'il y en avoit anciennement." (Pyrard, p. 72.)

(8)

Water.

WATER.—"Ils [isles inhabitées qui n'ont aucune verdure] n'ont point d'eau douce que rarement; les autres isles couvertes, et habitées ou non, en ont; excepté quelques-unes où les habitans sont contraints d'en aller chercher aux isles circonvoisines: aussi ils ont des inventions pour recevoir celle qui tombe du Ciel. Et encore qu'il y ait des eaux en ces isles, elles ne sont pas semblables les unes aux autres, estant bien meilleures en un endroit qu'en un autre. Toutes les eaux de puits ne sont pas fort douces ny fort salubres. Ils font leur puits de cette façon: c'est qu'en creusant trois ou quatre pieds en terre, peu plus ou moins, on trouve de l'eau douce en abondance, et ce qui est fort estrange, à quatre pas du bord de la mer, mesme aux lieux qu'elle inonde souvent. J'ay observé que leurs eaux sont fort froides le jour, principalement à midy, et la nuit fort chaudes." (Pyrard, p. 73.)

Farther on (p. 89) he states that the water of Málé Island was so bad, that the king and the chief people were forced to procure water from a neighbouring island in which no interments were made—perhaps "*Bandos*" [*Bados*] where the water was "plus salubre" (p. 62).

Christopher, however, in commenting on Laval's opinion, remarks:—"We found wells very common all over the islands, few compounds being without one; but we never heard that the natives entertained such an opinion as he has expressed respecting the quality of the water. Our host, the Vizier, and his family used the water of the well in the yard, and we followed their example."*

From the following report made last year (December 5th, 1879) on a sample of the ordinary well water of *Gaufaru* Island (lat. 4° 42′ N.) it would appear that the Máldive Islanders are better off in this respect than is generally believed:—

"I have analysed very carefully the water sent me. It is a great deal purer than most of the water drank in Colombo. It had a rather clayey colour, due probably to its being so long [a fortnight] in the India rubber bottle, or to its percolation through a clay bed.

	Grains per gallon.
Total solids	56·2
Oxygen used to oxidise organic matter	2·380
Chlorine as chlorides, &c. ...	16·
Ammonia:	
Saline	·0056
Albuminoid ...	·0042

	Degrees.
Hardness (Clarke's scale):—	
Total	8·
Permanent	4·5
Temporary	3·5
	Grains.
Equal to carbonate of lime in a gallon	7·

"Professor Wanklyn allows that a water should not be condemned unless it contains ·10 parts of Albuminoid Ammonia in a million parts. This water contains ·06 parts per million of Albuminoid Ammonia, and is therefore perfectly fit for drinking. The large amount of solids is due to the presence of sand in considerable quantity in the specimen." (*Report of an analysis of water from the Máldive Islands* by T. F. Garvin, M.D., Public Analyst, Ceylon.)

---

* Trans. Bombay Geo. Soc. 1836-8 (1844) p. 58.

II.—CLIMATE,

AS AFFECTING HEALTH.

Climate.

The climate* of the Máldive Islands as regards the feeling is neither oppressive nor disagreeable.

Thermometer.

The range of the *thermometer* is moderate. In December, January, and February, the coolest season, it averages from 80° to 84° during the day: at night it falls to 78°. In April it varies from 85° to 90° in the daytime, and generally falls to 80° in the night. The winds moderate the solar heat, and prevent its being so oppressive as might be supposed from the height of the thermometer.

Winds & Weather.†

"As the Máldives occupy a space of nearly 8 degrees of latitude, and are partly South of the Equator, it may be expected that their climate will be influenced on the one hand by the N.W. monsoon of the Chagos and Seychelles, and S E. trade when it blows up to the line: on the other hand, by those atmospheric disturbances which usher in the N.E. monsoon of Hindústán and Ceylon.

"NORTHERN MÁLDIVES. At Ihavandiffuḷu Atol, the head of the Máldives, the N.E. monsoon is steady from mid-December to the end of February, between N.N.E. and E.N.E., moderate and light breezes, with slight showers of rain about every fortnight. In March and April the winds incline more from N. and N.W.—with gales and squalls from uncertain directions in the latter month—until in May the S.W. monsoon commences, and lasts four months only. In September the winds become N.W., but occasionally West squalls accompanied by rain. In October the winds are moderate and variable from W. by S. to N. by W., when the weather is cold and pleasant, but occasionally hard squalls occur with heavy showers of rain at about the same period as the Bombay *elephanta.* In November the winds are light between N.N.E. and N.N.W., with occasional Easterly squalls; after the middle of the month there occurs a period (about one week) of dark cloudy tempestuous weather, with long-continued rain from the West; this seems to be at the same time as the change of monsoon in the Gulf of Mannár; after which the N.E. monsoon is fairly established, and throughout December is steady at E.N.E., with pleasant and clear weather, but occasional squalls and rain from about E.S.E.

"MÁLE ATOL, the central part of the Máldives, marks a great difference in the weather during the N.E. monsoon, for the Southern groups then experience frequent squalls and rain with variable winds: whereas to N. of Mále, that is the season (as at the Lakkadives) of fine weather and generally moderate breezes. There is no such marked difference in the S.W. monsoon.

"SOUTHERN MÁLDIVES. Aḍḍú-Atol, being 40 miles to the S. of the Equator, is almost without the influence of the regular Indian monsoons; the winds and weather being very variable, subject to squalls and rain. The N.E. monsoon is felt in January, February, and March; the winds generally from N. and N.E., but occasionally from W. of North, and the weather is less cloudy and rainy than when the S.W. monsoon prevails N. of the line. In April and May the winds are variable, but mostly from the Westward. From May to December the winds are from W. by S., to S. and S.S.E., with much rain and squalls. About the middle of the latter month, which is about the time that the S.E. trade finally retires Southward, and the N.W. monsoon commences below the Equator, hard squalls and fresh gales from W. to W.N.W., with heavy showers of rain, occur at the Equatorial Channel, lasting for about a fortnight."‡

Most rain falls in the Southern Atols, and the decay of the rank vegetation, engendered in the light sandy soil, breeds much sickness.

Health.

The climate cannot be considered salubrious even for the natives, judging by its influence on them. Its unhealthiness for Europeans has become notorious, and has undoubtedly been a great obstacle to foreign intercourse and internal improvements.

---

* Note (1). † Note (2). ‡ Taylor's Sailing Directory, Part I., p. 653-4.

Dr. Campbell attributes the cause of strangers losing their health partly to the lagoons and marshes formed throughout the Islands, and partly to the unvarying temperature of the climate, due to the absence of the influence which the continent of India has in cooling the air at night, and increasing the heat during the day.* Additional cause may be found in the ubiquitous growth of low jungle, allowed to spring up unchecked round habitations to the exclusion of the sea-breeze and inducing of malaria, and in the want of any attempt at systematic drainage.

Diseases.

Among the natives *intermittent fever* and *ague* (*M. huma, hung*) are very prevalent, and are said to be difficult to shake off †—resulting in, if not accompanied by, *disease of the spleen* (*M. buriturá*—Pyrard, "*ont cory,*" p. 93, "*on cory,*" p. 133) and *ulcers* (*M. fággaḍu*), both attributed to bad water.

Small-pox (*M. karhivaduri*) has occasionally visited the Islands, though stringent quarantine laws have for centuries been in force to prevent its importation.‡

Itch (*M. kas*) is very common; as are *coughs* (*M. kessang*), and *colds* (*M. adidafus*), natural to a humid atmosphere.

Dysentery (*M. béra' kingun*) is not unknown, but cases are somewhat rare.

"The sickness to which strangers are most liable is a bowel complaint, which appears peculiar to these Islands. The only remedy is immediate departure for the continent. Dr. Campbell has collected many cases in which the destructive effects of the sickness upon foreigners is shown; but the natives also appear liable to it, for in one instance nearly the whole population of an island was carried off. There appear to be few other diseases of importance, with the exception of *beri beri.*"*

A curious *sun blindness*—apparently somewhat similar to the *snow* blindness of the Arctic regions—affects, after sunset, the natives who have been much exposed to the dazzling glare during the day. Pyrard, who calls it *rosnans* [*M. rekanu*] did not escape (p. 132).

It was noted in 1834-6 that many of the Islanders in the Huvadú (Suvádiva) Atol suffered from *elephantiasis* [*M. barosbali*].

The mortality among children is said to be above the average, not more than one in five attaining maturity. But this high death rate may be fairly doubted; grey heads are not uncommon, nor do the aged in general appear emaciated. Seventy is not considered an unusual age.§

NOTES.

Notes.

(1)

Climate.

CLIMATE.—"Par ce que j'ay dit que ces isles sont si proches de l'equinoctial, de çà et de là, on peut juger quelle est la qualité de l'air, qui est fort intemperé, et la chaleur excessive. Toutefois le jour et la nuit y sont égaux en tout temps, et les nuits y sont fort fraisches, et amenent force rosée. Cette fraischeur, est cause qu'on peut habiter le pays moins incommodement, et que les herbes et les arbres foisonnent, nonobstant l'ardeur du Soleil. L'Hyver commence au mois d'Avril, et dure six mois, et l'Esté au mois d' Octobre, qui dure six autres mois. L'Hyver est sans gelée, mais continuellement pluvieux. Les vents sont aussi pour lors fort impetueux du costé de l'Oüest; au contraire l'Esté est extremement chaud, et il n'y pleut jamais. Les vents sont du costé de l' Est." (Pyrard p. 78.)

It should not be forgotten that the above remarks apply to the weather experienced mainly at *Mále Atol*—about the centre of the chain—where Laval spent most of his time.

(2)

Weather.

WEATHER.—"Les vents sont assez souvent fixes, comme les Courants du costé de l'Est ou de l'Oüest; mais ils varient bien davantage, et ne sont pas si reglez, biaisans quelquefois vers le Nord ou vers le Sud." (Pyrard, p. 76.) "Ces *Monssons* ou *Muessons*, sont vents qui changent pour l'Esté ou l'Hyver de six en six mois; et qui trompent le plus souvent quand on part trop tard,

---

* Trans. Bombay Geo. Soc. 1836-8 (1844) p. 106. † Note (3). ‡ Note (4).
§ Trans. Bombay Geo. Soc. 1836-8 (1844) p. 68.

THE MÁLDIVES.

CLIMATE.

Notes.

et le vent contraire vient eependant qu'on est lá ; aussi trompent ils encore, en ee qu'ils sont par fois plus eourts ou plus longs l'un que l'autre : et eeluy qui est propre sera plus eourt, et son contraire plus long d'un mois ou six semaines, et quelquefois de deux mois plus qu'on ne pense. Cela contraint par fois de sejourner sept ou huit mois plus qu'on ne veut, eomme j'ay veu arriver assez souvent." (Pages 199-200.)

(3)

Máldive fever.

MÁLDIVE FEVER.—Europeans seem especially liable to this fatal scourge of the Islands. Many have been the ill-fated survivors of wreeks on the Atols who have but exehanged "a watery grave" for a slower death from this insidious pest. "All the British offieers and men, who remained on the island of Málé during a part of the S.W. Monsoon, at the time of the survey (1834-6) were prostrated by it and eompelled to leave." (Taylor's Sailing Direetory, Part I., p. 569.) "On la eonnoist par toute l'Inde," observes Pyrard—who himself nearly sueeumbed to a severe attaek of the malady—"sous le nom de fiévre des Maldives. Ils l'appellent *Malé ons* [*Málé hung*]. C'est de eette maladie que la pluspart de mes eompagnons estoient morts, *comme tous estrangers ne manquent pas d'en estre bientost atteints.*" (Page 63.) "La fiévre y est fort eommune, qu'ils appellent *homan* [*huma*] ; *mais elle est fort dangereuse aux estrangers qui abordent là, et elle les consomme en peu de jours.*" (Page 132.) And later (p. 199) he speeifies "Málé fever" as dreaded by traders no less than the eurrents and reefs of the group.

It appears, however, not to be an altogether "unmixed evil" for residents :—"Quand on en reschappe, on peut s'asseurer qu'on guarira des autres maladies ausquelles l'air du pays est sujet : d'autant que l'on tourne l'air du pays et la maniere de vivre en habitude, et eomme si eette maladie avoit fait un eorps nouveau, on s'y sent du tout aceoustumé. Et de fait un estranger qu'ils appellent en leur langage *Pouraddé* [Christopher, *furadi mtha*] s'il en guarit, ils disent qu'il est *dives*, comme qui diroit naturalizé et non plus estranger." (Page 63.)

(4)

Small-pox.

SMALL-POX —"De dix ans en dix ans il vient une maladie appellée *carivadiri* [*karhivaduri*], pour laquelle ils s'abandonnent les uns les autres, eomme si e'estoit la peste. Ella ressemble à la verolle des petits enfans de deça, et de eette maladie il meurt beaueoup de peuple." (Pyrard, p. 132). It is greatly dreaded. On small-pox breaking out among the erew engaged in operations eonneeted with the wreek of the S. S. "Sea Gull" (December, 1879) the inhabitants of *Gaufaru* island are said to have forthwith fled *en masse* to another island.

III.—POLITICAL DIVISION.*

THE ATOLS.†

THE Máldive group is divided politically into thirteen *Atols* (*M. Atoḷu*), as follows:—

1.—TILADUMMATI' ATOL.
- *a.* Ihavandiffuḷu Atol.
- *b.* Tiladummatí Atol.

2.—MILADUMMAḌULU ATOL.
- *a.* Makunudú (Malcolm Atol).
- *b.* Miladummaḍulu Atol.

3.—FÁDIFFOḶU ATOL.

4.—MÁḶOSMAḌULU ATOL.
- *a.* North Máḷosmaḍulu Atol.
- *b.* South Máḷosmaḍulu Atol.
- *c.* Goidú (Horsburgh Atol).

5.—MÁLE ATOL.
- *a.* Kaharidú (Kardiva Island).
- *b.* Gaufaru Reef, and Island.
- *c.* North Mále Atol.
- *d.* South Mále Atol.

6.—ARI ATOL.
- *a.* Toḍḍú Island.
- *b.* Rasdú (Ross Atol).
- *c.* Ari Atol.

7.—FELIDU ATOL.
- *a.* Felidu Atol.
- *b.* Waṭṭaru Reef.

8.—MULAKU ATOL.

9.—NILANDU ATOL.
- *a.* North Nilandu Atol.
- *b.* South Nilandu Atol.

10.—KOḶUMAḌULU ATOL.

11.—HADDUMMATI' ATOL.

12.—HUVADU' (SUVÁDIVA) ATOL.

13.—AḌḌU' ATOL.
- *a.* Mulaku Island.
- *b.* Aḍḍú Atol.

Málé Island.—The capital, where the Sultan resides, is situated in lat. 4° 10′ N., long. 73° 30′ E., at the South extreme of the North Mále Atol.

1.—TILADUMMATÍ ATOL.

(a.) IHAVANDIFFUḶU ATOL, the head of the Máldive group, lies off the N.W. side of Tiladummatí Atol, from which it is separated by the deep *Gallandú Channel* [*Gallandú kaḍu*], wide at the E. mouth, but narrowing to less than 3 miles on the W. In length N.W. and S.E. the Atol is 12 miles; crosswise it measures 7 miles. It has 24 islands, lying all round the boundary reef, but the principal ones are on the S.W. and N.E. sides. Only seven were inhabited (1834-6) by a population of 760 souls. Wood, water, and some supplies are procurable. Ihavandiffuḷu Atol.

Ihavandú, towards the S., was the chief island, from being the residence of the *Atoḷuveri*. It is nearly one mile in length, and planted with cocoanut, breadfruit, yams, and nacherin *(M. bimbi)*. This island is well adapted for a coal depôt.

Turákunnu, the most Northerly island of the whole of the Máldives, is in lat. 7° 7′ N., long. 72° 53′ E.

One long barrier reef forms the W. side of the Atol. Its South extreme is another barrier reef. Along the E. margin there are nine islands. Between most of this Atol's islands there are passages for ships. The general soundings in the centre are 20 to 30 fathoms, with several coral patches dotted about.

(b.) TILADUMMATI' ATOL stretches S.S.W. for 30 miles, and contains nearly 40 islands generally of a fair size, and some distance apart; those at the N. and E. extremes are largest and inhabited, affording good water and some supplies. *Kelai*, the North island (lat. 6° 59′ N., long. 73° 12′ E.), covered with cocoanut trees, forms a very prominent point to the Atol. The West boundary has fewer islands, but more reefs. Safe passages occur between all. Tiladummatí Atol.

The coir yarn made in Tiladummatí Atol ranks highest in the market.

---

* The description of the several Atols is for the most part condensed from Taylor's Sailing Directory, Part I., pp. 570-85, which should be consulted for fuller particulars regarding tides, currents, channels, anchorage, &c.

† Note (1).

THE MÁLDIVES.

POLITICAL DIVISION.

2.—MILADUMMAḌULU ATOL.

Makunudú (Malcolm Atol).

(*a.*) MAKUNUDU' (MALCOLM ATOL), a large lagoon reef, 15 miles long by only 3 miles broad, lies 10 miles W. of the N.W. part of Miladummaḍulu group, and 24 miles N.W. of *Powell Islands*, at the North of the Máḷosmaḍulu Atol. It is said to have been unknown to Europeans previous to the survey of the Máldives in 1834-36. According to native information many ships have been lost on its barren reefs with all hands, scarcely a vestige of the wrecks remaining after a few hours, from the violence of the surf and the perpendicular sides of the reef. The lagoon is deep, but full of coral patches, and has two boat passages along the E. barrier. Except *Makunudú* island (lat. 6° 25′ N., long. 72° 41′ E.), inhabited, on the N.E. point, and a small island on the N.W., there is nothing but the surf to mark the reef.

Miladummaḍulu Atol.

(*b.*) MILADUMMAḌULU ATOL is in reality a continuation of Tiladummatí, being on the same plateau of soundings, and the frontier islands of both being visible one from the other. This Atol contains 101 islands, principally along the E. and S.E. parts of the boundary, extended over a space 55 miles in length N.W. and S.E., by not quite 20 miles in breadth. In 1834–6 there were 29 islands inhabited by a population of 1,700 or 1,800. Along the W. frontier are not many islands, but more detached lagoon reefs. Ships can easily pass through this group in the daytime, as the islands and reefs which form the boundary are separated by broad passages into the interior, where the general depths are from 20 to 25 fathoms, sandy bottom.

The principal islands are *Manadú* and *Kedikoḷu*. *Kaḍudú*, the S. island, is in lat. 5° 39′ N., long. 73° 17′ E. *Manadú*, at one time the residence of the *Atoḷuveri*, is a beautiful island, with groves of breadfruit and other trees, a fine pathway, and good landing places.

On some islands a little cotton is grown; good water and some supplies may be obtained.

3.—FÁDIFFOḶU ATOL.

Fádiffoḷu Atol.

FÁDIFFOḶU ATOL lies 10 miles S.E. of Miladummaḍulu, N. of Kaharidú (Kardiva) island, and E. of Máḷosmaḍulu Atol. Of a square shape, with its N.E. and S.W. sides pressed in, and the others rather convex, it presents four prominent corners. At the S. corner stands *Aligau* island (lat. 5° 15′ N., long. 73° 29′ E.), 16 miles N. by E. of Kaharidú (Kardiva), marked by high trees; at the W. corner is *Kanifurhi* island (lat. 5° 20′ N.), bearing N.E. 10 miles from the E. point of South Máḷosmaḍulu Atol. The *Atoḷuveri* resided at *Máfurhi* (lat. 5° 26′ N.). Passages into the interior occur between all the islands on the N.W. side, and between several islands on the S.W. side; along the N.E. concave face only a few openings are found, and those in the N. half; thence nothing but an extensive barrier reef, 18 miles in length, stretches round the E. extreme and down the S.E. face, on which the N.E. monsoon breaks with violence. Within the Atol the general depths, on a sandy bottom, are from 25 to 30 fathoms, but many coral patches and sunken reefs exist. There are upwards of 20 islands, but only four were inhabited in 1834-36 by 550 persons. The N.W. islands can furnish good water and some supplies.

4.—MÁḶOSMAḌULU ATOL.

Máḷosmaḍulu Atol.

MÁḶOSMAḌULU ATOL. This West Atol, lying only 7 miles S.W. of Miladummaḍulu Atol, is upwards of 50 miles in meridional length, and is divided into *two* distinct groups by a narrow, but deep passage, called by the surveyors *Moresby Channel (M. Dekunu kaḍu.)*

North.

(*a.*) NORTH MÁḶOSMAḌULU is 35 miles in length N. and S., and 15 miles across at its broadest part. Its W. side is composed of a series of round or oval reefs irregularly placed, some prominent, others retiring—a feature peculiar to all these Northern Atols—with little to mark them, whilst the E. side is a gentle curve with a series of islands, 20 in number, between which good passages lead into the Atol. No vessel could navigate through the intricacies of the Atol's centre; but its N. end is narrow and clear of reefs. The general depths are from 23 to 27 fathoms, water. *Ettigili* and *Alifurhi*, the two *Powell*

Islands (lat. 5° 59′ N., long. 72° 54′ E.), inhabited, standing on a detached reef of their own with no soundings off it, mark the N. end of the Atol.

None of the islands have good water, except *Fainu* (lat. 5° 27′ N.), where (1834-6) the chief of the Atol lived.

South.

(b.) SOUTH MÁḶOSMAḌULU differs in shape from the N. group. Its E. point is prominent, and in the same latitude as the S. point of Fádiffoḷu Atol, which is distant nearly 20 miles. The length of this group is 26 miles from E. to S.W., and most of the islands border the S.E. face. The W. side is similar to that of the N. group, being composed of large, separate, lagoon reefs, with scarcely any islands to distinguish them. Passages into the interior occur between all the islands, and reefs, on the W., S.E., and N.E. boundaries.

Hitadú island (lat. 5° 1′ N., long. 72° 50′ E.) marks the S. point of the group. It contained (1834–6) 250 inhabitants.

The *Atoḷuveri* resided at *Daravandú* island. Wood and water are procurable. Cloth is woven in this Atol principally.

Goidú (Horsburgh Atol).

(c.) GOIDU′ (HORSBURGH ATOL)—a lagoon reef distant 25 miles W. by S. from Kaharidú (Kardiva) island, and the same distance N. from Toḍḍú island—marks the N. side of the W. entrance of *Kardiva Channel* [*Kaharidú kaḍu*] and is separated from Máḷosmaḍulu Atol by 6 miles deep water. This Atol is oval in shape and small, its greatest length E. and W. being 10 miles, and its breadth less than 5 miles. Its three large islands, on the N. and E. parts, were inhabited in 1834-6 by a population of 200. They afford wood, water, and some supplies. *Goidú* is the largest (lat. 4° 53′ N., long. 72° 58′ E.) The only entrance into the lagoon, called *Doru kaḍu*, is on the S. side of the Atol. In the interior there is fine anchorage in 17 to 20 fathoms, sandy bottom mixed with mud and clay, and free from rocks in the centre.

5.—MÁLE ATOL.

Kaharidú (Kardiva island).

(a.) KAHARIDU′ (KARDIVA ISLAND) (lat. 4° 58′ N., long. 73° 26′ E.), lies towards the E. end of the *Channel* to which it gives its name. It is covered with a dense mass of high cocoanut trees: contained (1834-6) 200 inhabitants: and can supply good water and some provisions.

Its S.E. side is convex and sheer, having no soundings in 240 fathoms, water, close to the beach. A circular lagoon reef on the N.W. side provides a snug anchorage for the islanders' boats. There is generally a heavy surf round the island, except at the sole boat passage through the fringing reef near the N.E. point. The natives are famed for their manufacture of excellent cordage.

Gaufaru island.

(b.) About 15 miles south of Kardiva lies the ISLAND and lagoon REEF of GAUFARU, separated from Mále Atol by a narrow, but deep, channel, 1½ to 2 miles wide, with no soundings. It is as much a separate Atol as the similar lagoon reefs called Goidú (Horsburgh Atol) and Rasdú (Ross Atol).

Gaufaru island stands at the E. extreme of its own reef, and is approachable only through two narrow openings on the N.E. and N.W. faces, which are difficult to descry. It is inhabited by about 100 souls (32 houses), who are supported by fishing.

They possess not more than two or three fishing boats *(M. mas-oḍi)* and are poor. Rank jungle covers most of the island, but there are some cocoanut trees, and a few breadfruit, limes, and plantains, round the houses. From having no landmarks on its N., and W., sides, Gaufaru reef has proved very disastrous to vessels making a cut through the Máldives by the Kardiva channel.

Mále Atol.

MÁLE ATOL. Both N. and S. groups are included by the natives under one name, but being separated by a channel without soundings, they are really *two* distinct Atols.

North.

(c.) NORTH MÁLE ATOL is of irregular shape, taperingat the N., S., and E. ends, convex on the W., and concave on the N.E. and S.E. faces. In length 32 miles N. and S., it has a central width of 23 miles. It contains about 50 islands, (of which 12 were

THE MÁLDIVES.

POLITICAL DIVISION.

inhabited in 1836,) and innumerable coral reefs. The general depths in the interior are from 25 to 35 fathoms, sandy bottom, but so numerous are the sandbanks and coral patches, that it can be traversed safely only in the daytime with a sharp look-out. All the openings into this, and other Atols, cannot be distinctly seen three or four miles off, the barrier reef presenting apparently one continuous threatening line. The passages are numerous on all sides. Lagoon reefs occur along the N., N.E., and S.W. faces. Some of the more important islands—after *Málé* or *Sultan's Island*—are *Diffurhi* (E.), *Girávaru* and *Hebadú* (W.), and *Makunudú* (W. centre).

Málé, or Sultan's Island.

Málé, or *Sultan's Island* (lat. 4° 10′ N., long. 73° 30′ E.), at the very South of this Atol, is the *capital* of the Máldive group.

It is oval in shape, low-lying like all these islands, and about one mile in length by ¾ mile in breadth. (Pyrard, "de tour environ une lieuë et demie," p. 89.) An unbroken reef, just awash, renders its South side inaccessible; but the rest of its circumference has a lagoon or harbour, formed by an artificial bank of coral three to four feet above water, and six to eight feet in width, roughly renewed from time to time, which serves as an effective breakwater against the monsoon storms. As the depth of the water inside is from six to fourteen feet, this harbour gives excellent shelter to both the trading *gundara (M. daturu oḍi)* and fishing boats *(M. mas oḍi)* of the natives. The only entrance, about 30 feet in width, is on the N. side, where the coral bank approaches the breach to within 60 or 70 yards.

At some period the island must have possessed a substantial *fort*. The remains of the stone wall, still solid in parts, shew that it was enclosed (except on the S. or barrier reef side), and strongly defended, by regularly designed bastions at various points. A few pieces of ordnance are still mounted at intervals along the fort wall, chiefly on the N. face, but rusted, choked with coral, and unserviceable.

The main bastion fronts the entrance to the harbour, and commands all approach from the North. It is 20 feet at least in height and faced with solid masonry. In 1835, according to Christopher, this fort was "a solid mass" filled with earth.* It must have been partially excavated since, as 10 or 12 steps now lead from the ground level, (where the old flagstaff still stands), to the upper tier, which is seven or eight feet below the top of the wall. The embrasures are bare, the iron guns lying unlimbered, and half buried in the grass, at the rear of the bastion. This fort was probably erected by the Portuguese, as Christopher supposed, for Pyrard mentions (p. 170) that on one of their temporary occupations of Málé in the 16th century, "ils firent une forteresse."

The Sultan's Palace *(M. gaḍuvaru)* is a large upper-roomed house, with sloping roof in a high-walled enclosure, comprising an area of about a quarter of a mile. "Within this space there is also a well-built magazine, besides several houses—one said to contain a variety of arms and relics taken from wrecked vessels—and a neat building raised on stone arches, from which the ladies witness the games exhibited before the court on festivals."* [See also Pyrard, p. 155.] The shallow moat, 12 to 15 feet broad, which formerly surrounded the Palace walls, is now nearly choked with scrub and rank vegetation. A few brass cannon of small calibre still guard the entrance ("A' l'entrée du Palais...... on void quelques pieces de canon"—Pyrard, p. 155), but are only used for firing salvoes on State occasions. The Palace stands back about 150 yards from the chief gateway through the fort wall on the North.

In the town are two chief, and several minor mosques *(M. miskitu)*: a tower or minaret *(M. munnáru)*, 40 feet high, from which "the faithful" are called to prayer:† a public office for the transaction of revenue and other business: a mint: and a house set apart for the use of visitors or shipwrecked persons.

The town is somewhat regularly laid out with broad streets, straight and long. running in attempted parallel lines, intersected by others at right-angles. It was formerly divided into five municipal wards called "*avares*," each of which had its headman, "*Mouscouly Avare*, l'ancien du quartier." (Pyrard, p. 146.) There are now only four

---

* Trans. Bombay Geo. Soc. 1836-8 (1844) p. 57. † Note (2).

such divisions *(M. mádún)*, called respectively, *Galolugé*, *Hemvéru*, *Machchangolí*, and *Máfannu*,—the last containing the Palace. The houses (generally of wattle and daub, or cocoanut thatch) have as a rule a yard or compound attached, where fruit trees and some flowers are cultivated. A *cadjan* fence five or six feet high shuts out all the houses from the road. Apparently only one stone-and-brick-built private house now exists, which is owned by a rich *Dídí;* but in Pyrard's day the nobility and richer inhabitants commonly occupied houses built of madrepore (p. 89)—the ruins of some of which were noticed by the Indian Navy Surveyors in 1834-6.* The streets are shaded by a variety of fruit trees, such as cocoanut, breadfruit, biling, areka (rare), plantain, &c., and are neatly kept.

Málé† must contain between 2,000 and 3,000 inhabitants, and has for two centuries at least been over-populated, rendering it even in 1602–7 "la plus mal saine" (Pyrard, p. 89) of all the islands, owing chiefly to the numerous graveyards, which at the present day meet the eye at every turn. Many of the inhabitants are traders, but the most common employments are fishing, gathering cocoanuts, drawing toddy, and collecting cowries. The whole foreign trade of the several Atols is conducted at Málé under regulations imposed by the Sultan. Good water and supplies may be obtained.

There are no soundings to the S. of Málé, but round the inner side of the island the depths are from 25 to 28 fathoms, sandy bottom. *High water* on the F. and C. occurs at Málé at 12 h. 30 m.; rise and fall of *tide* three feet, and sometimes four feet.

South.

(d.) SOUTH MÁLE ATOL is separated from the N. group by *Wádú Channel* [*Wádú kaḍu*] which, though less than 2½ miles wide at its narrowest part, has no soundings at 200 fathoms. Oblong in shape, this Atol is 20 miles in length N. and S., by 12 in greatest breadth. It contains 22 islands, nearly all situated along the E. boundary, but only three, counting 200 persons, were inhabited in 1834-6. None afford good water or supplies. There are safe passages on one, or both sides of nearly all. Inside the Atol the general depths are from 25 to 32 fathoms, sandy bottom, full of reefs and little coral patches not difficult to avoid.

6.—ARI ATOL.

Toḍḍú Island.

(a.) TOḌḌU' ISLAND (lat. 4° 23′ N., long. 72° 56′ E.), situated 5½ miles N. of Rasdú (Ross Atol), is a solitary island at the W. entrance of Kardiva Channel. The reef is steep and safe to approach to within a cable's length of the high trees, which cover the island and make it visible 20 miles from a mast-head. It contained (1834–6) about 250 inhabitants, principally employed in fishing. Possesses good water and some supplies.

Rasdú (Ross Atol).

(b.) RASDU' (ROSS ATOL) is a large lagoon reef distant 4½ miles from the N.E. point of Ari Atol, and connected with it by a plateau having soundings of 100 to 140 fathoms. The diameter of this miniature Atol, which is circular, is only 4½ miles. The N. and W. sides are one continuous barrier reef, and the E. side is another, but entrances occur at the N., E., and S. extremes of the Atol. The interior has soundings from 15 to 20 fathoms, but abounds in detached coral patches.

Ari Atol.

(c.) ARI ATOL.—This West Atol is situated about 10 miles N. of Nilandu Atol, and to the W. of Felidu and Mále Atols. It is oblong in shape, 48 miles in length N. and S., by 17 miles in E. and W. breadth, and contains some 50 islands, generally small, which lie chiefly along the E. boundary. Except a small space on the S., Ari Atol, in common with those further North, has no continuous barrier reef round it. On the W., N., and E. sides are numerous good passages for ships into the Atol. In the interior the general soundings are 30 to 40 fathoms, interrupted by many large coral reefs not all dry at low-water. The N. extreme of this Atol is in lat. 4° 17′ N., long. 72° 45′ E.

Between Ari and Nilandu Atols, and W. of Felidu Atol, lies *Ariyadú Channel* [*Ariyadú kaḍu*]. In width 10 miles, with no soundings, it is free from danger.

---

* Trans. Bombay Geo. Soc. 1836-8 (1844) p. 108.

† An outline map of Málé, shewing the general position of the old Fort, is annexed. This tracing has been enlarged in the Surveyor-General's Office, Colombo, from Admiralty Chart, 66 *b m* = 0·25—the approximate position of the chief buildings being inserted from memory (Visit, November, 1879). There is said to be a plan of Málé in Charton *(Voyageurs Anciens et Modernes*, Vol. IV., Paris, 1856.)

THE MÁLDIVES.

POLITICAL DIVISION.

7.—FELIDU ATOL.

Felidu Atol.

(*a.*) FELIDU ATOL, separated on the N from South Mále Atol by *Fuḷidú Channel* [*Fuḷidú kaḍu*] 8½ miles wide, has a very irregular outline. Its shape has been compared to a gouty foot and leg. This Atol has only 10 islands, of which five were inhabited (1834–6) by a population of 320. The *Atoḷuveri* resided at *Tinadú* near the centre of the deep bight on the Atol's N.E. side. Many openings occur on the S.W., N.W., and N.E. faces: but none on the S. and E. sides, which are one continuous barrier reef. The water of the islands is brackish and unwholesome. Of supplies, a few fowls, turtle, and some fruit are obtainable, and firewood is plentiful. The islands of *Fuḷidú* (lat. 3° 41′ N., long. 73° 24′ E.) and *Rakídú* (lat. 3° 19′ N., long. 73° 27′ E.) mark the N. and S. extremes of this Atol, and *Fotteu* its E. point, or toe.

Waṭṭaru Reef.

(*b.*) WAṬṬARU CHANNEL and REEF. *Waṭṭaru Channel* [*Waṭṭaru kaḍu*], which separates Felidu and Mulaku Atols by a space of eight miles, has in its centre a circular lagoon reef, four to five miles in diameter, dividing it into *two* deep passages, 2 and 2½ miles wide. The strength of the tides and currents, and the absence of land marks, render both passages dangerous. There is only one entrance into the lagoon, in which soundings give 12 to 20 fathoms, sand.

8.—MULAKU ATOL.

Mulaku Atol.

MULAKU ATOL lies about 20 miles E. of the Nilandu group, and 15 miles N.N.E. from Koḷumaḍulu Atol. It is of irregular form, prominent towards the N.E. and S., but very straight on the W. In length it is 25 miles, and contains altogether 21 islands, nine of which were inhabited (1834–6) by a population of 980. All are on the boundary reefs (most on the S.E. quarter), except *Mulaku*, the largest, which stands nearly one mile within the principal entrance. In the interior of the Atol there are many coral patches, and the depth of the water varies from 28 to 40 fathoms, sandy bottom. Many safe openings occur, chiefly on the W. side. Good water, plenty of wood, and a few supplies can be obtained at *Mulaku* island (lat. 2° 57′ N., long. 73° 35′ E.) The *Atoḷuveri* lived at *Muli* island.

9.—NILANDU ATOL.

Nilandu Atol.

NILANDU ATOL—the most Southerly of those that lie in double rows—is 40 miles in length N. and S., and is in reality *two* Atols, separated by a channel, 3½ miles wide, without soundings.

North.

(*a.*) NORTH NILANDU ATOL is a perfect semi-circle on the E., but its W. side is rather indented. There are not many islands on its boundary. In the interior, where the general soundings are 25 to 35 fathoms, are four islands, and several large coral reefs dry at low water. *Nilandú*, the S. island (lat. 3° 4′ N., long. 72° 53′ E.), inhabited, affords some supplies and good water. From this island the double Atol takes its name. *Himiti*, the W. island, though small, is important in the group. In 1834-6 it contained 200 to 300 inhabitants, who were great traders and navigators, sending annually five or six vessels (80 to 100 tons burden) to Bengal, and having schools for instruction in navigation.

South.

(*b.*) SOUTH NILANDU ATOL is of somewhat oval form, flattened slightly on the E. and W. sides. In meridional length it is 21 miles, by 13 miles E. and W. Many passages admit of vessels entering the Atol, but it is least accessible on the S.W. The general depths in the interior are from 27 to 35 fathoms, but studded by many coral reefs, large and small, some dry at low-water and all easily avoided. About 20 islands lie within the Atol: two or three on the W. side boundary: most on the E. boundary reef. A number of jewellers live on the two islands *Ribudú* and *Huludeli* ("Doorais Island"—Taylor's Sailing Directory, Part I., p. 576), and travel periodically among the different Atols in pursuit of their calling. At *Kuḍa-huvadú* island (lat. 2° 40′ N., long. 72° 53′ E.) some supplies of wood, water, and poultry can be procured.

It gives its name to *Kuḍa-huvadú Channel* [*Kuḍa-huvadú kaḍu*], a narrow but safe passage, which separates Nilandu Atol from the Koḷumaḍulu group. The W. entrance is only 10 miles wide. The Atol on the S. (Koḷumadulu) is soon past, but the two Atols on its N. side (Nilandu and Mulaku) give this channel a length of over 30 miles.

10.—KOLUMADULU ATOL.

Koḷumaḍulu Atol.

Koḷumaḍulu Atol is of somewhat circular form—its greatest measurement from E. to W. being 29 miles, and from N.W. to S.E. 23 miles. It is principally surrounded by barrier reefs, and in the whole circumference there are a dozen openings. There are many islands along the S. boundary: a few on the N.: and in the interior only six. Within the Atol lie numerous coral patches dry at low-water, but the general depths are from 32 to 42 fathoms. The chief islands are *Hirilandú* and *Kaḍudú* (W.), separated by a passage two miles wide, *Véimandú* (S.), *Fálu*, nearly four miles in length (E.), and *Buruní* (N.) in lat. 2° 34′ N., long. 73° 6′ E. From these islands, and some others, good water, firewood, and some poultry, are procurable.

Véimandú Channel [*Véimandú kaḍu*], 25 miles in length N.E. by E. ½ E., and 16 or 17 miles in breadth, divides Koḷumaḍulu and Haddummatí Atols. It may be traversed by vessels at night.

11.—HADDUMMATI′ ATOL.

Haddummatí Atol.

Haddummati′ Atol. This small Atol, in shape said to resemble a leg of mutton, lies lengthways N.E. and S.W. for 26 miles: its greatest breadth is 15 miles. The boundary reef—more regular in outline than that of any other Atol—has six gateways or openings *(M. kaḍu)*, four of which are available for large ships—one on each side of the boundary. Coral patches, not difficult to avoid, stud the interior. Wood, water, and poultry are to be obtained at *Mowa* [? *Mávaru*] (lat. 1° 54′ N., long. 73° 14′ E.), the chief island, at the W. extreme. It contained (1834-6) from 300 to 400 inhabitants, who traded in their own vessels—three or four of 80 to 100 tons burden—to India annually. At the N.E. point of the Atol—the narrow end—stands the large island *Isdú* (lat. 2° 7′ N., long. 73° 35′ E.) two miles in length, and covered with cocoanut trees.

The *One-and-a-half Degree Channel*, comprehending the space between Haddummatí and Huvadú (Suvádiva) Atols, is 50 miles broad, and free from dangers. It is adopted by vessels from the Westward bound to Ceylon, in the months of October and November.

12.—HUVADÚ (SUVÁDIVA) ATOL.*

Huvadú (Suvádiva) Atol.

Huvadu′ (Suvádiva) Atol, one of the largest of the Máldive group, is 42 miles in length N. and S., by 34 miles in breadth. Fine broad passages into the interior occur on all the sides. There are 30 islands in the centre of this group, which has both a greater depth of water (35 to 40 fathoms) and fewer coral reefs than other Atols. The aggregate population was about 2,000 in 1834-6. The men are principally employed in fishing, whilst the women weave a rush which grows in this Atol (dyed black, brown, and yellow) into the pretty and valued "Máldive mats." The inhabitants of this Atol are said to be much subject to *elephantiasis*.

The chief islands are:—*Hundadu* (lat. 0° 27′ N., long. 72° 56′ E.) at the W. extreme, on the N. end of a barrier reef which is 19 miles in length and forms the S.W. side of the Atol. In 1834-6 it contained 200 inhabitants, and was the residence of the *Atoḷuveri*.—*Mátura*, the Southernmost isle, consisting of a number of little islets on one coral reef.—*Wádú*, about 1½ mile long E. and W. and half as broad, said to have been once a very fertile, thriving island, with 1,200 inhabitants, but contained in 1834-6 not more than 100. Some ancient mosques, and burial places, render the island interesting to the antiquary.—*Gaṇ*, the largest of the group, shows plenty of trees on more than 1½ mile of sea frontage. A fort was erected on this island against the Portuguese in the 16th century.†—*Gaddú*, the principal island of the mat manufacture.—*Máfurhi* at the N.W. projecting angle of the Atol.—*Tenadú* (W.), about one mile in extent, contained 200

* Note (3).

† Gray, J. R. A. S., Vol. X., p. 197, quoting Pyrard.

inhabitants (1834-6). Good water, wood, and supplies are furnished by most islands. An impassable barrier reef, 11 miles in length, forms the N.E. boundary of the Atol; and on its N. and N.W. sides are many irregular detached coral reefs. Some of the royal lineage either voluntarily emigrated, or were banished, to this group, at a former period.* Their descendants, styled *Dídí*, still reside there, as well as in the island of Mulaku and Aḍḍú Atol.

The *Equatorial Channel.*—By this name navigators in general know the entire passage between Huvadú (Suvádiva) and Aḍḍú Atols, 46 miles in breadth, but Mulaku island lies athwart the way 31 miles S. of Huvadú Atol, and it is this latter space which properly constitutes the Equatorial Channel. This channel is free from danger.

13.—AḌḌÚ ATOL.

A little to S.E. of the centre of the Equatorial Channel lies :—

Mulaku Island.

(*a.*) MULAKU ISLAND (erroneously called *Addon Island* by navigators formerly), in lat. 0° 17′ S., long. 73° 23′ E., two miles in length N.W. and S.E. by an average breadth of ¾ mile. The N.E. and W. sides are precipitous, with no soundings close to the beach; but off the S. side a shelving bank extends for 1½ mile, on which the surf breaks very high. The inhabitants are principally employed in fishing and weaving cloth, and numbered in 1834-6 between 300 and 400. They can provide turtle, fowls, eggs, some fruit, firewood, and fresh water.

Aḍḍú Atol.

(*b.*) AḌḌU′ ATOL (named *Phoolah Moloque* in error by the old navigators) is the South termination of the Máldive chain, and the smallest of all the Atols. It is shaped like a half-moon, concave on the N. side, and is only 10 miles from E. to W., and seven miles from N. to S.. There are nine large and several small islands—over 20 in all—which contained 500 persons in 1834-6. The two chief islands are *Hatadú* (N.W.) and *Mídú* or *Huludú* (N.E.). *Gaṇ* Island (lat. 0° 42′ S., long. 73° 6′ E.) is the most Southerly of the whole Máldive group. The islands afford a few supplies of fruit, limes, poultry, eggs, &c., and firewood and water in abundance. The natives, though timorous, are civil and obliging, and will exchange their products for money, rice, or provisions. They possess some trading boats—one or two of which visit Ceylon annually—and their principal occupation is making cotton cloth, dyed by themselves white, red, chocolate, and black, neatly blended, which realize a good price in the other Atols.

There are four gateways into this Atol, two on the N., and two on the S. side—the broadest and deepest. No soundings are obtainable outside the Atol, but within the general depths vary from 20 to 25 fathoms.

Defence.

DEFENCE.

The importance of the Máldives in the event of maritime war in Indian seas in which England was involved, might be made considerable. Lying within two to three days' steam of Ceylon and the Coast of Hindústán—and therefore within easy reach of supplies—they could advantageously be selected as a *rendezvous* and temporary station, or as a *point d'appui* for war-vessels destined to harass the marine of the enemy in the East.

History affords at least one instance of the recognition by a European power of the utility of these Islands in time of war. Their admirable position did not fail to attract the watchful eye of the shrewd *Dupleix*, who occupied Málé (Sultan's Island) in 1754 with a detachment of French troops when engaged in the struggle against the English for supremacy in Southern India.

---

* Note (4).

THE MÁLDIVES.

Political Division.

Defence.

Numerous secure roadsteads and landing places abound throughout the group. Supplies are not abundant ; but there is no lack of vessels—both large and small craft—and rafts peculiarly suited for navigation and landing troops in the dangerous waters of the Atols.

As far back as 1836 Lieut. F. T. Powell, I.N., proposed *Ihavandú* island, at the head of the Máldives, "as better adapted than any other for a coal depôt. It lies nearly in a direct line between Point-de-Galle [426 miles distant] and Socotra [1,173 miles distant], at about one-third of the whole distance from the former place : is easy of access in every direction : and possesses safe anchorage for ships and steamers in all seasons. During the S.W. monsoon a vessel could anchor at the East side of the island between it and a small reef dry at low water ; in the N.E. monsoon the best anchorage is in the channel between the island and the South barrier reef in 16 or 17 fathoms, sand and rock. Opposite both the anchorages there are good landing places for boats, which are procurable for the landing and shipment of coals, &c. The natives, who are civil and peaceable, might, I think, be induced to work for a small hire, such as rice, tobacco, &c., or any other remuneration they might consider adequate."*

Equal facilities exist for the establishment of coal depôts at Kardiva Island *(Kaharidú)* about the centre of the group, and on Suvádiva (Huvadú) or Addú Atols at the South.

Owing to their low-lying nature, the great extent of coast line, and the want of stone suitable for fortification, it may be doubted whether the Islands could be strongly defended except at a cost clearly prohibitive. The old Portuguese fort at Málé is, however, a standing proof of the practicability of erecting fairly substantial works at important points, capable of offering some resistance.

Upon emergencies, a battery of Artillery with one or two companies of Marines, aided by a vessel of war, would probably suffice to hold the Islands against the sudden descent of an enemy's rovers.

Peaceable and timid by nature, but amenable to discipline, there is every reason to believe from their past history that the Máldivians could be relied on at least in defensive operations affecting the safety of their Islands. Though constitutionally lazy, they are likely to prove sufficiently alive to their own interests to co-operate in carrying out ordinary undertakings, if adequate inducement is held out.†

NOTES.

Notes.

(1)

The Atols.

The Atols—of which there are more than twenty physically distinct—have for centuries been divided by the Máldivians into *thirteen* chief groups, forming the entire realm of the Sultans.

"Elles sont divisées," says Pyrard (p. 71), "en *treize* Provinces, qu'ils nomment *Atollons* qui est une division naturelle, selon la situation des lieux : d'autant que chacun Atollon est separé des autres, et contient en soy une grande multitude de petites Isles" ; and he proceeds to speak of the Máldive sovereign, "*Sultan Ibrahim*," as ' king of 13 provinces and 12,000 islands *(dolos assa ral tera atholon)*." As though this title was not sufficiently pompous, on their coins the Máldive Sultans are described as 'lords of land and sea' (*assulṭánul bar wal bahr*, السلطان البر والبحر)—in other words, 'rulers of the world !' Βριάρεως φαίνεται ὢν λαγώς.

Laval (p. 74) enumerates the Atols "in order from the North" thus :—(1) *Tilla dou matis*, (2) *Milla doue madoue*, (3) *Padypolo*, (4) *Malos madou*, (5) *Ariatollon*, (6) *Malé Atollon*, "qui est le principal où est l'isle de Malé capitale des autres," (7) *Poulisdous*, (8) *Molucque*, (9) *Nillandous*, (10) *Collo madous*, (11) *Adou matis*, (12) *Souadou*, (13) *Addou* and *Poua Mollucque*, "qui en sont deux petits distinguez et separez ensemble comme les autres, mais fort petits, pour raison de quoi ils ne sont comptez que pour un. Toutefois *Addou*, comme le meilleur, donne le nom à l'autre." "These atolls with Suadiva were sometimes considered as a sub-kingdom, apart from the other atolls. The dethroned king *(Dom Manuel)* who lived at Cochin entitled himself 'king of the Maldive islands and of the three atolls of Cuaydu *(rei das ilhas de Maldiva e de tres Patanas de Cuaydu, &c.'—Documento*, 1560.*)*"‡

---

* J. R. A. S., Bengal, Vol. IV., p. 322. † Note (5). ‡ Gray, J. R. A. S. Vol. X., n. s. pp. 196, 200.

THE MÁLDIVES.

POLITICAL DIVISION.

Notes.

"This division into thirteen Atolls is political rather than physical: thus, *Tilla dou matis* [Tiladummatí] includes what is really the Northernmost atoll, *Heawandu Pholo* [Ihavandiffoḷu], and does not include *Mille doue Madoue* [Miladummaḍulu], though both form one long straggling Atoll intersected by no deep soundings. *Malcolm Atoll* (so called by the English surveyors) is taken to belong to *Mille doue Madoue: Horsburgh Atoll* to *Malosmadou* [Máḷosmaḍulu—itself consisting of two Atols]. *Malé* [Mâle] has three Atolls ; *Ari*, [*Nilandu*], and *Addou*[Aḍḍú] each two."*

Ibn Batuta (middle of 14th century) gives the following as among the provinces (Arabic, *aklím*) which are distinguished :—(1) *Pâlipour*, (2) *Cannaloûs*, (3) *Mahal*, 'which gives its name to all the islands,' (4) *Télâdib*, (5) *Carâïdoû*, (5) *Teïm*, (7) *Télédomméty*, (8) *Hélédomméty*, (9) *Béreïdoû*, (10) *Candacal*, (11) *Moloûc*, (12) *Souweïd*.†.

"The French Editors identify [some of] these names with those given by Pyrard as follows :—*Pâlipour*—'Padypolo' : *Mahal*—'Malé' : *Carâïdoû*—'Caridou' : *Télédomméty*—'Tilla dou matis' : *Hélédomméty*—'Milla doue madoue' : *Béreïdoû*—'Poulisdous' : *Moloûc*—'Molucque' : *Souweïd*—'Souadou.' The *Cannaloûs* of Ibn Batuta, they add, is perhaps the 'Collomadous' of Pyrard, or, as Horsburgh writes it, 'Colomandous.'"‡

The majority of the above "are easily recognisable," but five (viz., *Cannaloûs, Télâdib, Teïm, Hélédomméty*, and *Candacal*) present more difficulty,—some, indeed, being shaped, *more Arabico*, out of all but unsatisfactory conjectural recognition.

As regards *Hélédomméty*, the French translators would appear to be at fault. It may perhaps with more reason be taken as equivalent to *Hela-du*(*m*)*-matí* (S. *hela*, හෙළ, 'white,' or even *sela*, සෙල = Javanese *sela*, 'rock' + *dúva*, දූව, 'island' + *matu-piṭa*, මතුපිට 'above') passing by contraction into *Had-dummatí*. *Aḍḍu* may similarly be a contracted form of *Hela-dú* or *Huludú*—the name of one of the islands in that Atol.

If it be open to question the orthography of the MS. and, supposing an error of the copyist, read *Nélâdîb* for *Télâdîb*—*t* and *n* are not unlike in Arabic—it can be at once fitted to *Nilandu* Atol. Even accepting the received form as correct, the identification may possibly be not considered too far-fetched. Cf. *Tojaree* = ? *Nausâri; Accanee* and *Kaluftee* islands (Lakkadive group) = *Aucutta, Kalpeni*, Adm. Chart. (Col. Yule in Indian Antiquary, Vol. III., pp. 212–4, on "Names in the *Tohfat-al Majâhidîn*.") *Nilandu* may, however, perhaps = 'the lotus island' (S. *nelum*, නෙළුම්, 'lotus' + *dúva*, දූව, 'island' ; but cf. also *Pulo-nila*, 'indigo' or 'blue island' in the Molucca Sea.

To attempt to twist the rest into probable coincidence with the modern names of the remaining Atols seems hopeless. But the identification of *Carâidoû* with *Caridou* [*Kaharidú*]—if accepted—suggests a likely clue to their origin. Admitting that this island—now-a-days of comparative insignificance—was of sufficient importance in the 14th century to be classed as a "province," it is not improbable that other islands would have been taken as representative of whole groups or Atols.

Télâdîb, if not *Nilandu*, might then be *Toḍḍú*, on the analogy of *Haddummáti* from *Hélédomméty: Cannaloûs—Kinaḷos*, 'Kenoorus,' Admiralty Chart, (Máḷosmaḍulu Atol) : *Candacal—Kedikoḷu*, 'Kaindecolos,' Admiralty Chart, (Miladummaḍulu Atol). *Cannaloûs* and *Teïm* should lie *North* of Mále. Ibn Batuta, crossing from the Malabar coast, landed first at the former, "an island fair to behold, where there are many mosques," and touched later at *Teïm* "after four days' cruise" when bound for *Mahal* (Málé).‡

The ephemeral prominence that individual islands may assume is well illustrated by Pyrard. Thus he particularises *Maconnodou* [*Makunudú*, Mále Atol] the property of the "High Admiral" : *Misdoue* [? *Midú*, Nilandu Atol] and *Gooradou* [*Gurádú*, Fádiffoḷu Atol] where a former Sultan's brother-in-law, and a powerful chieftain, respectively raised the standard of revolt at different times : *Game* [*Gaŋ*, Huvadú Atol] on which a fortress was erected : *Maspillaspoury* ['the city of the Mápiḷḷa (Moplas)' ? *Máfurhifaru*, Miladummaḍulu Atol.]

Many of the names occurring throughout the Máldive Archipelago are of simple explanation, and find their counterpart in Ceylon (North and South), and on the South Coast of India : of others—some apparently heterogeneous compounds—it would be premature to offer more than a possible solution. Pure Aryan derivatives prevail, but the Dravidian element is not absent. Of words chiefly recurring as terminations, the following are most common :—

(a.) M. *ḍú* ; S. *dúva, diva*, දූව, දිව ; Sans. *dwípa*.

---

* Gray, J. R. A. S., Vol. X., n. s. 1878, p. 196, Note 1.

† *Voyages d'Ibn Batoutah* par Defrémery et Sanguinetti, IV., 111, 112, (2° tir.) Paris, 1879; Gray, J. R. A. S., Vol. X, n. s. 1878, p. 196, Note 1.

‡ Gray, Translating from *Voyages d'Ibn Batoutah* par Def. et Sang., IV., 455.

(b.) M. *furhi, fujja, fuḷu, foḷu*, and *koḷu ;* S. *piṭiya*, පිටිය ; T. *paṭṭaṇam*, பட்டணம், *paḷḷi*, பள்ளி; Sans. *pattana, palli ;* but cf. Malay *pulo*, 'islet.'

(c.) M. *faru, varu, hura ;* S. *pura*, පුර ; T. *puram*, புரம், *chéri*, சேரி, *úr*, ஊர் ; Sans. *pura*. But with M. *varu* cf. also Sans. *vára*, 'multitude,' and *váṭa* 'enclosure,' 'district' (*e. g. Márwár*).

(d.) M. *maḍulu ;* S. *maṇḍalaya*, මණ්ඩලය ; T. *maṇḍalam*. மண்டலம்; Sans. *maṇḍala*.

(e.) M. *atoḷu ;* S. *ẹtuḷa*, ඇතුළ 'inside.'

(f.) M. *kaḍu*, 'channel,' 'sea' cf. (i) T. *kaḍi*, கடி 'to cut ;' (ii) T. '*kaḍal*, கடல், 'sea.'

If Pyrard is right, *Tiladummatí* is a hybrid ("commençant à la pointe du Nord, qui en est la teste, que les Portugais appellent à cause de ce *Cabexa des las ilhas*, et en langue Maldivoise *Tilla dou matis* en meme signification, c'est à dire la pointe d' enhaut"—p. 74) from Mal. *tala*, T. *talai*, தலை, 'head,' or T. *tolci*, தொலை, 'limit,' 'end,' and S. *dúva*, දූව, 'island,' + *matu-piṭa*, මතුපිට, 'above.' Compare *Taleimaṇṇár* (N. Province, Ceylon) ; but also *tala*, (Sans. Mar.) 'low ground.'

Miladummaḍulu and *Kaharidú* may be equally conglomerates :—*mila du(m)maḍulu* = T. *mullai*, முல்லை, + S. dúva, දූව, + S. T. maṇḍalaya, මණ්ඩලය, maṇḍalam, மண்டலம் ; *kahari* = T. *kárai*, காரை, + S. dúva, දූව. Cf. *Mullaitívu* (N.E. coast, Ceylon) and *Kárativu* (Amsterdam Island, N.W. coast, Ceylon).

Máḷosmaḍulu—perhaps = 'the country of the large *ḷos* (M.) tree.'

Fádiffoḷu (Ibn Batuta, '*Pálipour*,' Pyrard, '*Padypolo*')—compare *Pulas-ti-pura*, the modern *Polonnaruwa*, (Ceylon) and *Pudupaṭṭanam* (on the Malabar coast) the Ποδοκέρουρα of Ptolemy and Πουδοπάταυα, of Cosmas Indicopleustes (Caldwell, Dravid. Gram. 1875, p. 105.)

Mulaku—probably another form of *Máliku* (Minakaï) the *Mulkee* of the *Tohfat-al-Majâhidîn* (Ind. Ant. Vol. III., p. 213). Cf. Mar. *Mulúk* 'kingdom' *Mâlaka*, (Malacca), and *Maluka*, Port. *Maluca* (Moluccas).

Koḷumaḍulu—Cf. *Chola* (Sans.), *Chóṛa* (T.) or *Chôḷa* (Tel.)—*maṇḍala*, 'the country of the Chólas, Chóḷas, or Chóṛas, whence *Coromandel*.

It remains to notice that the natives customarily affix the term *atoḷu* only to the Atols *Mále, Ari, Nilandu, Felidu*, and *Mulaku*, shortening their final vowel, or even, as in *Mulakatoḷu*, altogether eliding it, and appear to use *maḍú* or *maḍulu* synonymously, as *Miladummaḍú* or *Miladummaḍulu*,—*Koḷumaḍú* or *Koḷumaḍulu*.

(2)

" The Muezzin's call doth shake the minaret :
'There is no god but God !—to prayer—lo ! God is great !' "

Ces quatre Moudins [*M. Mudimmu*] montent tous ensemble sur un bastiment de pierre fort haut élevé, qui est tout joignant le Mesquite [*M. Miskitu*]. Ils mettent les mains à leur oreilles, et ils crient par trois fois de toute leur force, d'une voix effroyable tous ensemble, ces paroles en langue Arabesque, *Alas Alas aquebar* [*Allah*—pronounced *Allāhŭ—akbar :* should be repeated *four* times] c'est à dire *grand Dieu :* et puis adjoustent quelque chose de Mahomet." (Pyrard, p. 98.)—See Stobbart, 'Islam,' 1876, p. 117.

(3)

HUVADU' (SUVÁDIVA) ATOL.—The following recent notes regarding the islands of *Viligili*, *Tenadú*, and *Hitadú*, in this Atol, made, at request, by the Captain of the S. S. "*Consett*" (wrecked on the Suvádiva reef, May 7th, 1880), are of interest :—

Huvadú (Suvádiva) Atol.

" The population of the three islands, which are small, is about 1,000. The inhabitants live within small *kraals*, each containing an indefinite number of huts. These huts are built of sticks, thatched and covered with *cadjans*, are low, and small (about 7 feet by 9). The natives were very obliging, kind, and friendly, did not seem ignorant, having books of their own languages [probably treatises on the *Kurán*], but were extremely inquisitive. Those who have been abroad to Calcutta, Ceylon, &c., can speak a little Hindústání, Arabic, and Siṇhalese. The supplies obtainable are dry fish, fish blood, fowls, eggs, cocoanuts, breadfruit, and jaggery. The manufactures consist of coir yarn and rope, finest fancy rush mats, fans, and tats. Trade is done mostly by barter, though cowries and Máldive copper coins are in circulation. Prices could not be ascertained, as provisions were obtained *gratis*, and were freely given.

" The island of *Viligili* is one of the most cleanly kept islands ever visited. The inhabitants are very industrious, civil, and obliging. The women are extremely shy and bolt like antelopes [*sic*] at the sight of Europeans. Their costume is pretty, and resembles that of Arab or Persian women. The morality is good. Children are taught to learn their own dialect from a young age. The men are noted for their power of *sástras* (magic), and the whole race is very superstitious. The climate is unhealthy for European constitutions. Fever and bowel complaints are the chief disorders prevalent, probably due to the brackish water. From India and Ceylon are imported

THE MÁLDIVES.

POLITICAL DIVISION.

Notes.

silk and cotton goods, rice and other grains, medicinal roots and drugs, and such luxuries as tea and sugar. It was noted that some men understood the intrinsic value of English money, and accepted it in exchange for goods."

(4)

" C'est le lieu où le Roy envoye en exil ceux qui luy ont dépleu, d'autant que c'est une isle fort éloignée de sa Cour, où les navires estrangers n'abordent jamais, et dont les habitans sont fort peu courtois, fort rudes et grossiers. (Pyrard, pp. 68-9.) Accordingly three of Laval's companions were deported to "*Souadou*" [*Huvadú*] to prevent concerted plans for escape (p. 69) ; and he further mentions (p. 176) that the Sultan's mother-in-law and her brother were mutilated ("ils eurent tous les poings coupez") and banished thither for high treason.

Suvádiva Atol was ever a favourite 'penal settlement.' Ibn Batuta (A.D. 1343-4) mentions the banishment to "the islands of *Souweïd*" of '*Abd-Allah* by his step-son, Sultan *Chihâb-ed-dín* [*Shiháb-ul-dín.*]* The present Sultan's grandfather (*Sulṭán Hassan Núr-ul-dín*) is also said to have been temporarily banished (1790 ?) to this Atol, and, on obtaining the throne, to have similarly retaliated upon the relations of the Sultan whom he succeeded.

See too Pyrard (p. 170) regarding the voluntary exile of two Máldive nobles (ultimately joint Sultans) who, "unwilling to submit to the Portuguese yoke," retired to Huvadú Atol, where the enemies never dared venture, and defied their arms.

(5)

Defence.

DEFENCE.—The question of the potential capabilities of the Máldive group, as of possible future service to the Imperial Government on military and commercial grounds, assumes the more interest at the present time from the recent official inspection of *Diego Garcia* (lat. 7° 26′ S., long. 72° 23′ E.), the principal island of the Chagos Archipelago (*Basses de Chagos*), lying above 400 miles directly South of the Máldives.

The surveyors' report has yet to be published ; but meanwhile the following extracts from the notice by the local press of the visit of H. M. "Eclipse" bear so closely on the above remarks, as to warrant insertion :—

......" The examination of the harbour itself and its shore showed that there was deep water throughout and most suitable localities for *coal depôts* as well as commanding positions for the erection of one or more *batteries*.† It is of course natural that the Government in establishing a depôt of coal for the Navy would desire to have it protected from robbery, and no doubt private steam companies connected with the Australian lines, viâ the Red Sea, would likewise be glad to coal their steamers here, seeing that it is in the direct line to the South, instead of going out of their way for other coaling stations. *We believe it is understood that one battery and a small force of Artillery, with a company of Infantry, would amply suffice for all purposes of protection.*" —*Ceylon Times*, July 13, 1881.

" The opening of the Suez Canal and the consequent rapid development of steamer traffic between Great Britain and Australia has naturally directed attention to this group, lying, as it does, in the direct passage between the Red Sea and Australia, and the "Eclipse's" mission may be looked on as a harbinger of Diego Garcia becoming a large coaling station, and, consequently, obviating the necessity which at present exists for steamers to Australia proceeding directly out of their course to Point-de-Galle for coals. A lighthouse placed on Diego Garcia would be of great service to ships outward bound to India and Ceylon, and an important landmark for the correction of their chronometers, when making the South passage to the Persian Gulf and Red Sea during the prevalence of the South-West monsoon. The harbour of Diego Garcia is admirably adapted for a *coaling station*, being large, well protected from the prevalent winds, and uniformly deep, except at certain portions where coral reefs have arisen.......It seems quite impracticable to entertain the idea of making it a strongly fortified depôt, except at an enormous expense, as, although the harbour would admit of being strongly fortified, the extreme narrowness and length of the island would allow of its being attacked and taken in the rear by a hostile squadron, unless the whole of its coast line were defended by a succession of forts which would have to be erected at an enormous expense and heavily garrisoned.......The fact of a British man-of-war being sent to enquire into the feasibility of an almost unknown island being made into a large coaling depôt may be taken as an assurance that the Admiralty are becoming alive to *the necessity of establishing some large stores of coal, properly defended by fortifications, from whence we might draw a supply in war time*, instead of being to a large extent dependent, as in the case at present, on neutral States for our supplies."—*Ceylon Examiner*, July 8, 1881.

---

* *Voyages d'Ibn Batoutah* par Def. et Sang. IV., 131.

† Vide *ante* p. 4, Note (3).

IV.—HISTORICAL SKETCH.

1.—EARLY PERIOD.

"THE story of a people who have no history can only be gleaned from the records of strangers, who have settled among them, or by an examination of their own language."*

The early history of these Islands is buried in obscurity—the natural result of their complete isolation and comparative insignificance. Indeed, except for scant glimpses afforded by the accounts of a few casual travellers, whom accident has taken thither from time to time, the world, in this the latter half of the 19th century, knows little or nothing of the whole past history of the Máldives. The Máldivians themselves possess no known historical records of any antiquity,† and would seem to be utterly ignorant of their antecedents, beyond such vague and unreliable shreds of information as may have been handed down by tradition.

Origin of race.

It is difficult, perhaps impossible, to state with certainty the exact origin of the Máldivian race. There can, however, be little doubt that the whole group—including *Maliku (Minakai)*‡—was occupied either directly from Ceylon, or about the same time as this Island, by a people of A'ryan stock and language. This supposition is greatly supported by the known kinship between the Máldive and Siṇhalese languages.

Gradually, from contact and intercourse with strangers of the coasts of India—chiefly Malabar Mápiḷḷas—the influx of pure Arabs, and the occasional importation of African slaves, many characteristics of the original type have been modified. More particularly is this the case in the Northern Atols, which have necessarily been more exposed to foreign influence than those lying further South.

When colonised.

"'They' [the natives], says Pyrard (p. 78), 'hold that the Maldives were formerly peopled by the *Cingala*, for so the inhabitants of Ceylon are named; but I find that the Maldivans do not at all resemble the *Cingala*, who are black and ill-shapen.§ The former are well-shaped and proportioned, and differ but little from ourselves, except in their colour, which is olive. Yet it may be believed that the climate and lapse of time have rendered them more fair than were those who first colonised the islands' "‖ "Added to the fact," he continues, "that there is incorporated a large number of strangers from all parts, who have settled there, besides many of the natives of India *(Indiens)*, who have been wrecked from time to time, as we were, and who are constantly being cast away there and remain. On this account the inhabitants [of the islands stretching] from *Malé* and its vicinity up to the Northern limit prove to be more polished, courteous, and civilised."
"Again (p. 185): 'They say that the Maldives began to be inhabited only about 400 years ago [*circa* A. D. 1200], and that the first who came and peopled them were (as I have already said in passing) the *Cingalles* of the Island of Ceylon, which is not far distant, and were idolators, but have since changed their religion.' "‖

Mr. Gray seems right in conjecturing that "if the Siṇhalese were the first colonists, they were probably there as far back as the beginning of the Christian era, when Ceylon was a powerful monarchy." It can hardly have been much later than this period that *Eḷu* (the pure Siṇhalese) was the vernacular of Ceylon, unadulterated by Sanskrit and Páli infusions. And it is to this form of Sinhalese that the Máldive language approaches nearest. Indeed it may be preferable to assign to the original colonisation of the group a date synchronic with that of Ceylon itself (viz., several centuries before the Christian era) by a distinct isolated party of the same A'ryan adventurers, and to presume a subsequent direct immigration from this Island.¶

* Crawfurd, Dictionary of the E. Indian Islands, 1856, p. 17. † Note (1). ‡ Note (2).

§ Gray fancies that Pyrard could only have seen the *Tamiḷs* of Ceylon.—J. R. A. S. Vol. X. n. s., pp. 178, 183.

‖ Gray, J. R. A. S., Vol. X. n. s., p 177.

¶ According to the *Dípawaṇsa, Rája Ratnákara, &c.*, Ceylon bore the name '*O'jadípa*' during the time of Kakusanda, the first Buddha of the present *kalpa* or period, the commencement of which cannot be fixed for want of historical data. At the present day this Island is called by Máldivians "*Oḷudú-kara*" (cf. S. මුදු කර, *múdu kara*, and T. கரை, *karai*, 'sea-shore'.)

THE MÁLDIVES.

HISTORICAL SKETCH.

Early references to the Islands.

Among the general allusions to the islands lying off the coast of Ceylon by the early travellers and geographers whose writings have as yet become known to the world,* some at least may reasonably be taken to include the Máldives, though specific mention of these Islands scarcely once occurs. Nor is this surprising, in spite of their central position in the track of the trade with India carried on by the Greeks and Romans, and later by Persians and Arabs, considering the uncoveted nature of their products, their unfertile soil, and, above all, the dangers of navigation among the coral reefs—those mythical 'loadstone rocks,' the dread of Ceylon seas—added to the deadliness of the climate, all of which would combine to cause the Máldive and Lakkadive archipelagos to be carefully shunned.

Pappus.

In any case "the date given by Pyrard must be put back several centuries."† "*Pappus* of Alexandria (about end of the 4th century) says :—'It [Taprobanê] is one of the largest islands in the world, being 1,100 miles in length by 1,500 miles broad, and reckons 1,370 adjacent islands among its dependencies,'"‡—probably following *Ptolemy* (A.D. 160) who places before Ceylon a group of 1,378 islands (Geog. VII. c. iv. p. 213).

Scholasticus.

About the same time (*circa* A.D. 400) *Scholasticus* the Theban,§ who visited India in company with a priest and reached Muziris (Cranganore) on the Malabar coast, mentions the thousand islands, Maniolae (Μανιόλης), and the loadstone (μαγνῆτις) rocks which attract iron-bound vessels to their destruction. Lt.-Col. W. H. Sykes‖ and Sir E. Tennent¶ identify these islands with the Máldives, but Ptolemy, who limits their number to 10, throws them forward some degrees East of Ceylon (Geog. VII. c. ii. p. 21.)

Fah-Hian.

Fah-Hian (in Ceylon A.D. 412) records :—"On every side [of '*Sse-tseu-koue*'=*Siṃhala*] are small islands perhaps amounting to 100 in number. They are distant from one another 10 or 20 *li*, and as much as 200 *li*. All of them depend on the great island. Most of them produce precious stones and pearls"**—a description which, it must be admitted, applies more naturally to the islands closely skirting Ceylon, chiefly round the North coasts, than to the distant Máldives as supposed by Landresse†† and Tennent.

Kosmas.

Kosmas Indicopleustês (*circa* A.D. 535), on the information of Sopater who had visited Ceylon 30 years previously, says :—"Around it [Σελεδῖβα : Ταπροβάνη] there are a multitude of exceedingly small islets. All contain fresh water and cocoanut palms (ἀργέλλια ; Sans. *nárikela* ; Arabic, *nárghyl*). These islands lie as close as possible together."‡‡

The early political dependency of the Máldives on Ceylon may be doubted. It must at least have been merely nominal, unless it existed in those 'palmy days' of Hindú legend when *Ṣri-Laṅká-pura* (long. 75° 53′ 15″ E.)—the prehistoric capital of the kingdom of Laṅká—remained unsubmerged by the ocean which now rolls far to Eastward of its computed site.§§ It is otherwise difficult to account for the total silence of the chief

---

* Early Chinese historical literature particularly offers still a vast unexplored field of likely value.

† J. R. A. S. Vol. X. n. s. 1878, p. 178.

‡ Tennent, Ceylon, 1860, Vol. I., p. 571, note, quoting Moses Chorenensis, edit. Whiston, 1736, p. 367.

§ A contemporary of Palladius, Bishop of Helenopolis in Bithynia, and quoted in the tract "*De Moribus Brachmanorum*," and its Greek version "Περὶ τῶν τῆς Ἰνδίας ἐθνῶν καὶ τῶν Βραγμάνων;" *Pseudo Callisthenes*, edit. Müller, Lib. III. c. vi., vii.—Tennent, Ceylon, Vol. I., pp. 562-3.

‖ J. R. A. S. Vol. VI. o. s. 1841, p. 393.

¶ Tennent, Ceylon, Vol. I., p. 563, Note 2.

** Beal, Buddhist Pilgrims, p. 148, quoted by Gray, J. R. A. S. Vol. X. n. s., p 178. Five *li* (1643 *mètres*) are a little more than an English mile (1,069 *mètres*)—Stanislas Julien, "*Mémoires sur les Contrées Occidentales*," Tome II. p. 259.

†† *Foĕ-kouĕ-ki*, translated by Remusat, ed. by Klaproth and Landresse, Paris, 1836, English Trans. by J. W. Laidlay, Calcutta, 1848, p. 332.

‡‡ Tennent, Ceylon, Vol. I., p. 567.

§§ "[Eustathius], the scholiast of Dionysius, (translated) thus speaks :—'Others on the contrary have it, that Maldivia was originally one vast island, but that a resistless ocean burst in upon it far and wide, and formed a countless number of islets (νήσους ἀπειρέσιας)'"—Pridham, Ceylon, &c., 1849, Vol. I. p. 17; Forbes, Eleven Years in Ceylon, Vol. II. p. 259. See too *ante* p. 3, Note (1).

Siŋhalese historical books regarding these Islands.* Certainly at a later period among the territories claimed as subject to the Rájás of Ceylon the Máldives are not included ;† and even in the 4th century the "*Divi*"—probably 'the Islanders' of the Máldive (M. *Divehi mihun)* and Lakkadive groups—are distinguished from the "*Selendivi,*" or 'Ceylonese,' by Ammianus Marcellinus, in his account of the Indian embassy to the Emperor Julian (A. D. 361.)‡

2.—ARAB AND PERSIAN PERIOD.

Arab enterprise.

The spirit of enterprise and trade had led the Persians and Arabs to the far East very early in the Christian era. Within a few centuries were added the burning ardour of propagandists and the ambition of conquerors. "The enthusiasm inspired by Mahomet converted the Arabians into a nation of military apostles, whose successive conquests furnished a succession of armed proselytes sufficiently numerous to extend and confirm their empire, and at the same time to engross the entire commerce of Asia: their commercial navy was spread over the whole expanse of the Indian Ocean, and its shores were generally covered by their factories, and subject to their influence."§ In the islands that lie scattered in this Ocean their success was particularly rapid. "The want of commerce procured them the best reception both from Princes and their subjects. They soon rose to the highest dignities in these petty States, and became the arbiters of government. They took advantage of the superiority of their knowledge and the support they received from their country to establish a universal dominion. The despots and their vassals, in order to ingratiate themselves with them, abandoned a religion to which they had no great attachment, for new opinions which might procure them some advantages. This sacrifice cost them the less, as the preachers of the Koran made no scruple of admitting ancient superstitions into an alliance with those they wished to establish."‖

Their trading settlements.

The Muhammadans first made their influence felt in Southern India and Ceylon—if their traditions be held reliable, possibly as early even as the 8th century—by planting many trading emporia on the coast ¶ On Ceylon, Maṉṉár and "Mantotte" (Mántai)—as on the Malabar coast, Calicut—appear to have been the chief entrepôts of traffic for the Moorish merchants, who received from agents at various ports the produce of different parts of the East.**

Máldivians converted to Islám.

The Máldives, lying in the direct route to Malacca and China, must soon have shared their attention. Peaceable 'squatting' of "Moors" from all parts, in annually increasing numbers, countenanced by successive autochthonous Sovereigns, would be followed naturally by a gradual process of intermarriage with the natives, and smooth the way towards the firm establishment on the Islands of the faith and power of Islám.††

---

* No mention of the Máldive Islands occurs in the *Dípawaŋsa, Mahâwaŋsa, Thûpawaŋsa, Rája Ratnákara* or *Rájáwali*, nor, it is believed, in any of the older Siŋhalese poets.

† *E.g.*, titles of Rája Siŋha II. (1632-1687):—"Syn tytel was Raya Singa, Keyser van het Eyland Ceilon; Konink van Kandy, Zaitavaca, Cota, Lanbadaon, Amorayapore, Jaffanapatnam; Prince van Ove, Mature, Dinavaca, de Vier Provintien; Groot-Hartogh van de Seven Provintien; Grave van Cotiar, Batacalo, Vitana, Panoa, Putelaon, Bellingamma, Gale; Marquis van Duranura, Rotemira, Tinipana; Heer van de Havenen van Ceylon, den Peerl-visschery, en van de Gulde Sonne."—Wouter Schoutens, *Oost-Indische Voyagie*, Tweede Boek, 311, 3rd ed. Amsterdam, 1745. See also Dutch Records (Colombo) 17th century *passim.*

‡ Perinde timore ejus adventus ...... legationes undique solito ocius concurrebant...... nationibus Indicis certatim cum donis optimates mittentibus ante tempus *ab usque Divis et Serendivis* (XXII. L. 7, c. 10 §.)—J. R. A. S, Vol. XIX., o.s., 1862, p. 274.

§ Quarterly Review, Vol. VIII., 1812, p. 118.

‖ History of the Settlement and Trade of the Europeans in the East and West Indies, translated from the French of Abbé Raynal by J. Justamond, Vol. I., Book i., p. 49, London, 1776.

¶ See Tennent, Ceylon, Vol. I, p. 631.

** Sir A. Johnston, Transactions R. A. S., Vol. I., Art. 32.,* 1827.

†† "Inde *a seculo Hedschrae secundo* Arabes Musḷemi Indiam peragrarunt superiorem, mediam, et inferiorem, sedesque ibi fixerunt: et non solum libera mercatura, *sed etiam sacris, legibus, institutisque* patriis usi, mox in oris maritimis Indiae ingentem in numerum congregati sunt. Ipsi Indorum principes

From Ibn Batutá's narrative it is reasonable to deduce the approximate date of the Muhammadan conversion of at least the Northern Atols, including Málé, viz., about the beginning of the 13th, or close of the 12th century. Pyrard, indeed, writing *circá* A.D., 1611, records the native belief that "about 150 or 200 years at most [have elapsed] since they received Mahometanism through the Moors and Arabs, who, while trading over all the continent and islands of India, brought there also their law, which has since remained in most of those parts."* But, allowing for the slowest rate of progress southwards, the most distant group would not escape the "accursed and false doctrine of Mahomet," for so long a period as from two to two and-a-half centuries, *i.e.*, until A.D., 1400—1450.†

Influenced by Malabar States.

Everything points to a close connection at this time between the Máldives and the flourishing and powerful Muslim settlements on the Malabar coast, notably Cananore, not improbably resulting in a feudatory subjection of the Islands to that State during the course of the 14th and 15th centuries. At any rate their proximity and defencelessness could not fail to induce frequent incursions by the restless coast pirates, rendering the sway of the native Kings qualified and precarious. The commercial prosperity and political influence of the Moorish traders, which attained their highest degree in the 12th and 13th centuries, remained considerable until the end of the 15th century, at least, when they were destined to wane and finally disappear before the all-absorbing powers of the West, heralded by the Portuguese.

During this period notices of the Máldives occur in the accounts of a few Arab and Persian travellers.

Two Muhammadans.

In the travels of *The Two Muhammadans*‡ (9th century) allusion is made to the "many islands" [*Dybadjat*] lying between the seas of Herkend and *Delarosi*, which were then "governed by a Queen" and "all inhabited." The wealth of the inhabitants, who were "skilful in all workmanship," consisted in shells (*kaptage*), of which the treasury was full, whilst "ambergris in lumps of extraordinary bigness, as also in lesser pieces resembling plants torn up," was found in the surrounding seas.

Albyrúny.

Albyrúny (11th century) again calls the Islands "*Al Dybadjat*," alludes to their alleged gradual upheaval and disappearance, and divides them into two classes according to the nature of their chief products,—"*Dyrah-kouzah*," (Cowry Islands,) "from the cowries which are collected on cocoanut boughs placed in the sea," and "*Dyvah-kanbar*," (Coir Islands.)§

Ibn Batúta.

Ibn Batúta,‖ the Maghrabin traveller, crossed to the Máldives (*Dhîbat al Mahal*) from the continent of India about the commencement of A.D. 1343, and remained at Málé (*Makal*) 18 months. Connecting himself with the noblest families by marrying four wives, he rose into great consideration, had pressed upon him the office of Kázi (*Fandayarkâloû*), but ultimately deemed it prudent to leave in order to escape the jealousy of

---

haud pauci, Calecuti Samorinus, Reges Cambajae, Hinaur, Maabari, *et insularum Maldivarum Radscha*, Islamismum amplexi, Arabum leges et mores suis in terris divulgarunt ...... *Primo mercatum instituerunt singuli, mox propagando Islamismo operam navarunt denique rerum publicarum administratione potiti sunt.*" —Kosegarten, *De Mohammede Ebn Batuta*, p. 4, Jena, 1818.

* Gray, quoting Pyrard, p. 185.—J. R. A. S. Vol. X. n.s., 1878, p. 177.

† See Note to section V. on the "Date of the Muhammadan conversion."

‡ "As to the first of these Voyages ...... it appears clearly that it was written [by Sulieman, the Persian traveller] in the year of the Hegira 237 (A.D. 851). The latter, which is no more than a commentary or discourse upon the former, appears to have been the work of Abu Zeid [on the authority of Ibn Wahab, who travelled in A. H. 157 or A.D. 870] about the year of the Hegira 303 (A.D. 915)."—Pinkerton, "Voyages and Travels," Vol. VII., pp. 181-2; Gray, J. R. A. S. Vol. X. n.s., 1878, pp. 178-9, quoting Reinaud, "*Relation des Voyages faits par les Arabes, et les Persans dans l'Inde à la et Chine dans le* IX.e *Siècle*."

§ Reinaud, "*Fragments Arabes et Persans inédits relatifs à l'Inde antérieurement au* XI.e *Siècle*." Paris, 1845, pp. 93, 123-4.

‖ "Ibn Batouta," says Burckhardt ("Travels in Nubia," App. III., 534), "is perhaps the greatest land traveller who ever wrote his travels." His proper name was Abú 'Abd-Allah Muhammad. A native of Tangiers, he travelled for 30 years —*i.e.*, from the year 725 of the Hijra (A.D. 1324) to 755 (A.D. 1354). In the course of that period he several times traversed Egypt, Syria, Arabia, Persia, the coast of the Red

the Sultana's second husband, *'Abd-Allah,* who was also Chief Vizier. He describes in considerable detail the condition of the Islanders and their administration (which he honestly set himself to ameliorate), gives the quaint legend of their conversion to Islám, and specifies the export trade "to India, China, and Yemen" in dried fish *(koulb almâs)* cocoanuts, fabrics, cotton turbans, cowries *(wada'),* coir *(kanbar),* and even copper vessels. Cowries formed the currency.

Owing to failure of male issue, the eldest sister of the late Sultan had succeeded to the throne. A.D. 1343-4. "One of the marvels of the Máldives is that they have for their sovereign a woman, by name Khadîdjah [KHADI'JAH], daughter of the Sultan Djélâl eddîn 'Omar [JALÁL-UD-DI'N 'UMAR], son of the Sultan Salâh eddîn [SALÁH-UD-DI'N] Sâlih Albendjâly. The kingdom had at one time been possessed by her grandfather, then by her father, and, when the latter died, her brother Chihâb eddîn [SHAHÁB-UD-DI'N] became King. He was a minor, and the Vizier 'Abd-Allah, son of Mohammed Alhadhramy, espoused his mother and assumed authority over him .... When Chibâb eddîn attained full age he ousted his stepfather, 'Abd-Allah, and banished him to the islands of Souweïd. He was then left in sole possession, and chose as Vizier a freedman named 'Aly Calaky [? *'Alí-Kalége*] whom he deposed at the end of three years and banished to Souweïd."* To his scandalous profligacy Shahâb-ud-dín owed his own subsequent deposition, banishment "to the province of Hélédoutény" [? Haddummatí Atol], and violent death.

"There then remained of the royal family only the sisters of the deceased—Khadîdjah, who was the eldest, Miryam [*Maryam*], and Fathimah [*Fátimah*]. The natives raised to the throne Khadîdjah, who was married to their preacher, Djémâl eddîn [*Jamál-ud-dín*]. The latter became Vizier and Prime Minister, and promoted his son Mohammed to the office of preacher in his own stead; but orders were promulgated only in the name of Khadîdjah."† After the death of her first husband, the Sultana Khadíjah married 'Abd-Allah, who had been recalled from exile. The army of this queen consisted of about 1,000 men of foreign birth, though some of the soldiers were natives.

Between Ibn Batúta's visit and the advent in Eastern seas of the Portuguese—an interval of a century and a half—the history of the Máldives is as yet a blank page, with A.D. 1350–1500 *circa.* no 'foot-prints on the sands of time' to mark its course. Whatever tributary connection,

---

Sea, and the East coast of Africa. He then visited Bokhára, Samarkand, Balkh, Kábul, and Delhi, where he spent eight years. Separated from an embassy to China, he reached Cambay and Calicut, crossed to the Máldives, and thence to Ceylon, Southern India, and Bengal; passed the mountains of Tibet, and embarked for Java. After visiting China, he returned by Calicut, Yemen, Baghdád, and Damascus, to Cairo. Again he set out to perform the Hajj, and, returning to Tangiers, visited Spain, re-crossed to Morocco, and penetrated through the desert into the Soudan, whence he finally returned to Fez.

"*Mohammed Ebn Batuta* auctor nobis videtur fide omnino dignus; multa eorum quae notavit, mirifice congruunt cum iis quae viatores recentiores consignaverunt; quae non ipse spectavit, ea tanquam ab aliis sibi relata refert."—Kosegarten, *De M. Ebn Batuta,* p. 8, Jena, 1818.

* Gray, translating "*Voyages d'Ibn Batoutah*" par Def. et Sang., pp. 130–2.

† SALÁH-UD-DÍN may have succeeded Sultan "Dâoud" [DÁU'D] whose great-granddaughter was one of Ibn Batúta's wives whilst at Málé. Sultan DÁU'D was himself the grandson of Sultan "Ahmed Chénoûrâzah" [AHMAD SHANU'RÁZAH], the first royal convert on the Islands to Islám. (*Voyages d'Ibn Batoutah, p.* 154.) The genealogical succession would then be as follows :—

1. S. AHMAD SHANU'RÁZAH
2. S. ....
3. S. DÁU'D
4. S. SALÁH-UD-DI'N
5. S. JALÁL-UD-DI'N

6. S. SHAHÁB-UD-DI'N | 7. Sa. KHADI'JAH | *Maryam* | *Fátimah*

if any, may have existed with Cananore for some portion of this period, there would seem to be nothing at present to support the assertion of Barros,* that the Islands were involved in the vassalage to China, under which Ceylon was bound for 50 years between A.D. 1410 and 1460.

3.—PORTUGUESE PERIOD.

Before the arrival of the Portuguese the fusion on the Máldives between the natives and Musalmán settlers was probably complete. Muhammadanism was at any rate paramount throughout the group.

The Máldives must have been sighted by the Portuguese and fairly well known some years prior to the date of their discovery of the Islands usually accepted, viz., A.D. 1506–7.† Gaspar Correa relates how Vicent Sodré, Chief Captain of the Fleet, after the departure home of Vasco da Gama in 1502, captured four Máldive vessels *(gundras)* laden with coir, cowries, silk stuffs, and gold-woven cloths, which he sent to Cananore to be sold.‡

A.D. 1502.

A.D. 1506.

In 1506 Don Lorenzo d'Almeida was despatched by the Viceroy at Goa to the Máldives to intercept many ships from Pegu, Siam, and Bengal that used to pass through the Máldives to Mekka. The expedition consisted of two large ships, two *caravelas,* one *gale,* and a new *bargantim,* fully equipped and carrying 300 persons well armed. It left Cochin on August 1st, but, owing to treacherous currents, was carried to Ceylon.§ The Islands must, however, have been subjugated soon after, for Almeida appears to have restored the King of the Máldives in 1512–13, making him a vassal of Portugal.‖

A.D. 1512–3. Máldives tributary to Portugal.

Barbosa. (A.D. 1501–17.)

Duarte Barbosa, who sailed with Joao de Nova in 1501, and was out in the East till 1517, calls the Islands "*Palandura.*"¶ Ten or twelve were then inhabited by "light-coloured Moors" *(Mouros pardos)* of small stature.** The King, a Moor, resided at "*Mahaldiu*" and paid tribute "in coir rope and other products of the country" to some Moorish merchants at Cananore, by whom he was elected or removed at pleasure, and whose vessels he was forced to load with cargoes free of expense.

Barbosa mentions the "many kinds of dried fish" *(muyta moxama)* which the Islands provide—their export trade in cowries *(buzios pequenos)* to Cambay and Bengal, and tortoise shell *(alquama)* to Guzerat—the Island manufacture of cloths, of cotton, and of silk embroidered with gold, with "very fine head handkerchiefs"—and the existence of ambergris *(ambre)* "in large pieces" of two sorts *(ponambar, minambar).* The Islanders used no fire-arms and were timid, but very ingenious and great sorcerers *(grandes encantadores).*

A.D. 1517.

At this time Moorish vessels used to frequent the Máldives to avoid the Portuguese. In 1517 Don Juan de Silveira obtained permission from the Máldive King to erect a factory†† on the Islands. The King who then ruled had a rival who had a possession of some of the Islands, and also assumed the title of King. He was a wealthy Moor of Cambay, named "*Mamale,*" and lived at Cananore on friendly terms with the Portuguese.* Prior to 1510 this Mamale had held nearly the whole trade between Southern

* De Barros, *Asia, &c.,* Dec. III., Tom. iii., pt. ii., ch. i., p. 3, quoted by Tennent, Ceylon, Vol. II., p. 175. (Note.)

† In 1506 by Suarez, or, according to other accounts, in the following year by Lorenzo d'Almeida.

‡ Gaspar Correa, *Lendas,* Tom. I., cap. i., p. 341. The same year the Captain and crew of a Portuguese vessel, accidentally driven to the Islands, suffered much from bad water and over-indulgent living—Tom. I., cap. iii., p. 347.

§ *Idem,* Tom. I., pp. 643–4.

‖ *Indice Chronologico das Navigaçao & das Portuguezes (do secolo* xv.) p. 122. Lisboa, 1841.

¶ *Collecção de Noticias para a Historia e Geografia das Nações Ultramarinas,* Tom. II., p. 351–2. Lisboa, 1812.

** Barbosa (p. 351) evidently confuses the Lakkadive and Máldive groups:—"There is one Archipelago of Islands, which the Moors say are 12,000 in number ...... The first four are small and flat, called *Maldio,* and inhabited by Malabar Moors." See also Stanley's Barbosa (Hakluyt Society), p. 164. London, 1865.

†† Faria y Sousa, Translated by Stevens, Vol. I., p. 219. London, 1695.

India and the Máldives in his own hands upon an exclusive contract with the reigning King to exchange at settled prices the Island products and manufactures for rice, salt, and earthenware, in which they lacked. Mamale had his own agents *(feitors)* on the Islands and at Cananore, and supplied "all the coir for the use of India." From this Moor, Afonso de Alboquerque, second Viceroy at Goa, exacted, as a condition of his retaining the monopoly of the Máldive trade (the Portuguese excepted), an annual payment of 1,000 cords of coarse coir and 1,000 of fine coir, delivered at his own charges to the Portuguese at Cananore.† To counteract the influence of Mamale, the real Máldive King also sought the alliance of the Portuguese, and undertook to render them tribute on condition that they would compel Mamale to renounce his pretensions. Under pressure from Alboquerque Mamale yielded for a time, but soon, stung by the derision of his enemies, desired to regain his rights supported by the Portuguese. This disgusted the Máldive King exceedingly.‡ Mamale.

On the information given by Alboquerque to the Court of Portugal regarding these Islands, and the advantages to be derived from them, Lopo Soares, his successor in the Government of India, received orders from home to come to terms with the real King and to form a solid establishment in his kingdom. He had been instructed to promise all that was desired, and obtained what was wished.§

During this period the Máldives must have suffered considerably from the frequent descents not only of Malabar corsairs but of Portuguese cruisers carrying on a system of virtual piracy. Thus, in 1517, Dom Fernando de Monroys and Joao Gonçalves de Castello Branco, under the authority of the Viceroy Soares, proceeded to the Máldives to intercept Jeronyms de Sousa who was "playing the pirate" among the Islands, but, ignoring their mission, commenced filibustering on their own account. The following year‖ Joao Gomes Cheiradinheiro was also despatched to the Islands to build a fort and take command. After roving among the Atols and robbing according to his fancy, he landed at "*Mafacolou*," where the King resided, and strongly fortified himself. The exactions and conduct of the Portuguese garrison became so intolerable that the Máldivians invoked the aid of one of the powerful coast rovers, a Moor of Cochin named "*Patemarcar*," who sailed with 12 *paroas* and made a sudden attack on the Portuguese encampment. The defenders (including Gomes) were killed to a man, and their vessels looted.¶ A.D. 1518.

According to Barros, Simao Sodrè was sent, a few years later, by Vasco de Gama (3rd voyage, *circa* 1524) from Cochin to the Máldives to attack the Moors, who intercepted supplies for the fleet, chiefly coir rope.** A.D. 1524-5.

In 1525 Mamale, "the most honoured Moor in India"—"a titular King of the Máldives"—was chased by Vicent Sodrè with four vessels, captured, and put to death.††

Notices occur in the Portuguese historians of the continuance of this period of *quasi* legalised piratical expeditions proceeding to the Islands almost yearly;‡‡ and it is probable that the Portuguese retained their hold on them, unopposed by the Máldivians at least, until the middle of the 16th century, exacting, directly or indirectly, an annual tribute. A.D. 1526-8.

---

* Lafitau, *Histoire de Découvertes et Conquestes des Portugais dans le Nouveau-Monde*, Vol. I., p. 552. Paris, 1733.

† Gaspar Correa, *Lendas*, Tom. II., p. 129.

‡ Lafitau, *Découvertes et Conquestes des Portugais*, Vol. I., p. 552.

§ *Idem*, Vol. I., p. 522. ‖ Correa, *Lendas*, Tom. II., p. 508.

¶ *Idem*, p. 568; Faria y Souza, Translated by Stephens, Vol. I., pp. 225, 229.

** Stanley's *Three Voyages of Vasco da Gama* (Hakluyt Society), p. 404. In 1777 the "Nine-Degrees Channel" between the Lakkadives and Minakai was still known as "the channel of Mamala" *(canal de Mamale)*. See Stavorinus' *Voyages to the East Indies*, Vol. III., p. 280. (Wilcocke's Translation, London, 1798.)

†† Lafitau, *Découvertes et Conquestes des Portugais*, Vol. II., p. 54.

‡‡ *E. g.*, George Cabral (Correa, Tom. III., p. 79) and Martin Alphonso Insarte (Stephen's *Faria y Sousa*, Vol. I., p. 299) in 1526; Simao de Mello (Correa, Tom. III., p. 228) in 1528.

THE MÁLDIVES.

HISTORICAL SKETCH.

A.D. 1540-5.

On occasions they did not hesitate to assert their authority. In 1540 a Moor lord was seized, put in chains, and full penalty exacted for the murder at the Máldives of some Portuguese;* and five years later the offer of the title and privileges of 'Lord of the Máldives' was made to "*Pocoralle*," brother of Mamale, on certain conditions.†

Sultan Hasan. A.D. 1552.

Pyrard (pp. 169–174), on hearsay, carries back the history of the Islands some 50 years prior to his captivity. The King then ruling at the Máldives, named HASAN,‡ who was of pure and ancient race, finding his authority qualified by the influence of a near relative called 'ALÍ,‡ a rival to the throne—or as Laval rather thinks, "inspired of Heaven"—voluntarily abdicated, and crossing over secretly to Cochin with his wife and some of his suite embraced Christianity under the name of *Dom Manuel* after the reigning King of Portugal.§

Sultan 'Alí.

His rival was at once elected King by the Máldivians.

The ex-King, however, sent to demand his accustomed tribute, and to counsel his late subjects to become Christians. But they rejected alike his claims and his advice, replying that they "would die sooner than change their religion." Dom Manuel then sought and obtained the support of the Portuguese at Goa to enforce his asserted rights.

The first expedition of the Portuguese to the Islands was disastrous, resulting in the loss of a *galere*, three other vessels, and many lives; but the following year they returned with a larger force and better pilots, defeated the Máldivians, and put to death their brave King, who "preferred to fall fighting than basely fly."‖ Málé was occupied and fortified, whilst other Islands also felt the invader's sword.

Ultimately all the assembled chiefs were informed that the Portuguese had no wish to coerce them into a change of religion or ought else, but insisted on the payment of the ex-King's dues. A Máldive agent¶ with limited authority, appointed by the Portuguese, was to be stationed at Málé, and the trade of the Islands conducted exclusively with that nation.

A.D. 1563 *circa*.

For 10 years this Portuguese yoke was quietly borne. But meanwhile two brothers, MUHAMMAD BOḌU TAKURU** and HASAN KILÉGE,** though each but the humble *Katibu* of his own island, unable to brook the sway of 'the infidels,' had retired to the distant Huvadú (Suvádiva) Atol. Gradually strengthening themselves in their fortress of Gaṇ,†† they at length virtually held the Portuguese at Málé in a state of siege, and harassed them incessantly. This continued for eight years, when, with the aid of four pirate vessels from the coast ("*Corsaires Malabares*"), the brothers made a well-timed attack on Málé, carrying the fort by a night escalade and killing 300 of its defenders. This successful *coup* they crowned by the immediate rout of their quondam allies, and the recovery of their share of the booty.

Sultans Muhammad and Hasan.

The brothers then established themselves conjointly as "absolute Kings," marrying, respectively, the wife and daughter of the Sultan executed by the Portuguese—a politic step which tended to avert the animosity of nobles of higher birth.

A.D. 1566 *circa*.

Three years were spent by the Portuguese in repeated efforts to retrieve their fortune, but every expedition was repulsed.

---

* Correa, *Lendas*, Tom. IV., cap. xii, p. 152.

† *Idem*, Tom. IV., cap. xii.

‡ Pyrard.—"*Assan*," "*Haly*."

§ The exact date was A.D. 1552. See Note (3).

‖ 'Fleeing in battle before the face of an infidel' is classed among the 17 *Kabíra*, or "great" sins.—Hughes' "Notes on Muhammadism," p. 140, London, 1877.

"Who falls in battle 'gainst a Giaour
Is worthiest an immortal bower."

Paradise is guaranteed as the reward of those who fall fighting against 'idolaters' (*Kurán*, Sura, xlvii, 4–7).—Stobbart, "Islám." p. 155.

¶ The first "agent" was grandfather of the Sultan's wife of Pyrard's day.

** Pyrard.—"*Mohamed Bode ta couru*," "*Assan Quilague*." Tradition, according to Christopher, (Trans. Bombay Geog. Soc., 1836–8, p. 74) assigns the glory of the deliverance from the Portuguese thrall to a Tiladummatí chief.

†† Pyrard.—"*Game*." See *ante* pp. 15, 18.

At length, wearied with the protracted struggle and mutually desirous of peace, a treaty was concluded, by which independence was accorded the Máldivians under certain restrictions:—viz., a fixed annual tribute, as his sole claim on the Islands, payable at Cochin to the Christian ex-King, his heirs, and successors :* the Island Ruler to have in future an inferior designation (*e. g.*, Prince, Duke),—the title of "*Quilague*" [M. *Kilage-fánu*] being limited to two nobles bound to superintend the tribute payment jointly with the ex-King's own agent: and, lastly, trade to be conducted solely with the Portuguese unless by express permission.

"Notwithstanding this peace," sententiously remarks Pyrard half a century later, "the Máldivians bear the Portuguese deadly hatred."

The brothers continued to reign together for 25 years, though not without internal troubles fostered by fractious nobles of purer blood. Muhammad survived his younger brother three years, and was succeeded by his son IBRÁHI'M, the Sultan in whose reign occurred the wreck of the "Corbin." S. Ibráhím. A.D. 1591 *circa*.

"François Pyrard of Laval in Bas-Maine was one of a company of French adventurers, who, incited by the reports of great discoveries made and vast wealth gained by the mariners of other countries in the 16th century, equipped two vessels which left St. Malo in Normandy in the year 1601. Pyrard was on board the 'Corbin.' Both vessels rounded the Cape and left Madagascar in safety; but the 'Corbin,' piloted by an Englishman who had lost his bearings in the Indian Ocean, was wrecked on the Malosmadou Atoll [Málosmadulu Atol] of the Máldives on the 2nd July, 1602. The crew [about 40 in all] were taken captive, and the goods recovered from the wreck became, by the Máldive law [then in force], the property of the King. F. Pyrard.

"The subsequent history of the captives bears a strong resemblance to that of Knox's crew in Ceylon.†" So long as the Frenchmen were thought to have money they were compelled to buy provisions at so high a rate as to reduce them at length to great extremities. The Captain, with many others, died of sickness or starvation: two parties (of twelve and four persons) escaped at different times: whilst four more of the crew were executed for an abortive attempt. Laval and his three remaining companions were then interned in separate islands, but, subsequently reunited, shared a joint deliverance after five years' captivity. Captive at the Máldives. A.D. 1602–7.

"Pyrard, by learning the language and conducting himself discreetly, won, as Knox did, the favour of his guardians, and finally of the King; and in the same way was allowed to go from island to island for purposes of trade."† This indulgence, coupled with the reliance of foreign traders at Málé, rendered him "somewhat rich according to the notions of the country."‡

Of the social economy and customs of the Islanders, Pyrard has drawn a picture in detail exact and full—brightened throughout by touches striking and *bizarre*—which, in spite of the lapse of 2½ centuries, stands out still a fresh and faithful portrait of the Máldivians at this day. Neither in moral characteristics, nor—until very recently, and that but partially—in political administration, have they suffered change. Time has but softened down the blemishes of a petty Oriental despotism and obtrusive licentiousness into the hues of purer and more civilised *régime*. Pyrard's narrative.

In the month of February, 1607, Málé was startled by the sudden appearance in the offing of a powerful fleet of 16 sail ("*galiotes*") manned by Mukwas ("*Moucois*")§ which had been despatched with hostile intent by the "King of Bengal." A.D. 1607. Expedition of the "King of Bengal."

There was no thought of resistance. Every one strove to hurry off with such property as the emergency allowed and, thanks to their swift-sailing boats, most contrived to escape. The King, less fortunate, embarked at the last moment with his three wives on board his slower "*galeres*," and, the wind falling, was easily overtaken by the eight vessels the enemy detached in pursuit. The King and a few attendants were cut down, and the *galeres*, and afterwards the palace, looted.‖

---

* Note (3). † Gray, J. R. A. S., Vol. X., n. s., 1878, p. 174. ‡ Pyrard, p. 70.

§ Note (4). ‖ Pyrard, pp. 222–30.

Character of S. Ibráhím.

"His hour was come," says Pyrard (p. 226), "and he well deserved his fate for the great cruelties he had committed"—a fate which, even in death, (having fallen at the hand of Muslim foes,) denied him the honours due to a martyr (*Sháhid*—Pyrard, "*Chayde*"), consigning him a lowly grave in a distant isle (*Gurádú*) with the meanest of his subjects instead of a stately burial in his self-built mausoleum at Málé.* Sensual, heartless, and unscrupulous to a degrée, he yet possessed some redeeming qualities which command respect. Industrious and passionately fond of art in every branch, he encouraged, both by personal example and Court favour, the development of artistic taste in his kingdom. A disposition naturally ready, combined with keen sagacity, prompted him ever to grasp fresh knowledge likely to benefit his realm and people.†

After a short stay of ten days to load their vessels with the booty, including some five and twenty cannon, the fleet slowly returned to the Continent (after visiting the Northern Atols) carrying with them the four Frenchmen, as well as the step-brother and brother-in-law of the late Sultan.‡

Pyrard "underwent many further adventures and more captivity [in India], and it was not till 1611 that he once more set foot on the beloved soil of France."§

Ranna Badéri Takuru. A.D. 1608 *circa*.

Of what transpired at the Máldives after his deliverance, Laval heard at Goa (p. 231) that the four chief nobles disputed the succession, each fighting 'for his own hand' (Sultan Ibráhím having left neither children nor nephews to succeed him),‖ and that after this internecine war had lasted some time, 'Alí Rájá¶ of Cananore intervened, defeated the other aspirants, and by securing the kingdom for the late chief Queen's brother, RANNA BADÉRI TAKURU,¶ as his Vice-Regent, re-established peace.

A.D. 1610–1710.

For another century the veil that shrouds the history of the Islands can at present be lifted only at rare intervals, disclosing glimpses so meagre as but to tantalise from their faintness.

4.—DUTCH PERIOD.

No show of force was needed on the part of the Dutch in Ceylon to secure a recognition of their inherited suzerainty over the Máldives. With a wise discretion the Máldive Sultans, for at least two and a half centuries past, have voluntarily placed themselves under the protection of the dominant European power in this Island, and courted its alliance.

A.D. 1640.

It was worthy the mercenary spirit of the Dutch, that hardly had they obtained a footing in Ceylon, than they despatched a vessel to ascertain the nature and prospects of trade at the Islands.**

A.D. 1645.

Five years later occurs perhaps the first record of the annual Embassy from the Sultans to the Governors of Ceylon, which has been continued uninterruptedly to the present day.††

Wreck of the "Persia." A.D. 1658.

The first Englishmen (with the exception of the pilot of the "Corbin") to land on the Máldives were, as far as is known, the unfortunate Captain and crew of the merchantman "Persia," which sailed from England and was wrecked on the Atols in 1658.

All hands reached the shore in their boat, but as this was too small to allow of their crossing the sea in it, a vessel was purchased from the Islanders. Captain William Vassal and twelve others put to sea in their boat, accompanied by the vessel, and steered for Ceylon. They made land at Puttalam, but were at once seized, plundered, and "carried up before" Rájá Sinha II. at Kandy, where they shared the fate of Knox and the crew of the "Ann." Knox gives the names of all and some account of their treatment

---

* Pyrard, p. 230. † *Idem*, p. 159. ‡ *Idem*, 231–4.

§ Gray, J. R. A. S., Vol. X., n. s., 1878, p. 175.

‖ Pyrard adds: "*Et le royaume ne tombent jamais en quenouille, non plus qu'en France*"—a statement at least thrice refuted in the history of the Islands.

¶ Pyrard (pp. 231–2), "*Ali Rhadia*"; "*Rana Banduy Tacourou.*"

** Dutch Records (Summary of Resolutions of Council) Galle, Nov. 30th, 1640.

†† *Idem*, Galle, Dec. 21st, 1645.

and conduct. Two, Hugh Smart and Henry Man, came to a violent death.* In 1683, after 25 years' captivity, two others, Thomas Kirby and William Day, managed, with much difficulty, to reach the Dutch outpost at Sítáwaka and effect their escape,† as, four years previously, Knox and Rutland had safely traversed the forests separating Anurádhapura from Arippu on the N.W. Coast.‡ Vassal was still a prisoner at Kandy in 1696.§ The fate of the rest remains unknown.

Dutch survey of the Máldives. A.D. 1671.

Instructions were issued in 1671 by the Dutch Government in Ceylon for an accurate survey of the Lakkadive *(Baxos de Padua)* and Máldive *(Maldives)* groups, to better secure the navigation of "the Company's costly ships" to and from Persia and the Netherlands. Governor Rykloff Van Goens took advantage of the opportunity to send by the hands of the Surveyors a letter and presents to the Máldive Sultan, MUHAMMAD IBRÁHI'M, in courteous acknowledgment of his good treatment of some Dutch and native sailors, the crew of a Jaffna vessel wrecked in his dominions.‖

S. Muhammad Ibráhím.

A.D. 1688.

The Sultan in 1688 also bore the name MUHAMMAD IBRÁHI'M,—probably the same Ruler who was reigning seventeen years previously.¶

The local Dutch Records furnish a clue to the regular succession of the Sultans from 1711.

S. Muhammad 'Imád-ud-dín Muzaffar. A.D. 1711.

In that year Sultan MUHAMMAD 'IMÁD-UD-DI'N MUZAFFAR was on the throne, and it was marked at the Máldives by a sudden and unprovoked attack of some "enemy" (probably Malabar pirates) who withdrew unexpectedly within a month—'by the interposition of Providence,' writes the Sultan.**

S. Ibráhím Iskandar. A.D. 1721.

Muhammad 'Imád-ud-dín died in 1721, and was succeeded by his son IBRÁHI'M ISKANDAR,†† whose reign of 30 years is noteworthy from the close and friendly commercial connection established between himself and the Dutch. Sultan Ibráhím proved himself an enlightened, humane, and liberal ruler. He steadily encouraged intercourse with foreigners, removed obstacles to trade with his subjects, and won the confidence and regard of his powerful allies, the Dutch. English, French, and Portuguese vessels frequented Málé, whilst the Dutch sent over from Ceylon one or two vessels in several years to negotiate for cowries.‡‡

A.D. 1726. Wreck of the "Ravestein."

The survivors of the Dutch ship "Ravestein" wrecked among the Islands in May, 1726, with a valuable cargo of gold, received every attention at the hands of this Sultan, whose generous action throughout under most trying circumstances justly evoked the gratitude of the Dutch Governor at Colombo.§§

The same year a scare of impending war with Cananore was made the excuse for a small supply of cowries to the Dutch‖‖ who, alarmed at the possible cessation of this profitable source of revenue, lost no time in guaranteeing the Sultan assistance—significantly pointing out that the Cananore King in his wisdom knew better than to become the enemy of "the Company's friend."¶¶

---

* "An Historical Relation of the Island Ceylon in the East Indies, &c.," by Robert Knox, a captive there near Twenty years, Part IV., ch. iv., London, 1681.

† Dutch Records (Miscellaneous), Colombo.

‡ Knox, Ceylon, Part IV., ch. x., xi.

§ There is extant a letter in Portuguese from "*Gulielmo Vassall o Feitor Engles*" (Dutch translation dated March 21st, 1696) imploring the Dutch to obtain his release from captivity.

‖ Dutch Records (Resolutions of Council), Colombo, 1671.

¶ *Idem* (Miscellaneous), Colombo, 1688.

** Sultan's letter to Governor H. Becker, dated October 19th, 1711 (Dutch translation) :—"*Nu heeft God gementioneerd vyand weder van heer verdreven.*"

†† Sultan's letter to Governor T. A. Rumpf, dated October 26th, 1721.

‡‡ The Portuguese and French especially seem to have ingratiated themselves into the Sultan's favour, judging from the fact that some of the annual letters to the Dutch Governors in Ceylon are in those languages, viz.: —Portuguese, May 1st, 1723 ; May 9th, 1734 ; May 19th, 1735 : French, June, 1726.

§§ Note (5).

‖‖ Sultan's letter dated October 31st, 1726.

¶¶ Reply of Governor P. Vuyst, dated January 7th, 1727.

THE MÁLDIVES.

HISTORICAL SKETCH.

In October, 1733, a cyclone visited the group, devastating and laying under water many islands (particularly among the Northern Atols), and causing great loss of life and property. The Sultan, with Muslim resignation, accepted the disaster as "the will of God."*

A.D. 1750.

Sultan Ibráhím died in 1749, having previously installed his brother as his successor—his own son being still a minor and ineligible.†

S. Muhammad 'Imád-ud-dín Mukkarram.

The new Sultan assumed the title MUHAMMAD 'IMÁD-UD-DI'N MUKKARRAM. He did not long enjoy his honors.

In 1753 occurred perhaps the most stirring revolution that has ever marred the peaceful history of the Máldives.‡

A.D. 1753. Revolution at Málé.

Fadiáru Kalóge-fánu, the Prime Minister, dissatisfied with the Sultan's administration, and aided by a small faction, secretly entered into communication with 'Alí Rájá of Cananore with the avowed object of handing over the Islands to him. Armed vessels were to be sent to Málé under pretence of an Embassy, and suddenly seize the Island. The scheme succeeded fully. Three vessels with *lascarins* and munition of war were despatched from Cananore and anchored peacefully before Málé.§ The same night the gates of the Fort were treacherously thrown open by the Fadiáru's party. Before the Sultan, hastily roused from sleep, could collect together a handful of followers and oppose the invaders, the powder magazine and warehouses had been fired, and the town was in the hands of the enemy. Ultimately yielding to the advice of the Fadiáru (who still feigned loyalty) that resistance was useless, the Sultan, accompanied by his nephew, met the Mápillas to arrange terms of peace. Thereupon he was seized and taken on board the Cananore vessels, which sailed away at once.

Abduction of the Sultan.

His subsequent fate.

The misfortunes of the luckless Sultan did not end here. On the return of the victorious fleet to Mangalore 'Alí Rájá presented his captive, whose eyes he had cruelly put out, to Haidar 'Alí. That Prince "was so irritated at the barbarity of Ali Raja, that he instantly deprived him of the command of the fleet; which he afterwards gave to an Englishman named Stanet. Shocked at the inhumanity of Ali Raja, he entreated the King of the Maldives to forgive the outrage his Admiral had been guilty of, and after expressing how much he was afflicted at the event, and using every argument in his power to console him, he gave him one of his palaces for a retreat, with a revenue sufficient to procure all the pleasures his situation permitted him to enjoy."‖

Meanwhile, at the Máldives, the traitor Fadiáru soon had his reward. Immediately after the abduction of the Sultan, he claimed from 'Alí Rájá the vacant throne, but the Cananore Court, considering that equal harm would be likely to accrue to their garrison by admitting or rejecting the Fadiáru's claim, wisely avoided the dilemma by directing that he should be bound hand and foot, placed in a sack, and thrown into the sea. The order was promptly executed. The Mápillas then temporarily assumed the Government, but harassed the Máldivians to such an extent, that they shortly rose suddenly in the night and overpowered their oppressors. Houses were re-built, the Sultan's wives and suite allowed to cross the sea to him, and the Government carried on by the Ministers in his name. Warned by recent events, application was further made to the Dutch for a supply of ammunition on payment.

Mápillas ousted from Málé.

---

* "*Mas com tudu consollo com a vontade de Deos.*"—Sultan's letter (Portuguese) dated May 9th, 1734.

† Statement of *Ahmad Kévi* made at Galle April 11th, 1750.

‡ Letter to Dutch Governor from the Ministers of the abducted Sultan, 1753.

§ "Ali Raja having formed a fleet, at the commencement of the fair season made the conquest of the Maldive Islands, under the pretence of some in justice done to his nation...... This conquest was made in the name, and on the account of Hyder ['Alí], whose colours were borne by the fleet. Ali Raja had embarked on board a number of Sepoys, or disciplined soldiers; so that Hyder's colours had no sooner appeared at sea, but they enforced respect."—*The History of Hyder Shah, &c.*, by M. M. D. L. T., p. 97, London, 1784 (Reprint, Calcutta, 1848).

‖ *Idem*, p. 98. "The courtiers and poets of [Haidar's] court, little acquainted with Geography, having learned that their master was become King of 12,000 islands, added to his titles that of 'King of the Islands of the Sea.'"

It is curious that the same year (1753) which witnessed for the Máldivians the temporary deprivation of a Supreme Ruler, should usher in the era of their historical existence as a race. The letter from the Sultan's Ministers to the Ceylon Government, conveying details of the *bouleversement*, also intimated the extension by the Chief Government at Batavia of the privilege to fly a flag and pennons—a virtual recognition of the *quasi* independence of the Máldives.*

Dutch recognise Máldive flag. A.D. 1753.

The interregnum lasted six years, during which period the Government was administered by *Hasan Raṇṇa Baḍéri Maṇiku-fánu* on behalf of the absent Sultan, in the name—for two or three years at least—of his daughter A'MINÁ RAṆI KILAGE-FÁNU.†

Interregnum. A.D. 1753–1759. Sa. A'miná Raṇi Kilage-fánu and Hasan Raṇṇa Baḍéri Maṇiku-fánu.

The year succeeding the revolution a small detachment of French troops under a Corporal was dropped on the Máldives by the great Dupleix,‡ the opponent of Clive in the Carnatic, where hostilities were being actively carried on between the English and French.

No sooner had the French raised their flag on the Islands, than they found it necessary to send over to their Dutch allies at Colombo for supplies.§

French occupy Málé. A.D. 1754-9.

Dupleix was recalled soon after the conclusion of the Provisional Treaty of Peace in December, 1754 ; but the *corps-de-garde* at Málé was not relieved by M. de Lally, his successor, until 1759.‖ Some may have remained, as within two years of their arrival (1756) the interim ruler Hasan was reported to have 20 Frenchmen in his service.** The same year 'Alí Rájá of Cananore,¶ anxious to restore the blind Sultan to his subjects (presumably under pressure from Haidar 'Alí), wrote to Málé desiring that four persons should be sent over to India to act as escort.** He appears, however, never to have returned, and probably died shortly afterwards.

At any rate, in 1759 Hasan Raṇṇa Baḍéri had acquired sufficient popularity and influence to secure the Sultanship for himself. He took the name GHA'ZI' HASAN 'IZZ-UD-DI'N.††

S. Ghází Hasan 'Izz-ud-dín. A.D. 1759.

The following year the Islanders had to repel another raid of the Mápiḷḷas. The Malabar fleet, manned by 700 "*Turken*" seized the uninhabited island of Funadú, and commenced to bombard Málé. The Máldivians hastily equipping some vessels, attacked, and finally drove off the invaders, with the loss of five prisoners.‡‡

Mápiḷḷas attack Málé. A.D. 1760.

Sultan Ghází Hasan 'Izz-ud-dín died in February, 1767, during *Ramazán*, restoring the throne before his death to the former line, by appointing the son of Sultan Ibráhím his successor—his own children being minors.§§ The new Sultan, MUHAMMAD GHIYÁS-UD-DI'N, seems to have commenced his reign well. "He managed the affairs of the

S. Muhammad Ghiyás-ud-dín. A.D. 1767.

---

* Letter from the Ministers of the abducted Sultan, 1753. The Máldive flag as displayed on modern *gundras* is the ordinary plain Muslim *red*, rarely relieved by a white crescent.

† "Dat nooyt voor deezen hunne Eylanden gereegeerd is door een vrouw als zedert de wegvoering van de voorwart gementioneerd Koning" [S. Muhammad 'Imád-ud-dín Mukkarram].—Statement of *MuhammadKévi*, *'Alí Kévi*, and *Kásim Kévi*, made at Colombo, 18th November, 1756. *Vide ante*, pp. 24, 25, 30.

‡ "Dupleix was a vain, ambitious man, possessed of very considerable ability, and burning with desire to extend the French power in India. With all his vanity, however, he united profundity as a politician, while he was possessed of rare address in the management of Indian affairs. He saw clearly that on the one hand the existence of any other Europeans in India, and particularly of the English, would be perilous to his hopes; and on the other, that he never could succeed but through alliances with the native princes, and by simulating adhesion to the cause of some powerful chief."—Parliamentary Papers ('Nawanbs of the Carnatic') May, 1861. A remark of M. Sonnerat ("*Voyage aux Indes Orientales, &c.*," Tome II., 84, Paris, 1782) sufficiently explains Dupleix's occupation of Málé :—"Pour se soutenir dans cette riche contrée [l'Inde], il faut nécessairement un port à la côte de Malabar, d'où nos escades puissent observer en tout tems celles des ennemis : on sait que deux fois on n'a dû la perte de Pondichéry qu'à l'abandon des escadres qui quittèrent la côte de Coromandel pour revenir à l'île de France."

§ Note (6). ‖ Sonnerat, "*Voyage aux Indes Orientales, &c.*," Tome II., 97. ¶ Note (7).

** Said, however, to have been enlisted from successive private rice vessels, and certain to be dismissed should the exiled Sultan get his own again.—*Vide* † *supra*.

†† Sultan's letter dated 22nd day of *Ramazán*, A. H. 1174 (1760).

‡‡ Statement of *Tuládú Katibu* made at Colombo, November 17th, 1761.

§§ Sultan's letters, 1767.

THE MÁLDIVES. — HISTORICAL SKETCH.

Kingdom with strict uprightness and impartiality, to the contentment and prosperity of his subjects. Moreover, he rendered assistance and support to the wife and children of the late Sultan. For all these blessings we adore the Almighty God."* However, three brothers of the Sultan did not share in the general enthusiasm, for within a few months they conspired to dethrone him. The plot coming to light, they were banished to a neighbouring island, and subsequently persisting in their treasonable designs, to a distant Atol. Here they were followed secretly by their wives and children, who contrived to carry off much State property. The rebels then altogether disappeared, though the Dutch Governor was asked to arrest and hand them over to the Sultan's Ambassador, in case they reached Ceylon.†

A.D. 1771. It would appear that in 1771 the Máldivians were again threatened with an invasion by the Mápiḷḷas—ever their inveterate foes‡—and the Dutch assented, as an exceptional indulgence, to supply the Sultan with a mortar and ammunition on payment.§

A.D. 1772. In 1772 the Sultan found it necessary to arrest eight malcontents, who, however, managed to escape from Málé in a fishing boat.‖

It is perhaps not unreasonable to hazard the conjecture that the storm of revolt, which had never ceased to lower from the day of his accession—gathering strength year by year despite all precautions—culminated (1773–4) in the overthrow and death of Sultan Ghiyás-ud-dín, the last of his line.¶

S. Ghází Muhammad M'uizz-ud-dín. A.D. 1774. The silence preserved by the new Sultan, GHA'ZI' MUHAMMAD M'UIZZ-UD-DI'N, elder son of Sultan Ghází Hasan 'Izz-ud-dín, the founder of a rival dynasty,** touching the fate of his predecessor and the circumstances attending his own assumption of the Sovereignty, viewed in connection with a tradition related by Christopher, still vaguely current, is ominous of ill. "We were told," says Christopher, "that a Sultan, who reigned about one hundred years ago, rendered himself obnoxious to the people by ridiculing their religion. He, however, undertook a voyage to the Red Sea on a pilgrimage to Mecca, and during his absence a nobleman, named Faruna Kalegefana [*Fáruná Kilagefánu*], who was a leader of the popular party, and had gained great influence, determined with others to prevent the resumption of the Sultanship by the absent prince by putting him to death, if he should return. Return he did; but before he could land the plot against his life was carried into execution. Some of the conspirators, without divulging their purpose, pushed off in a boat, under pretence of bringing the Sultan on shore. He entered their boat, and while returning they bound him hands and feet, and fastening stones to his feet, threw him overboard.

"On landing they announced the accomplishment of their purpose, and being now joined by the rest of their party, proclaimed their leader Faruna successor to the murdered prince, by the name of Sultan Mahomed Nooradeen. On his elevation he banished to Suadiva Attol the son of the man whose place he filled, but after a few months he himself was obliged to quit the station to which he had waded through crime, and to abdicate in favour of a Prince of the royal blood, in consequence of the people not wishing to have on the throne one who was not descended from the family which had so long commanded their homage and allegiance. The son of the Sultan who was murdered by drowning, and his offspring, lived nearly independent in the Southern Attols until the year 1831. Some of his decendants are still alive [1836–8], and are permitted to visit Málé."*

---

* Sultan's letter, 1767. A free translation of the Arabic. † *Idem.*

‡ Sultan's letter, 1771. (Dutch translation, dated August 27th, Colombo.)

§ Reply of Governor I. W. Falck, dated December 30th, 1771:—"Of schoon wy geen handel mogen dyven in ammunetsie van oorlog heb ik echter aan Uwer Hoogheids afgezant een mortier met de daer toe nodige bommen aengeboden; maer hy heeft zwarigheid gemaekt hetzelve om den hoogen prys aen te neemen."

‖ Sultan's letter dated September 25th, 1772.

¶ Last letters of S. Ghází Muhammad Ghiyás-ud-dín, dated 4th November, 1773 (Colombo); November 20th, 1773, (Galle).

** First letter of S. Ghází Muhammad M'uizz-ud-dín, dated November 2nd, 1774 (Colombo).

†† Trans. Bombay, Geog. Soc., 1836–8 (Reprint 1844) p. 73. See Note (8).

Whether or not the unexplained disappearance from history of Sultan Ghiyás-ud-dín be connected with the tragic event above related, it seems certain that in 1774 the throne passed finally to the descendants of Hasan Ranna Badéri (Sultan Ghází Hasan 'Izz-ud-dín), with whom it has rested to this day.

A.D. 1777.

A French vessel with some ladies was cast away on the Island of Himiti in 1777, and all on board met with the kindest treatment from the Sultan.*

S. Hasan Núr-ud-dín. A.D. 1779.

Sultan Ghází Muhammad M'uizz-ud-dín reigned from 1774 till his death on October 2nd, 1779, and was succeeded by his younger brother, HASAN NU'R-UD-DI'N.†

During the reign of Sultan Núr-ud-dín another French (or English) vessel, containing specie, was wrecked among the Máldives. When the crew had got all the dollars they could from the vessel's hold, into which the rock had worked, they were provided with a passage to the Continent. One man remained, however, from choice, turned Musalmán, married at Málé, and died in 1830 or 1831‡ after 40 years' residence on the group. After the departure of the French the natives appear to have continued the search for dollars with success, for it is said that with the plunder obtained from this vessel Sultan Núr-ud-dín made the pilgrimage to Mekka, where he died.

S. Muhammad M'uín-ud-dín. A.D. 1799.

His son, MUHAMMAD M'UI'N-UD-DI'N, succeeded him in 1799.

5.—ENGLISH PERIOD.

Upon the acquisition of Ceylon by the English in 1796 the inheritance of the suzerainty over the Máldives fell to them unsought, as it had to the Dutch, by the free-will of the Sultan. In the letter of 1798 to the English Governor (Sir F. North) the Sultan, Hasan Núr-ud-dín, expresses himself as follows :—

Máldives feudatory to the English.

"I inform you that I always lived in great friendship with the former Governors, and that they have always shown me many favours. I hope that the same will take place between us."§ To which Sir F. North replied :—"[The Ambassador] will inform Your Highness how sincerely I wish to preserve the good understanding and harmony, which so happily subsists between us."‖ Thus quietly was the feudatory connection with the English established, which has remained unchanged for upwards of a century.

Wreck of the "Tranquebar." A.D. 1797.

It is unfortunate for the character of Sultan Núr-ud-dín that another case of alleged improper treatment of a wreck occurred during his reign. In January, 1797, the "Tranquebar" (Messrs. Fisher and Overend), laden with cloth to the value of 12,898 star pagodas, was wrecked on the Máldives under circumstances, *primâ facie,* little to the credit of the natives. At the request of the Madras Government, Sir F. North called upon the reigning Sultan (Muhammad M'uín-ud-dín) in 1800 for an explanation. The Sultan's "friendly explanation of the case," however, "perfectly satisfied" the Governments of Fort St. George and Ceylon.¶

Wreck of the "Europa." A.D. 1812.

The conduct of the Máldivians in the case of the "Europa,"†† which occurred a few years subsequently, stands out in a far different light. This vessel foundered among the Atols in 1812, and the account of the outrageous proceedings of the Captain and crew,—particularly during their stay at Málé,—are a disgrace to the English name. It is impossible not to be struck by the forbearance exercised by the Sultan and his people under great provocation. Nothing but absolute necessity for the preservation of order in the capital, would have led to the incarceration of an Englishman, one of their powerful and respected

* Malte Brun's Geography, Vol. III., p. 252. Perhaps identical with the "Duras" of which Sonnerat (Vol. II., p 98) says : "Des débris du vaisseau le *Duras,* qui se perdit, sur une de ces îles en 1776, le Roi de l'Archipel vient d'en faire contruire un de deux cents tonneaux, qu'il expédie toutes les années pour les côtes de Coromandel et d'Orixa."

† Sultan's letter dated November 10th, 1779.

‡ Leaving an only daughter who was married in 1835. Trans. Bombay Geog. Soc. 1836–8 (Reprint, 1844) p. 65. Asiatic Journal, Vol. xix. n. s. (1836) p. 190.

§ Sultan's letter dated October 21st, 1798 (English translation)

‖ Governor Sir F. North's reply, dated December 26, 1798.

¶ Appendix B.

†† Note (9).

THE MÁLDIVES.

HISTORICAL SKETCH.

allies. Governor Sir R. Brownrigg considered it necessary to bring the matter to the notice of the Governor-General of India, Lord Minto, and the Sultan received cordial letters of acknowledgment from both Governments.

Threatened rupture with the Lakkadivians. A.D. 1828.

In 1828 the Máldivians "seemed likely to be involved in distress in consequence of the hostile disposition of their Northern neighbours, the Lakkadivians," and appealed to the Ceylon Government for aid. Sir R. Brownrigg undertook to refer the matter to the Madras Government, as the Bíbí of Cananore (under whose rule the Lakkadives* had been for centuries) was subject to the English at Fort St. George.† The matter must have quietly dropped, as there is no record of further steps.

English survey of the Máldives. A.D. 1834–6.

A survey of the Máldive Archipelago, lying in the direct track of our trade to India, had been for many years considered of the greatest importance to navigation in these seas. "Mr. Horsburgh, in particular, exerted himself to obtain this object for the interests of Geography; and through his instrumentality chiefly a survey was directed.

"Accordingly, the survey of the Red Sea having been completed in April, 1834, Captain Moresby was ordered to proceed in the H. C. Surveying Ship 'Benares,' having under him as tenders the 'Royal Tiger' schooner, in charge of Lieutenant F. T. Powell, Assistant Surveyor, and the 'Maldiva,' a large decked boat." Captain Moresby, at the request of the Bombay Government, received a special letter of introduction to the Sultan from the Government of Ceylon, clearly setting forth the object of his mission.‡

"The 'Benares' arrived at Malé on the 15th November, 1834, but her appearance excited among the natives such apprehensions as augured ill for any friendly intercourse."

Natural timidity of character and recent political circumstances combined to induce this feeling.

Ahmad Dídí.

"The tyrannies of the reigning Sultan and the misconduct of his Ministers had, two years previously, provoked a rebellion, headed by his younger brother, Hamed Didee [*Ahmad Didi.*]" An appeal was made by the Sultan for aid against his revolted subjects, but the Ceylon Government, strictly adhering to the law of nations as regards non-intervention in the internal affairs of foreign states, simply regretted the occurrence, and trusted that the rebels would return to their allegiance.‡

"The insurgents were successful; secured the person and threatened the life of their Sovereign, who procured his safety and release by promising to satisfy their demands. Hamed, nevertheless, dared not trust himself to the royal word, but embarked by night on board a large boat, and steered for the coast of Arabia; but in the Gulf of Aden his provisions had failed, his boat was leaky and so damaged, that there was little probability of escaping death either from famine or in the sea. In this distress the H. C. Surveying Brig 'Palinurus,' Commander Haines, came in sight, and supplied them with provisions as well as repaired their damages. Hamed was now enabled to reach Mocha and eventually Cochin, where he continued watching the course of events at home, and where he was supposed to be meditating the execution of a threat he had made before leaving his country, that he would revenge himself by a Malabar invasion, the horrors of which had been felt in former days by the Maldivians. Captain Moresby was naturally supposed to be the minister of Hamed's vengeance; and as soon as the 'Benares' anchored, a boat was sent off to demand the cause of coming. Their uneasiness was not removed by a request to survey.

"The suspicious nature of Captain Moresby's avowed object now co-operated with political circumstances upon minds whose characteristic trait is fearfulness.

"An interview with the Sultan being proposed, his Ministers came on board with unusual state, and apologised for delay, on account of their master's ill-health; but were very careful not to commit themselves by answering the questions put to them. Nothing could be obtained from them for many days. At length, the Sultan's health being improved, an interview was settled, but the appointed day being arrived, the Sultan nad a

---

* Note (10).

† Reply of Governor Sir E. Barnes (dated December 8th, 1828) to Sultan's letter of A. H. 1244.

‡ Governor Sir R. W. Horton's letters, dated October 31st, 1834.

relapse. Captain Moresby was compelled, ultimately, to inform them that he should commence the survey on a certain day with, or without, their consent; and operations commenced on that day without permission. The 'Benares' having quitted the Islands for the Coast, the Maldivians were again alarmed by a letter from the Bengal Government regarding the establishment of a coal depôt." The Sultan excused himself from acceding to the proposal on the grounds of indifferent anchorage and the bad disposition of his subjects.* "After the return of the 'Benares' the natives appeared more easy, although by no means free from apprehensions; for they objected to the surveying flags, and were not satisfied until they were permitted to set up their own also.

S. Muhammad 'Imád-ud-dín. A.D. 1835.

"The obstacles in the way of friendly intercourse were eventually removed by events consequent on the death of the Sultan [Muhammad M'uín-ud-dín] in January, 1835, and the accession of his second son [at the age of 17, under the title of MUHAMMAD 'IMÁD-UD-DÍ'N]. The distresses of the people were increasing, and the public voice demanded the recall of Hamed Didee. The young King accordingly invited his uncle to his Councils, and he became the most influential adviser, although he declined any official situation. He took advantage of his position to pay a debt of gratitude by supporting the wishes of the Company in effecting the survey. He represented to his countrymen the folly of opposing a Government which was so powerful, and from whose dominions they derived their staple food: on the other hand, he endeavoured to remove any bad impressions which the conduct of his countrymen might have given: and, lastly, he obtained permission for Lieutenant Young and Mr. Christopher to remain at Male after the departure of the 'Benares.'

Ahmad Dídí's influence.

"The importance of these services may be appreciated by considering the character of [the natives], and the popular belief in future events, whose close approach is indicated to them by circumstances which they observe. They have a tradition that they shall one day be subjugated to Europeans, the population shall diminish, and their Islands shall gradually sink down into the deep."†

Ahmad Dídí, endowed with larger and more enlightened views than his countrymen generally, remained steadfast in his predilection for the English, and continued to exercise at Málé a beneficial control in political affairs for several years, as adviser to his nephew the Sultan. His position, and the friendly services he had rendered, enabled him to correspond directly with the Ceylon Government, from whom he solicited and obtained personal indulgences which would hardly be extended now-a-days.‡

'Alí Dídí.

Much of his ability was inherited by his son 'Alí Dídí (recommended by the Sultan in 1850 to the notice of Lord Torrington),§ who became a domiciled Ceylon subject, and resided at Galle until his death, a few years ago.‖ Through keeping up his commercial intercourse with the Islands, he acquired considerable wealth. It is said, however, that some private misunderstanding with the Sultan had estranged the cousins for some years.

Wreck of the "Prazer e Alegria." A.D. 1844.

In March, 1844, the Portuguese Merchantman "Prazer e Alegria," bound from Lisbon to Goa with a large body of convicts, was totally wrecked on the Máldives. The tax on the resources of his little Island, caused by the sudden influx of 104 Europeans, must have been great, but the strangers were "kindly received" by the Sultan "and provided with houses and such food as could be had in the country."¶ Ultimately, 93 sailed for Goa in two hired vessels, whilst the rest (including Manoel G. Quinhones, Major and Governor of Bahia de Lorenso Marques) were conveyed in a native brig to Galle, and after a short stay in Colombo supplied with funds to reach Goa.

Wreck of the "St. Clare." A.D. 1851.

The Bombay Government, in 1851, forwarded to Sir Charles MacCarthy a complaint made by the Captain of the "St. Clare," wrecked on the Islands, regarding the alleged

* Asiatic Journal, Vol. VI. n. s. (1835) p. 22.

† Trans. Bombay Geo. Soc., 1836-8 (Reprint 1844) pp. 103-5.

‡ *Vide* Ahmad Dídí's letters of A. H. 1256-7, and replies of Governor Sir J. A. Stewart Mackenzie, dated December 16th, 1840, and December 1st, 1841.

§ Sultan's letter of August, 1850; Lord Torrington's reply dated October 4th, 1850.

‖ His son Hájí Ibráhím Dídí, now Turkish Consul, has just been honoured by a commission as Justice of the Peace. (*Ceylon Government Gazette*, April 21st, 1882.)

¶ Statement of Major Manoel G. Quinhones made at Galle, April 16th, 1844.

THE MÁLDIVES.

HISTORICAL SKETCH.

want of hospitality shown by the Sultan towards himself and the crew during their stay at Málé. The Sultan received a strong letter of remonstrance from Ceylon, but in his reply completely vindicated himself from the charges laid against him.*

Among recent wrecks on the Máldives, the most disastrous have been the S. S. "Aracan" in 1873, the S.S. "Sea Gull" in 1879, and the S.S. "Consett" the following year.

Sultan 'Imád-ud-dín, whose reign has lasted 46 years, is said to be in feeble health, and rarely, if ever, appears in public. For the last ten or twelve years the Government has been administered by his second son *Tuttu Manipul* or *Góma*, the Prince Regent, who is in all respects, except in title, *de facto* Sultan of the Islands. Frank and open in look and manner, he has acquired much popularity, and, as far as can be judged from outward appearances, is not averse to foreign improvements and the gradual introduction of European civilization.†

Annual Embassy.

The *Annual Embassy* from the Sultan of the Máldives to the Governor of Ceylon arrives at Colombo generally in the course of the last three months of the year.

During the Dutch occupation—and even as recently as 1844—a complimentary letter was sent annually to the Commandant at Galle, as well as to the Governor at Colombo—a striking instance of the conservatism and ignorance of events outside "their own little world" displayed by these Islanders, loath to break through a custom initiated at least as early as the Embassy in 1645 to Galle, then the chief seat of the Dutch Power in Ceylon.

There is rarely anything, save his superior rank, to distinguish the Ambassador from the ordinary Captains of the Máldive fleet.

Ceremonies at landing and reception.

The proceedings connected with the reception still retain much of the formality observed under the Dutch. On landing, the Ambassador is indulged with a non-commissioned officer's guard (furnished by the Police), and met at the jetty by a few specially deputed native headmen, under whose escort, preceded by the Mahá Mudaliyár's *lascarin* guard and native music, he makes his way slowly on foot to the audience with the Governor. Máldivian etiquette requires the Ambassador to bear with both hands on his head the silver salver containing his Sovereign's letter (in a double envelope of coloured silk and spangled muslin) and two tiny silk bags of ambergris and sea-cocoanut. The conference, conducted standing and through the medium of the Tamil and Moor Interpreters, is made as brief as possible.‡ Meanwhile "the Royal presents" are carried to Government House by Máldivian sailors.§

Purport of Sultan's annual letter.

The Sultan's annual missive (now written in Arabic) contains ordinarily a request for the continuance of friendship and favour of the English, for protection against all enemies, and for aid towards Máldive subjects who may be wrecked on Ceylon shores, and concludes with an apology for his Ambassador, and the tender of presents.|| These letters cling so closely to a stereotyped form, as hardly to differ during the course of nearly two centuries.

Governor's reply.

The same may be said of the replies, at least during the present century. The Governor promises to do everything in his power to promote the good understanding which subsists with the Sultan: undertakes to succour shipwrecked Máldivians, whilst stipulating for the same friendly office on the part of the Sultan towards British subjects wrecked on the Atols :* expresses his approbation of the conduct of the Ambassador : and offers return presents.

---

* Appendix B.

† As these pages are passing through the press news has reached Ceylon of the death of the aged Sultan on Tuesday, January 10th, 1882 (20th *Safar*, A. H. 1299). The ceremonies attendant on the installation of his younger son as Sultan, are deferred some months, according to custom. The elder son, *Dorhi Manipul*, is said to be a confirmed invalid.

‡ The Dutch Governors and Galle Commandants permitted the Ambassador to sit throughout the interview, and at its conclusion he was sprinkled with rose water, and offered betel—a delicate attention seemingly paid to all Ambassadors (*e. g.*, the Kandyan Embassy of August 3rd, 1705).

§ As illustrating the spread of Western conventionalism even to the Máldives, it is worthy of note that the last Ambassador, Ismá'íl Dídí—for many years a resident with his late uncle 'Alí Dídí at Galle, where he acquired a knowledge of Sinhalese, Tamil, and some English—discarded at the audience (March 9th, 1882) the turban, loose robe, and sandals of his country, for a fez, closely-fitting frogged uniform of grey tweed, and patent-leather shoes.

|| Note (15).

TABLE

OF THE

DUTCH AND ENGLISH GOVERNORS OF CEYLON, AND THE CONTEMPORARY RA'JA'S OF KANDY AND SULTANS OF THE MA'LDIVES, FROM THE 17TH CENTURY.

A.D.	Dutch Governors at Colombo.	Rájás of Kandy.	Sultans of the Máldive Islands.
1604	- - -	Senerat. - - -	Ibráhím.
1632	- - -	Şrí Rája Siṇha II.	
1656	A. Van der Meyden.		
1663	Rycklof Van Goens.		
,,	J. Hustar.		
1664	R. Van Goens.		
1671	- - -	- - -	Muhammad Ibráhím.
1680	Laurens Van Pyl.		
1687	- - -	Vimala Dharma Súriya II.	
1688	- - -	- - -	Muhammad Ibráhím.
1693	T. Van Rhee.		
1695	Paulus De Roo.		
1697	Gerrit De Heere.		
1702	N. Van Heuvel and Members of Council.		
1703	C. J. Simons.		
1707	H. Becker. - - -	Şrí Víra Parákrama Naréndra Siṇha.	
1711	- - -	- - -	Muhammad 'Imád-ud-dín Muzaffar.
1716	I. A. Rumpf.		
1721	- - -	- - -	Ibráhím Iskandar.
1723	A. Moll & Members of Council		
1724	J. Hertenberg.		
1725	J. P. Schaghen and Members of Council.		
1726	P. Vuyst.		
1729	S. Versluys.		
1732	G. Woutersz and Members of Council.		
,,	J. C. Pielat.		
1734	D. Van Domburgh.		
1736	J. Macare and Members of Council.		
,,	G. W. Van Imhoff.		
1739	- - -	Şrí Vijaya Rája Siṇha.	
1740	W. M. Bruynink.		
1742	D. Overbeck.		
1743	J. V. S. Van Gollenesse.		
1747	- - -	Kírti Şrí Rája Siṇha.	
1749	- - -	- - -	Muhammad 'Imád-ud-dín Mukkarram.
1751	G. J. Vreelandt.		
1752	J. De Jong and Members of Council.		
,,	J. G. Loten.		
1753	- - -	- - -	Ministers of Sultan.
1754	- - -	- - -	A'miná Raṇi Kilage-fánu. Hasan Raṇṇa Baḍéri Maniku-fánu.
1757	J. Schreuder.		
1759	- - -	- - -	Ghází-Hasan 'Izz-ud-dín.
1762	L. J. Van Eck.		
1765	A. Mooyaart and Members of Council.		
,,	I. W. Falck.		
1767	- - -	- - -	Muhammad Ghiyás-ud-dín
1774	- - -	- - -	Ghází Muhammad M'uizz-ud-dín.
1779	- - -	- - -	Hasan Núr-ud-dín.
1781	- - -	Rájádhi Rája Siṇha.	
1785	W. J. Van de Graaf.		
1794	J. G. Van Angelbeck.		

(continued over)

THE MÁLDIVES.

HISTORICAL SKETCH.

A.D.	ENGLISH GOVERNORS.	RÁJÁS OF KANDY.	SULTANS OF THE MÁLDIVE ISLANDS.
1796	Governor of Madras in Council		
1798	Sir F. North- - - - - - -	Şrí Vikrama Rája Sinha.*	
1799	- - - - - - - - - - -	- - - - - - - - - - -	Muhammad M'uín-ud-dín.
1805	Sir T. Maitland.		
1811	Maj.-Genl. J. Wilson, *lt.-gov.*		
1812	Sir R. Brownrigg.		
1820	Sir E. Barnes.	—	
1822	Sir E. Paget.	—	
,,	Sir J. Campbell, *lt.-gov.*	—	
1824	Sir E. Barnes.	—	
1831	Sir J. Wilson, *lt.-gov.*		
,,	Sir R. W. Horton.	—	
1835	- - - - - - - - - - -	- - - - - - - - - - -	Muhammad 'Imád-ud-dín.
1837	Rt. Hon. J. A. S. Mackenzie.	—	
1841	Sir C. Campbell.	—	
1847	Sir J. E. Tennent, *lt.-gov.*	—	
,,	Rt. Hon. Visc. Torrington.	—	
1850	Hon. C. J. MacCarthy, *lt.-gov.*	—	
,,	Sir G. W. Anderson.	—	
1855	Hon. C. J. MacCarthy, *lt.-gov.*	—	
,,	Sir H. G. Ward.	—	
1860	Maj.-Gen. H. F. Lockyer, *lt.-gov.*	—	
,,	Col. C. E. Wilkinson, *lt.-gov.*	—	
,,	Sir C. J. MacCarthy.	—	
1863	Maj.-Gen. T. O'Brien, *adm.*	—	
1865	Sir H. G. R. Robinson.	—	
1868	Lieut.-Gen. Hodgson, *adm.*	—	
1869	Sir H. G. R. Robinson.	—	
1872	Hon. H. T. Irving, *adm.*	—	
,,	Rt. Hon. W. H. Gregory.	—	
1874	Hon. A. N. Birch, *adm.*	—	
,,	Rt. Hon. W. H. Gregory.	—	
1875	Hon. A. N. Birch, *adm.*	—	
1876	Rt. Hon. Sir W. H. Gregory.	—	
1877	Hon. A. N. Birch, *lt-gov.*	—	
,,	Rt. Hon. Sir W. H. Gregory.	—	
,,	Hon. A. N. Birch, *lt-gov.*	—	
,,	Sir J. R. Longden.	—	
1881	Hon. J. Douglas, *lt.-gov.*	—	
1882	Sir J. R. Longden - - - -	- - - - - - - - - - -	Tuttu Manipul (*Sultan elect*).

* The last Rájá of Kandy, deposed in 1815.

TABLE OF DESCENT

OF

THE SULTANS OF THE MA'LDIVE ISLANDS FROM THE 18TH CENTURY.

1.—S. MUHAMMAD IMÁD-UD-DI'N MUZAFFAR.

2.—S. IBRÁHI'M ISKANDAR (1721)

3.—S. MUHAMMAD IMÁD-UD-DI'N MUKKARRAM (1749)

4.—A'MINÁ RANI KILAGE-FÁNU (1754)

Hasan Ranna Baḍéri raised to the throne as 5.—S. GHÁZI' HASAN 'IZZ-UD-DI'N (1759)

6.—S. MUHAMMAD GHIYÁS-UD-DI'N (1767)

7.—S. GHÁZI' MUHAMMAD M'UIZZ-UD-DI'N (1774)

8.—S. HASAN NU'R-UD-DI'N (1779)

9.—S. MUHAMMAD M'UI'N-UD-DI'N (1799)

10.—S. MUHAMMAD 'IMÁD-UD-DI'N (1835)

NOTES.

(1)

Tárikho.

HISTORICAL RECORDS.—In the Sultan's palace at Málé is said to be preserved a National Record styled *Tárikho* (Arabic, *Táríkh*, 'history') or *Mushuli foi*, in which all important events and matters of State have been faithfully noted for centuries in the old Máldive character *(Dives akuru)*, in Arabic, and in the modern native character *(gabali tána)*.

(2)

Minakaï.

MINAKAÏ—called MALIKU by the natives—lying between lat. 8° 14′ and 8° 19′ N., long. 72° 59′ and 73° 5′ E., is separated from the head of the Máldives by the Eight-Degree Channel, which is perfectly safe and adopted by vessels bound to the Malabar Coast or Ceylon during the S.W. monsoon.

The Island is a narrow strip of low land, seven miles long, in direction N.E. and S.W. From its N.W. face an irregular coral reef projects: on the S.E. side there is no reef. Within 100 yards of the reef no bottom is found. The land is less than a mile wide, the rest being a reef encircling a large lagoon, which has three entrances from the sea, one with a depth of two fathoms. It abounds in turtle and fish. The soil of the Island is coarse powdered coral with a little vegetable matter. It is quite flat, and no part is destitute of vegetation; the South side is thickly covered with tall cocoanut trees (visible from a vessel 10 or 12 miles) and underwood, the North more sparingly. Rats abound; there are some cats, a few cows and goats, large grey cranes, ducks occasionally, and swarms of mosquitos.

Though generally spoken of as one of the Lakkadive group, and, with the other "Cananore Islands, forming part of the Administrative District of Malabar," Minikaï on every ground properly belongs to the Máldives, distant only 68 miles South. Inhabited by a people of Máldive race and language,* it was formerly under the Máldive Sultans; but since the 17th century has been subject to the Rájás of Cananore, and is at present "the personal property *(jenmum)* of 'Alí Rájá." [For Administration, &c., *Vide* Note (10) "Lakkadive Islands."]

The population is about 3,000. The Islanders possess six large vessels fit for the Bengal trade *(boḍu oḍi)*, four for coasting *(bandar oḍi)*, and eight fishing boats *(mas oḍi)*. They export fish, coir, and cocoanuts to Goa, the Malabar ports, Ceylon, and Bengal, bringing home chiefly rice, salt, spices, and cotton cloth. The erection of a lighthouse on this Island is in contemplation by the Admiralty. The P. and O. Steamer "Colombo" was stranded there during a fog in November, 1862.†

(3)

Christian ex-King of the Máldives.

CHRISTIAN EX-KING OF THE MÁLDIVES.—Pyrard and his Portuguese editor (G. H. da Cunha Rivara) supply a few particulars touching the expatriated Christian Sultan, *Dom Manoel*, and his immediate descendants.

On the authority of Padre Lucena's 'Life of Francisco Xavier' (Lib. 9., ch. XV), Rivara‡ notes that in A.D. 1552 the King of the Máldives, a young man of 20, who had fled to Cochin and appealed to Garcia de Sá for help against his rebellious subjects, was baptised a Christian. "His conversion filled with joy the whole of India, exciting hopes that after the head all the members would be converted." He married a Portuguese girl of many virtues and noble blood, but died at Cochin, old, poor, and still an exile.

From contemporary correspondence between the Court of Portugal and the Viceroys of India,‖ it would appear that the Christianised Máldive Princes at Cochin were for years a constant source of trouble to the Portuguese authorities, owing to their restlessness and "follies of youth" *(mocidades)*.

---

* "La pesche y est tres-bonne, l'air y est fort sain et plus temperé qu' aux Maldiues, *et le peuple y a les mesmes coustumes, les mesmes moeurs et langages que ceux des Maldiues.*"—Pyrard, p. 232.

† Partially abridged from "Report during Fusli, 1268, on the Five Laccadive Islands" by E. G. Thomas (Madras Jour. of Literature and Science), and Article "Laccadive Islands" (W. W. Hunter's Imperial Gazetteer of India).

‡ *Viagem de F. Pyrard*, Goa, 1858.

§ Letter from the King of Portugal to the Viceroy Dom Duarte, dated Lisbon, January 10th, 1557.

‖ Chiefly in the *Livros das Moncoes*, which may be said to commence in A.D. 1584.

Dom Francisco, the eldest son of *Dom Manoel,* whilst still young contracted, against advice, a marriage with the sister of Antonio Teixera de Maçado (*circa* A.D. 1587),* and ended his days under an assassin's knife at Lisbon, whither he had betaken himself to air his grievances in person before Dom Philippe the Second.†

Another Prince, *Don Joao,* "King of the Máldive Islands" (*Rey das Ilhas de Maldiva*), also married a Portuguese wife, Dona Francisca de Vasconsellos, and obtained a reduction on his tribute to the Portuguese of 500 *pardaos* as her dowry.‡

It was probably this "Máldive King" who suffered imprisonment (*circa* A.D. 1591) for having scandalised India by putting away his wife and other misdemeanours,§ and who, with his brother *Dom Pedro,* was subsequently removed to Goa (A.D. 1597) but freely treated.‖

Ten years later, according to Pyrard (p. 210; Pt. ii., pp. 80–1), the rightful heir to the original Christian ex-king's dues was *Dom Philippe,* who resided at Goa with his Portuguese mother, and was in suit against his uncle, *Dom Paulo,* for forcible appropriation at Cochin of the tribute paid there annually by the Islanders, in terms of the old treaty of peace with the Portuguese.

This tribute consisted of cowries (Pyrard, p. 172, "*bollis;*" M. *boli*), and coir ("*cairo,* M. *rhónu*). The Máldivians every year despatched four vessels of 150 tons burden thus laden to Cochin, being liable to meet all charges and perils of the seas until the head of the Islands was cleared, after which the risk rested with the Christian king. From this tribute *Dom Manoel* and his son *Dom Francisco* delivered annually 500 *bares* of coir (*cairo*) to the Portuguese, and Pyrard says the payment in his day amounted to one-third.

(4)

Mukwas.

MUKWAS.—"The third class of inhabitants of Calicut and Malabar are the common people, who in every district are much despised, degraded, and contemptible, as slaves—the *Moucois* or *Poulia.* Their quarter is distinct, outside the towns, near the sea, and in other places at a greater distance. They differ in condition. Some dwell on the sea-board and are not permitted to live further (inland). These are properly named *Moucois.* They are all fishermen and salt workers, and throughout all the coast of Malabar no other people are employed as rowers or sailors, and they are hired for this purpose......... [In Malabar] the labourers (*Coulombin*) are the most honourable [class], the mechanics next, then the *Tiua,* and last—the meanest and most contemptible—the *Moucois,* who are fishermen."—Pyrard, pp. 277–8.

"[The Mukwa] of North Malabar follow the rule of descent *a matrice,* but those in the South allow descent of property to sons."—Balfour's 'Cyclopædia of India,' Vol. III. Madras, 1873.

(5)

Wreck of the "Ravestein."

WRECK OF THE "RAVESTEIN" (OR "RAVENSTEYN").—This Dutch vessel struck on a reef of the Máldive group, May 9th, 1726, when outward bound with a valuable cargo of gold. The Captain (Anthony Klink) and crew reached Málé (Sultan's Island), and were ultimately enabled to return to Ceylon with the gold chests and other property recovered from the wreck.

The attendant circumstances are well brought out in the following quaint, but forcible, letter of the Máldive Sultan :—¶

Seal of
S. Ibráhím
Iskandar.

A' Messieurs Les Gouverneur et Conseille des ville et forts et depandances
de La Conpagnie doliande en Celon,
A Colombo.

Messieurs par la voy des deux batiment qui ont partie de ce port leune le 8e et lautre le 9e de Juin, vous auré Jecroy ressus les deux lettre que Jay eu honneurl de vous ecrire, avec ausi les equipaze du vessaux Le Rauestin, qui comme je vous ay déja marqué sestois perdue daus ces Illes Jay, le Capitainne duquel vessaux enuoya tous le de monde, tous fort mal, en cette Ille, et me fit demander par le Commandeur quil auoit enuoyee avec ces gens des battaux pr pouuoir sauuer, si il estoist posible les effait de La Conpagnie, se quil ont fait de 9 caice neuf caice castée** des seau de La Conpagnie les ql mon éttée remie en mon Ille par Mr Busch, comme Jay

* Letter from the King of Portugal to the Viceroy, dated Lisbon, February 6th, 1589.

† Rivara (*Viagem de F. Pyrard*) quoting Padre Lucena's 'Life of Francisco Xavier.'

‡ Letter from the King of Portugal to the Viceroy, dated Lisbon, March 8th, 1589.

§ *Idem,* dated Lisboa, January 12th, 1591.

‖ *Idem,* dated Lisboa, February 13th, 1597.

¶ The French is an exact transcript of the original.

** *Castée* for *cachetées.*

deja en lhonneur de vous marquer, les ql Jaurois eu deja le soin de vous les enuoyer si les de Sr Busch y eut consentie, mes il me fit reponce quil ne pouuoit y consentir, que le Capitainne ne fusce prejant sequi na ettée que le 13e de ce mois Juin, le de Capitainne ayant restée dans lille de Matteuarie pres landroit ou sest perdue le vessaux tous ce temps sans auoir rien fait que je puisce connettre estre pr le seruisce de La Conpagnie, se pleignant fort des abittans* de la de Ille comme sil deuoit trauaillé commes des Mattele durope ne considerant pas que sont de pauure gens, les quels consider le moindre petie seruice quon exzize,† deux pr vne tres grandre opression Il est assée Messr a votre connessance seque ces que les gens des Illes de Maldiue.

Insi Messr vostre Capitainne nauoit aucun droit de se seruir des terme, et mouuemant dont il sest seruie a son arîuée a Maldiue deuant tous le Conseille, deune manier comme sil vencit fair la guer, et a son ariuée Jay ettée plus informée que tous se temps il nauoit veritablement rien fait pr le seruice de La Conpagnie nayant aportée que des guenille.

Ausitot que le de homme fut debarquée il me fit demander 50 hommes auec 4 grand battaux pr sauuer les effait de la Conpagnie, sequi me parue si extraordinair que Je ne luy fit point reponce Quar Messr il faut que vous sachiez que le vessaux est essouée dans vne androit aupres duquel il ne peut y aller quauec penne vn petie battaux leaux et le brigant passant passant par desus le vessaux, et dans cette moisson duv:‡ les mer son affruze dans cette androit.

Si Mr le Capitainne auoit voulue se donner vn peu peux plus de penne dans le commancement que le vessaux at ettée essouée on auroit Je croy sauuer quelque choze dauantage, mes Je vous auoüe cette vn brutalle qui ne prand conseill de personne, se qui á fait quil a resté dans de temps en cette Ille, Il poura vous rander contte de ce quil y á fait Je suie persuadée quil donne toutte la fautte a mon gouuernement, Ces la reconnessance que je resoit de ce brutalle le quel Je vous jur Messr que si senestoist et lestimme et respect que Jay eu et moy et mes entecesseurs pr La Conpagnie je laurois mie dans vne androit ou il auroit pue a loizir santir les insolance de sa brutalittée. Je nignor nullement Messr que ce de Capitainne ne vous assurrera quil est possible de pouuoit sauuer les effait de la Conpagnie, et que indubitallemt il ne vous fasce fair des pance§ tres inuttille quar je vous assur de rechef que dans la situation ou est le vessaux, il est impossible de rie fair a moins que le de vessaux ne sonnre;‖ quoy puisce sauuer les marchandize qui pouront flotter, si le temps permait au battaux de restter dehors et les marchandize pezante que pouront rester au font, la Conpagnie poura fair les deligence si elle juge a propos pr les sauuer denuoyer des occazion dans la moisson de feuuerir et mars quant de ma part Je vous assur, que si le vessaux sonnre,‖ et quil y est des marchandize qui flotte comme je vous marque sy deuant, et que nos battaux puisce tenir la mer Jaurie soin den fair vne exacte recherche pr vous les ranuoyer a la premier occazion.

Le 18e de ce mois des Juin le de Capitainne en Conpagnie de quelquevn de ces officiers sont venue a la porte de mon logie auec vne arogance qui ma Je vous assur outré au derniée point, Je vous le repette Messr si cenestoist les raison que jay deja ecrit sy deuant, il leurs seroit ariueé vne tres mauuais affaire esperant que vous me donneréе la satisfaction qui est a vn Roy.

Pretendant que Je lui eus remie cinq hommes quil dit luy manquer, ne mayant pas donné connessance dans la partie des 2 premiée vessaux quil manquoit, Comment pouuoire scauoir, si il estoist partie ou non, ou sil auoit restée dans le pay¶ Mes enfin Messr Jay voulue passer tous sans bruit a vos consideration, Je luy fit fair vne reponce pr luy fair antrer en luy meme quil deuoit bien considerée la mannier dont il parloit et des sestte dont il se seruoit, Sependant si ces hommes estois sur la terre, Je les ferois randre, et de plus que Jauois 3 batiment en rade sur leql il pouuoit en fair la cherche, se que sepandant il na voulue fair, et a retrouuée ces gens sur le vessaux de la Conpagnie de france auec le Capitainne duql il y a plusr parolle que Je nay point sceu.

Je vous ranuoy Messr le de Capitainne auec Mr Busch duql Je suie tres contant, pr estre veritablemt vne homme fort brudant, Le restant des officie vont jointement auec les 9 caice de La Conpagnie qui mauoit ettée remie par le de Mr Busch, le toutte enbarque sur mon nauir leql pr cet effait na pas eu le temps de dechargée, et suie obligée de le fair partir dans cette ettat pr au plutot vous donner la satisfaction de reseuoir et les gens, et les effait de La Conpagnie.

Vous mobligerez sansiblement de procurer au Nacoda de mon vessaux nomme Mamot Safie la vantte de la cargueson du nauir parse que luy meme en estoist chargée des Bingalle, et pr vniquement randre seruisce a La Conpagnie Je la fait partir dans le meme ettat pr y repasser tous generallemt se que Jay eu lhonneur de vous marquer sy deuant ausitost que la vantte de son rie

---

* *Abittans* for *habitants*. † *Exzize* for *exige*. ‡ *Duv*:—a doubtful contraction.

§ *Des pance* for *depense*. ‖ *Sonnre* for *sombre*. ¶ This sentence is very involved.

sera finie faites moy la grasce Messr de le depesché pr Bingalle le plustost que fair se poura pr ne point perdre son passaze Ces la grasce que vous demande Ce Luy qui veritablement soit estre vtille a La Compagnie.

Et suie veritablement
Amy
Ybraimme Chicondar
Roy De Larchipelle des Ille De Maldiue.

Seal of S. Ibráhím Iskandar.

Translation.

"To the Governor and Council of the Towns, Forts, and Dependencies of the Dutch Company in Ceylon, at Colombo.

"Gentlemen,—By the opportunity the two vessels afforded, which left this port on the 8th and 9th June respectively, I presume you have received the two letters I have had the honour to address to you, together with the crew of the vessel "Ravestin," which, as I have already mentioned, was lost among these Islands. The Captain of the vessel sent the whole of the crew in a wretched condition to this Island, and, through the Commander whom he had sent in company with the crew, asked from me boats to save, if possible, the effects of the Company. This they have done as regards nine chests marked with the Company's seal, which have been delivered to me in my Island by Mr. Busch, as I have already had the honour to inform you. I should ere this have taken care to send you these, had Mr. Busch consented, but he told me that he could not give his assent to it unless the Captain were present. This did not occur till the 13th June, as the said Captain had remained in the Island of *Maduvari*,* near the place where the vessel was lost, doing nothing the whole time, as far as I can ascertain, for the benefit of the Company, (but) complaining bitterly of the inhabitants of the said Islands, as if they could be expected to work like European sailors —not taking into consideration the fact that they are only wretched creatures who look upon the smallest service exacted from them as a grievous oppression. You are well aware, Gentlemen, of the nature of the Máldive Islanders.

"Accordingly, Gentlemen, your Captain had no right to make use of the terms, nor to resort to the actions he adopted on his arrival at *Málè* in the presence of the whole Council, just as though he had come to wage war. Since his arrival I have been further informed that the whole time he has actually done nothing for the Company's benefit, having only brought away some rubbish.

"As soon as this personage landed, he demanded from me 50 men and four large boats to save the property of the Company—a request which appeared to me so extraordinary that I gave him no answer. For, Gentlemen, I must tell you that the vessel is cast away on a place to which a small boat can approach only with difficulty, as the seas and the surf break incessantly over the vessel, and during this monsoon especially there is a terrible sea running at the spot.

"If, Gentlemen, the Captain had chosen to give himself a very little more trouble at first when the vessel was wrecked, some more property would, I fancy, have been saved; but, I assure you, this is a churl who will take advice from nobody, as proved by his staying so long in that Island. He will be able to render you account of what he has done. I feel convinced that he lays the whole blame on my Government. It is all the thanks that I shall receive from this churl, whom, but for the esteem and regard that both I and my predecessors have borne towards the Company, I should, I swear to you, have placed in a position where he would have had leisure to see the insolence of his outrageous conduct.

"I am very well aware, Gentlemen, that the said Captain will assure you that it is possible to be able to save the goods of the Company, and that, doubtless, he will cause you to incur very useless expense; but I tell you once again that in the place in which the vessel lies it is impossible to do anything unless she breaks up. In that case the cargo which floats might be saved if the weather allows of the boats remaining outside; and, as regards the heavy goods which would sink to the bottom, the Company, if it thinks fit, might endeavour to send over (workmen, &c.) at opportune times during the monsoons of February and March for the purpose of saving them. For my part you may rest assured that if the vessel breaks up and any of the cargo floats, as I have told you before, and our boats can keep the sea, I shall take care to make a careful search so as to send (it) to you at the earliest opportunity.

* As the "Ravestein" struck on a reef in lat. 3° 4′ N., this must be the island adjoining *Digguru* in Mulaku Atol.—See Admiralty Chart.

"On the 18th June the said Captain, accompanied by one of his officers, came to the gate of my Palace with an amount of arrogance which, I assure you, exasperated me to the last degree I repeat, Gentlemen, that if it had not been for the reasons I have stated above, it would have fared very badly with them. I trust that you will render me the satisfaction which is due to a Sovereign.

"He alleged that I had sent away five men, whom he said he missed, without having let me know at the time the first two vessels left that they were missing. How could it be known whether they had gone or not, or if they had stayed in the Island? But, briefly, Gentlemen, it was my desire to let all pass without making any fuss, out of consideration for you. I had an answer given him, calculated to bring him to his senses, that he ought to consider the manner in which he spoke and the terms he employed, at the same time that if these men were on shore I should have them sent back to him; and, moreover, that I had three vessels in harbour which he might search. This he did not chose to do, (but) he found his men on the ship of the French Company, with the Captain of which he had many words unknown to me.*

"I send back, Gentlemen, the said Captain and Mr. Busch, whom I am satisfied undoubtedly possesses much prudence. The rest of the officers leave also with the nine chests belonging to the Company, which had been sent to me by Mr. Busch.

"The whole have embarked in my ship, which, on this account, has not had time to discharge; and I am forced to let her start in this state the sooner to afford you the satisfaction of receiving the men and the effects of the Company.

"You will materially oblige me by enabling the *Nákhudá* of my vessel, named *Mahmúd Sháfa'í*, to sell the cargo of the vessel; because it was loaded from Bengal, and, merely to do a service to the Company, I ordered him to start in the same condition to enable all (your men, &c.) to return together, as I have had the honour of mentioning before. As soon as the sale of the rice is concluded, do me the kindness, Gentlemen, to despatch him to Bengal as early as you possibly can, that he may not fail in making a passage. This is the favour that he asks from you who may be of real service to the Company.

"Your sincere friend,

"IBRÁHI'M ISKANDAR,

"King of the Máldive Archipelago."

The concurrent testimony of the chief mate, Johan Busch, leaves no doubt of the magnanimity displayed from first to last by Sultan Ibráhím. Those of the crew who reached "*Maldiva*" [*Málé*] were "hospitably received by the King, who supplied them freely, as far as the resources of the country allowed, with rice, fish, and occasionally, flesh." "We met with every possible attention," writes Mr. Busch, "from the King. As soon as news of our stranding reached His Majesty, he was pleased to despatch two special men to the island of '*Mattuary*' [*Maduvari*] to render any help we needed in boats, provisions, and other requisites."†

Governor Vuyst, in replying to the Sultan's letter, expressed his "hearty thanks for all the aid afforded and kindness shown" to the Dutchmen, admitting "the generous and kindly spirit" which had ignored the unruliness of the Captain.‡

(6)

The French on the Máldives. A.D. 1754.

THE FRENCH ON THE MÁLDIVES, 1754.—The following is the letter of the French Corporal, Le Termellier, to the Dutch Governor :—

"A Monsieur le Gouverneur de Colombo.

"MONSIEUR,—Jay lhonneur de vous escrire pour vous marquer que la protection que Monsieur Le Marquis Duplaix a accordée aux Maldivois nous ont õbligés a mettre notre pavillion sur ses Islles et dy garder des troupe : La rarctté des vivre icy moblige à vous envoyer deux homes [?] pour ãcheter quellque pipe daraq et autre vivre Jespere Monsieur que vous voudrez bien ordonner qu'on ne les inquiette point et que vous voudréz bien les aider et vous õbligeré celuy qui a lhonneur d'estre avec respect.

"Monsieur

"Votre tres humble et tres õbëissant seruiteur

"A Maldive, le 20me Aoust, 1754." "LE TERMELLIER.

---

* The anomaly of the Sultan employing the French language, as well as the bitter tone of the letter, are thus easily accounted for. The French were much in favour at the Máldives at this time. *Vide supra*, p. 31, and Journ. R. Geo. Soc., Vol. II., p. 78 (1832) :—"Upon our showing *French* colours, a Máldive boat came alongside and supplied us with some fowls." (Log of the 'Rochester,' February 20th, 1716, in lat. 3° 52′ N.)

† Two letters (Dutch) dated *Maldiva*, June 7th, 1726. ‡ Letter dated Colombo, January 7th, 1727.

Translation.

"To the Governor of Colombo.

"SIR,—I have the honour to write to you to point out that the protection which Monsieur Le Marquis Duplaix has granted to the *Maldivois* has obliged us to hoist our flag on these Islands, and to station troops there. The scarcity of provisions here forces me to send you two men [?] to purchase some kegs of arrack and other provisions. I hope, Sir, that you will be so good as to give orders that they may not be molested, and that you will kindly assist them. In this you will oblige him who has the honour to be with respect,

"Sir,

"Your very humble and very obedient servant,

"Málé, August 20th, 1754." "LE TERMELLIER.

It is to be hoped that the Frenchmen were not in very urgent need of the required supplies, as the reply of the Dutch Governor (J. G. Loten), acceding to the Corporal's request, is dated February 11th, 1755.

(7)

'Alí Rájá of Cananore.

'ALI' RÁJÁ OF CANANORE.—The chief male representative of the Cananore Máppiḷḷa family always bore the honorific title *'Alí Rájá* or *Adi Rájá—i.e.*, "Prince of the Sea."*

Cananore *(Kannanúr)*, originally "included in the kingdom of the Kolástri or Cherakál Rájás," and partially feudatory "till the invasion of Haidar 'Alí,"† had become, by the middle of the 16th century, the chief seat of the Máppiḷḷas and a Muhammadan state of some importance on the S.W. coast of India.

Pyrard, writing *circa* A.D. 1613 of "the Malabars of Cananore," mentions that they had not long before thrown off their allegiance to "the Nair King" and set up one of their own. "This King of Cananore is very wealthy, and very powerful, for his subjects are numerous, including, if need be, the other Malabars who live along the whole coast. He is called *Aly Ragea*, and is a Muhammadan as are the other Malabars. Owning many vessels he is strong on the sea, and for the purposes of trade in India has many agents and factories."‡

The Lakkadive Islands *("Les isles de Diuandurou")* belonged to him,§ as well as some thirty of the Máldives,‖ and the Suzerainty over the entire group. "He is very courteous, benevolent, and affable, and, above all, he is fond of strangers. The Portuguese are at peace with him, and are allowed to occupy a small fort in Cananore where they have a church and College of Jesuits.¶ The other Kings of India, however, do not style the Ruler of Cananore 'King,' asserting that his title has accrued by force alone."**

A century later "Adda Rajah," according to Captain Hamilton, could, "upon occasions, bring near 20,000 men into the field." His "dominions" then reached "10 miles southward of Cananore to the Tellicherry river," near which was his harbour, "Dormepatam."‡‡

The particular 'Alí Rájá who captured the Máldive Sultan in 1753, supported the English cause against the French in Southern India. A treaty of offensive and defensive alliance between 'Alí Rájá and Thomas Hodges, Chief of Tellicherri, on behalf of the English East India Company, was concluded in 1759. The Máppiḷḷa Chief bound himself to assist the Company "readily with 300 men (or more if necessary) armed with my firearms at all times" upon request and upon similar payment as that received by other English troops. In consideration of the immediate loan of 13,000 rupees (Bombay silver), pepper to that value was to be delivered, at the price contracted for by the English with their own merchants, between January and March, 1760;

---

* Aitchison's "Treaties, &c., relating to India," Vol. V., p. 346. Calcutta, 1864.

† Hunter's "Imperial Gazetteer of India," Vol. II., Art. 'Cannanore.' London, 1881.

‡ Pyrard, p. 322.

§ *See* Note (10) "Lakkadive Islands."

‖ Ceded about 50 years previously [*circa* A.D. 1560] by a Máldive Sultan in return for aid against his revolted subjects.—Pyrard, p. 233.

¶ The Portuguese landed at Cananore A.D. 1498, and erected a factory A.D. 1505. The Dutch followed in A.D. 1656, but sold their fort about A.D. 1756 to 'Alí Rájá, whose avarice Haidar 'Alí had to curb. (M. M. D. L. T. "History of Hyder Shah," p. 101.)

** Pyrard, pp. 322–3.

‡‡ "A New Account of the East Indies," Edinburgh, 1727.—Pinkerton, Vol. 8, pp. 368, 370. At the present day the territory of the Rájá extends nowhere more than two miles from the *glacis* of the fort.

in default, the Company to have free liberty to take the Rájá's vessels to the amount of the said debt.*

In 1766 'Alí Rájá instigated Haidar 'Alí to his successful invasion of Malabar, and was entrusted with the management of all the conquered states from Cherakál to Cochin, except Cochin, Coringot, and Randeterra.†

On the capture of Cananore by the British in 1784 the Bíbí became tributary to the East India Company. It was taken again in 1791, and has since remained in British hands.‡

In the Cananore family, as usual in Malabar, the succession goes in the female line. "The last [male ruler] was succeeded by his niece, whose husband died during the siege of Cananore in 1790. This lady was succeeded by her daughter and granddaughter. The last died in October, 1861, and the Madras Government, mistaking the rule of succession, which requires that every heir must be descended immediately from a female, and imagining that females only could succeed, recognised her distant female relative to the exclusion of her son. But on the appeal of the son, Ali Rajah, and after further investigation of the case, his right to the succession was recognised."§

The *Máppiḷḷas*‖ (vulgarly *Moplás*) are all Muhammadans and descendants of Arabs who traded to or settled in Malabar from the 9th century.¶ The lax morality of the Indian women—particularly Tiyatti—favoured such casual or permanent connection with foreigners. "In the course of time the settlers, their descendants, and converts, became a power in the land......adding much by the industry to the material wealth of the country, and not a little to its social and political difficulties. To the arrogance of the strictly honest and austerely religious Nair, the Moplá—ignorant, bigotted, priest-ridden—opposed fanatical hatred, and, when driven beyond bearing [by agrarian grievances], open outrage and murder. Things are better now than they were. English rule has done much: the Moplá knife perhaps something: special legislation more than all."**

The Máppiḷḷas are all fine, sturdy, good-looking men, and, as a community, the most enterprising and industrious race to be found anywhere in India. Though disinclined to seek public service, they can prove themselves intelligent and hard-working.

The Labbays of the South-east Coast of India, the Moors of Ceylon, and a large proportion of the Máldive Islanders†† in the Atols as far south as Málé, have sprung from an origin similar to that of the Máppiḷḷas of Malabar.

(8)

Fate of S. Muhammad Ghiyás-ud-dín.

THE supposition that Sultan Muhammad Ghiyás-ud-dín met this violent death at the hands of his subjects should be received with much caution. The tradition "vaguely current" at this day rather favours the belief that it was a younger brother of Sultan Muhammad 'Imád-ud-dín Mukkarram, named *Sayyid Kaḷu Baḍára*, who thus perished. This Prince is said to have shared the captivity of the Sultan in India, and to have obtained possession of the throne on returning to Málé after an absence of some years. The two sons of Sultan Ghází Hasan 'Izz-ud-dín were thereupon banished to the Southern Atols. But during the *Hajj* of Kaḷu Baḍára, Fáruná Kilage-fánu, who had been banished with the ex-Sultan's sons, re-visited Málé and devised the scheme for the restoration of the former line (by the murder of the pilgrim Sultan), details of which Christopher relates. Fáruná then merely held the reins of government until the Princes could be recalled from their exile.

(9)

Wreck of the "Europa."

WRECK OF THE "EUROPA."‡‡—The facts of this case present features in many respects strikingly similar to those connected with the "Ravestein," a century earlier.

The British vessel "Europa," Captain J. Alwayn, apparently laden with arms, struck on a reef among the Southern Atols, May 23rd, 1812. Upon news of the disaster reaching Sultan

* Aitchison's "Treaties, &c.," Vol. V., pp. 357-8.

† Hunter's "Imp. Gaz. of India," Vol. VI., Art. 'Malabar'; Aitchison's "Treaties, &c.," Vol. V., p. 344.

‡ Hunter's "Imp. Gaz. of India," Vol. II., Art. 'Cannanore.' § Aitchison's "Treaties, &c.," Vol. V., p. 347.

‖ Perhaps from *má*, 'mother,' and *piḷḷai*, 'child.' (Wilson.)

¶ Il est bien certain qu'ils sont venus d' ailleurs, et on dit d'Arabie, mais il y a bien long temps."—Pyrard, p. 321.

** Hunter's "Imp. Gaz. of India," Vol. VI., Art. 'Malabar.'

†† Buchanan ("A Journey through Mysore, Canara, and Malabar," Jan. 12, 1801.—Pinkerton, Vol. 8, p. 745) observes that the Máldivians and their Sultan are "Moplays."

‡‡ Sultan's letters. The originals are unfortunately not forthcoming, and the translations (undated) must have been made by a native little acquainted with English.

M'uín-ud-dín, he "was pleased to despatch a *gundara dhony* from Maldive [Málé] to the rock the ship struck against," but the Captain and crew, including three women, had meanwhile started in another *gundara* for Málé, 300 miles distant.

On their way they foraged for supplies in the most reckless manner, shooting fowls and plucking cocoanuts wherever they landed. From one island 200 fowls were forcibly carried off after one of the natives had received a slight gunshot wound.

They were, nevertheless, landed at Málé with honours. "The colours were hoisted and a salute of guns fired from the fort. The Captain was provided with a house adorned with white cloth and every necessary article, &c.;" and the lascars quartered "in a suitable place and fed there properly." Before a vessel could be prepared for their conveyance to the Coast, the Captain and lascars had commenced an unseemly and serious quarrel in which blood was spilt—the latter demanding arrears of pay and their discharge, whilst the former insisted on their returning to the wreck and making some attempt to recover the cargo. The Vizier, appealed to by both parties, was in despair—"If neither of you will agree to deliver up your arms, what can I do?" The lascars had ultimately to be deprived of their arms. They then "began to trouble the Maldive Island as they had done the other islands, by seizing fowls, plucking young cocoanuts, breaking the olas with which the verandahs are covered, and letting dogs bite the inhabitants about the streets. The Pilot of the ship at 12 o'clock in the night had the audacity to enter the Sultan's Palace, but was stopped by the sentries and ejected. "The inhabitants, indeed, would not have been so patient if they had not thought that it was an honour to the Sultan, and the Sultan suffered himself to be thus treated merely for the sake of His Britannic Majesty."

The people came in a body before the Sultan, "and asked if it was proper that their country should be troubled by lascars, who were fed by the Sultan himself. The Sultan, however, pacified them."

Upon a complaint of killing a sheep, the Captain and Pilot, although summoned at "three different times," refused to appear before the chiefs, "observing that if they had anything to say to them they should come to their lodging." They were then rightly arrested, and the charge, though basely denied, having been clearly proved, were committed to prison for "two days and two nights;" and, after 15 days' surveillance "in a suitable house," "allowed to live in their former lodging."

The Captain and other Europeans reached Galle in a Máldivian vessel on August 18th with some of the cargo, which had been recovered from the wreck by the natives under the Sultan's orders. It is satisfactory to find that the Governor (Sir R. Brownrigg) expressed his concern for the misconduct of the officers and men of the "Europa" and his "best acknowledgments" of the Sultan's action.* The Provincial Judge at Galle was at the same time directed to hold a searching inquiry, calling upon the Captain "to answer distinctly to every particular of the charges."

(10)

The Lakkadives.

LAKKADIVE ISLANDS†—(*Laksha Dwipa*, 'the Hundred Thousand Islands'; also called the *Divi* or *Amindivi* Islands)—14 in all (9 inhabited, 2 uninhabited, 3 open reefs)—lie between lat. 10° and 14° N., and long. 71° 40′ and 74° E., about 200 miles West of the Malabar Coast.

The Islands, generally situated at the East end of coral reefs (which enclose on the West perfect lagoons). are from 2 to 3 miles in area, and only 10 to 15 feet above sea level. The surface soil being naturally barren, spontaneous vegetation is scanty. The cocoanut thrives well. In formation the soil differs little from that of the Máldives.‡ The well water is said to be not very wholesome. Climate healthy. Leprosy prevails, but the ravages of small-pox have been greatly minimised by vaccination, &c. Hurricanes occasionally visit the Islands, notably the storms of 1847 and 1867, which caused great loss of life. There are few animals, except rats which are a pest. Fish and tortoises are abundant.

These Islands (as distinct from Minakaí) were conferred in *jágir* on the Máppilla Chief of Cananore (*circa* A.D. 1550) by the Cherakál Rájá, subject to certain dues which were regularly

---

* Governor's reply of October 15th, 1812.

† Almost entirely extracted from the Article in Hunter's "Imp. Gaz. of India," Vol. VI., London, 1881. See too an interesting account of the group by Allan Hume in "Stray Feathers," Vol. IV., pp. 413–483, Calcutta, 1876.

‡ *Vide ante*, p. 2.

rendered to that State until the invasion of Haidar 'Alí. At the commencement of the 17th century the Lakkadives enjoyed a flourishing trade with India.*

After the storming of Cananore by the English in 1791, the Islands were sequestrated for the benefit of the East India Company. In 1799 the Bíbí obtained a remission on the tribute fixed by the Agreements of 1793 and 1796, reducing the *peshkash* to Rs. 10,000—at which amount it still remains. The Northern portion of the group is attached to the Collectorate of South Kanara : the remainder belongs to 'Alí Rájá, but was sequestrated for arrears of revenue between 1855 and 1860, and again in 1877, and placed under the direct administration of the Collector of Malabar.

South Kanara Islands.	*Cananore Islands.*
Amini or Amindivi.	Agathi.
Chetlat.	Kavarathi.
Kadamat.	Antrot.
Kiltan.	Kálpeni.
Bitra—uninhabited.	Minakaī.
	Suheli—uninhabited.

Total population in 1871, 13,495. The Kanara Islands are managed by a Sub-Magistrate and *munsif:* the Cananore group by *amins* (revenue agents). The Islands are from time to time visited by a European Officer.

The Islanders pay no land revenue, but in lieu the Government retains the *coir* monopoly—requiring the whole of this—the staple—product to be brought over to Mangalore, where it is paid for at fixed rates, somewhat below the market value. Payment is made partly in rice and partly in money, and, as the Islanders enjoy certain advantages with regard to salt, &c., the arrangement is still popular with them. Constant change of price and the exaction of other imposts by 'Alí Rájá has for years caused discontent and evasion of the monopoly by the Southern Islanders.

In Minakaī a more profitable arrangement for the tenantry exists, and few, if any, monopolies are enforced.

The people are all Musalmáns and, like the Máppiḷḷas, of Hindu descent ; they are of a peaceable disposition, with no little aptitude for self-government, and submissive to their own headmen. Monogamy is universal. The language of the group (Minakaī excepted) is Malayáḷam, written in the Arabic character.† The Islanders are bold seamen, and own 184 large and 719 small boats. The almost sole industry is the preparation for foreign sale of coir. Chief exports : coir, cocoanut, copra, and jaggery ; total annual value about £17,000.

(11)

Presents.

PRESENTS.—According to universal Oriental custom the tender of presents has always formed a necessary part of the ceremonial attending the annual Embassy from the Máldive Sultans, and is significant of their feudatory relationship with the Ceylon Government. It would be a departure from established usage for the Governor to receive the Ambassador with the Sultan's letter unaccompanied by presents. Thus in 1846 audience was denied the Máldivian Envoy until the presents (which had been accidentally left behind) could be brought from Galle.

(Colombo.) A.D. 1645–6.

On the occasion of the first recorded Embassy to the Dutch (A.D. 1645) from the Islands the return presents voted to the Sultan "to gain his friendship" (*ten eynde zyne vrundshap daar door mogen genieten*) were limited to two pieces and three rolls of satin.‡ The nature of the Sultan's presents at this time may be gathered from the list of those received the following year (A.D. 1646) :—

5 *bhar* [480 lb. the *bhar*] of fine coir.
12 Do. [do. do.] of coarse coir.
63 *parras* [40 lb. the *parra*] cowries, and some dried fish *(commelmas)*.

---

* "Ces *isles de Diuandurou* sont habitées de Malabares Mahometans, qui sont presque tous riches marchands, qui font un grand trafic par toute l'Inde, et specialement aux Maldives, dont ils tirent quantité de marchandises, et ils ont là des facteurs qui n'en bougent."—Pyrard, p. 233.

† "Ils ont les mesmes coustumes et langues que ceux de Cananor, de Calecut, de Cochin, et autres Malabares." —*Idem*, p. 233.

‡ Dutch Records (Summary of Resolutions of Council, Galle, December 21st, 1645).

In return for these the Sultan wished to obtain two cannon with ammunition, some grenades, and the loan of a Dutch gunner for a monsoon. The Council, however, decided to send instead, with profuse excuses, the following :—*

		Rds.		Rds.
3 pieces satin (at Rds. 25 each)	-	75	3 "grasshopper-guns" *(sprinkhanen)*	15
1 piece double red damask	-	40	1 match-lock *(lontroer)*, inlaid with silver	25
1 Japanese lacquered cabinet	-	34	6 Ceylon mats	6
6 muskets, with ammunition	-	18		
6 fine lacquered pikes	-	12	Rds.	231
6 grenades	-	6		

A.D. 1688.

Forty years later (1688) the Sultan sent :—†

2 cloths of silver, ornamented with gold and silk flowers.
2 Máldive mats.
2 Máldive turbans.
1,000 dried fish.

These were reciprocated by a present chiefly of spices,—the form it has continued to assume up to the present time :—

10 lb. (each) cloves, mace, and nutmeg.
50 lb. cinnamon
100 lb. Bengal powdered sugar.
10 yards red cloth.

A.D. 1706.

In 1706 the Sultan's presents were :—‡

1 female dress *(patta)* woven with Chinese gold thread.
3 pieces of Bengal cloth.
2 Máldive belts.
2 women's gowns *(rocken)*.
1 small piece ambergris.
1 piece of a sea cocoanut, "used for medicine."

The Dutch promptly sold all these "trifles" *(kleynigheden)* by auction to the highest bidder.

Ambergris and sea-cocoanut.

This seems to be the first record of *ambergris* (M. *goma*, *mávakaru)* and *sea-cocoanut* (M. *távakárhi)* being included in the presents. The practice was continued for more than a century at Galle,§ and is still in vogue at Colombo, where the Ambassador yearly hands over two tiny bags containing pieces of these rare and highly valued sea products with the envelope covering the Sultan's letter. The weight of the ambergris and sea cocoanut varied from Rs. 1 to Rs. 2½.

The same year Governor C. J. Simons returned :—‖

1 pair green Persian shoes.	3 lb. mace.
5 large bottles rose water.	10 ,, cinnamon.
5 pieces red cloth.	6 ,, cloves.
40 lb. sandal wood.	6 ,, nutmegs, and
1 bottle camphor oil.	3 *amuṇams* fresh Galle arecanuts.

Arecanuts.

Arecanuts were specially valued by the Sultans formerly. In more than one instance when they had been omitted from the list, either accidentally or owing to their scarcity, the reigning Sultan did not fail to bring the fact to the notice of the Dutch Governor, with the result of securing next year double quantities (*e. g.*, 1776, 1790, 1792).

In 1716 the Ambassador brought from Sultan M. 'Imád-ud-dín

1 piece ambergris.	1 large canister of sweetmeat cake.¶
1 piece of a sea-cocoanut.	1 bundle Máldive sugar candy.
2 silk cloths.	2 canisters Máldive pancake.
2 ornamented mats.	2 jars salt fish.
2 canisters of sweetmeat cake.¶	

---

* Dutch Records (Summary of Resolutions of Council, Galle, December 21st, 1646).

† Dutch Records (Miscellaneous), December 4, 1688.

‡ Dutch Records (Resolution of Council, Colombo, June 27th, 1706).

§ Bennett, "Ceylon and its Capabilities," p. 252, London, 1843.

‖ Dutch Records (Resolution of Council, Colombo, November 24th, 1706).

¶ The general Máldive term for these various sweetmeats is *avuru* (S. අවුළුපත්, *avuḷu pat*).

It was customary during the latter part of the reign of Sultan M. 'Imád-ud-dín and the commencement of that of his son Sultan Ibráhím Iskandar, for the wife, sister, or daughter of the Sultan to occasionally supplement the annual present to the Governor by a smaller one to the Governor's wife—a delicate act of courtesy, the lapse of which is to be regretted. Thus in 1718 the Sultan's daughter sent :—*

1 piece of ambergris of the weight of a rupee.
1 do. sea-cocoanut do. two rupees.
2 Máldive mats.
12 boxes of Máldive cake.
2 do. of *koliappam* (sweetmeat cake).

The Sultans' presents to the Governors at this time varied little from those of 1716 Cowries and dried fish were sometimes included ; cotton and silk stuffs never re-appear.

After 1736 no regular list appears to have been kept, nor, it is believed, is one kept now-a-days. As a matter of fact, however, the presents of this day do not differ in any material respect from those of 150 years ago.†

During the whole of the 18th century the return presents of the Dutch Governors consisted almost entirely of spices—between 1712 and 1735 generally, and after 1744 always—in the following quantities (*e.g.*, 1781) :— A.D. 1781.

To the Sultan :—			
8 *amuṇams* Colombo arecanuts	*f* 43	17	8
10 lb. cloves	3	6	8
6 „ mace	3	1	0
12 „ nutmeg	2	0	8
30 „ Malabar pepper	5	9	0
6 pieces sheeting, first quality	5	4	8
5 quires small medium paper	1	12	8
16 lb. cinnamon	4	0	0
To the Ambassador :—			
3 cubits red cloth	13	13	0
⅓ piece cloth for packing	2	18	8
	f 85	3	0

Except half a cask in 1712, 1714, and 1715, arecanuts do not figure in the list between 1712 and 1744. In the latter year 8 *amuṇams* were sent, and that quantity is still given to the Sultan year by year. (Galle.)

The Sultans' presents to the Commandants at Galle, judging by those of 1773, equalled, if they did not exceed, in value, those tendered to the Governors at Colombo. For in that year at the audience the Ambassador offered the Commandant from his Sovereign :—‡

24 boxes *boṇḍialuva* (sweetmeat).
1 box *koliappam* (do.)
1 box *alwa* (do.)
1 jar salt fish
1 bag of ambergris
1 do. , sealed up in white linen.

The presents of Bennett's day (*circa* A.D. 1725) were much the same.§

Between 1752 and 1792 the return presents from Galle were invariably as follows :—

3 lb. cinnamon.
½ „ (each) mace, cloves, and nutmeg.
10 „ pepper.
2 quires paper.

---

* In 1720, 1721, 1723, 1724, 1726, and 1727, the Sultana, and in 1725 the Sultan's sister, made very similar presents.

† The following constituted the entire presents received in November, 1880 :—10 small boxes sweetmeat (M. *boḍi*); 1 large Máldive pancake (M. *vedun gaḍu*) ; 1 bundle *koliappam* sweetmeat, 1 jar salt fish (M. *rhi hakuru*) ; 2 bags dried Máldive fish (M. *kaḷubili mas*) ; 1 small box of assorted shells ; 10 Máldive ornamented mats (M. *tuḍu kund*) ; 25 *koṭṭa* of cowries (M. *boli*).

‡ Dutch Records (Miscellaneous), Galle.

§ Bennett, "Ceylon, &c.," p. 252.

THE MÁLDIVES.

HISTORICAL SKETCH.

Notes.

The English Government in Ceylon have been no less conservative in this matter of return presents than were the Dutch, as the following comparative list will show :—

1800.	Rds.		1880.	Rs.	
8 *amuṇams* arecanuts	120	0	8 *amuṇams* arecanuts	184	0
125 lb. sugar candy	80	0	120 lb. sugar candy	45	0
30 „ pepper	10	24	1½ parra pepper	15	0
20 „ cinnamon	?*		20 lb cinnamon	13	70
1½ „ cloves	7	24	2 lb. cloves	2	0
1½ „ nutmeg	9	0	6 plates	3	0
1 „ mace	15	0	1 silk envelope (embroidered with gold thread) for H. E. the Governor's letter	10	0
6 dishes	3	0	2 yards broad cloth for Ambassador	20	0
5 quires gilt post paper	7	24	Cost of package	12	50
1 silk envelope (embroidered with gold thread) for H. E. the Governor's letter	—				
2 ells red cloth for Ambassador	16	0			
½ piece long cloth for package	3	0			
Rds.	271	24	Rs.	305	20

Fire-arms.

The Sultans have always been partial to gifts of fire-arms. In 1769 Sultan M. Ghiyás-ud-dín, in acknowledging a present from the Galle Commandant of two pistols with ammuniton, made a request for "a fire-lock *(snaphaan)* 6 or 7 palms long for my own use."†

Again, in 1831, Sultan M. M'uín-ud-dín reminded the Governor that he had asked to be provided with "a fowling-piece two cubits in length." A gun was accordingly sent the following year with an amusing apology, considered due to the backward enlightenment of the Máldive Ruler. "Your Highness is not to suppose," writes Sir R. W. Horton, "that the gun I send you in pursuance of my promise last year is less valuable from not being ornamented or from having been used. I have selected it because I know it to be an excellent one, worthy of Your Highness's acceptance. In England the guns which are used by persons of the highest distinction are never ornamented."‡

---

* Value not stated. The Ceylon Government cinnamon contract with the East India Company in 1802 made the price 3 shillings per lb. (See Bertolacci's Ceylon, p. 245, London, 1817.)

† Sultan's letter dated October 15th, 1769.

‡ Governor Sir R. W. Horton's letter dated December 14th, 1832.

V.—INHABITANTS.

PRESENT CONDITION AND ASPECT.

Briefly, the whole Máldive group may be said to be peopled at this day by a civilized race of A'ryan origin, professing the Muhammadan religion, who carry on a considerable trade with British India and Ceylon.

POPULATION.

Population.

There is no means of ascertaining, even approximately, the total population scattered over the Atols. It has been roughly estimated at 150,000 to 200,000 (Charton, Vol. IV., p. 255). On the other hand, Mr. Gray (J. R. A. S. Vol. X. n. s., 1878, p. 197) thinks 20,000 would be nearer the mark. This is perhaps too low an estimate, and a total of at least 30,000 may, with more probability, be assumed. That the population was in former days larger, is admitted by the Islanders themselves, who point with melancholy significance to islands in nearly every Atol now lying waste where homesteads stood of old. It is, however, satisfactory to find good ground for the belief that the gradual depopulation —mainly attributable to the proverbially unhealthy climate—has not merely been arrested, but that from the closer connection now yearly being established with the outside world, and the increased facilities for obtaining necessaries of life, a steady reaction is setting in. The Admiralty Chart, based on the Statistical Survey of 1835, gives the number of inhabited islands as 175; the present number may exceed 200.*

The annual census mentioned by Pyrard as taken at the close of *Ramazán* would appear not to be enforced at the present day.† The causes which have brought about on the Lakkadives the large proportion in the female population‡ are not likely to affect the Máldive group. Málé (Sultan's Island) contains between 2,000 and 3,000 inhabitants.

GENERAL CHARACTER.

General character.

The Máldivians are an inoffensive, timid, but—from their isolation—naturally a suspicious people. This reserve seems to be the effect of a vague feeling of apprehension, lest information given to foreigners may be used to their disadvantage.§ When confidence, however, has been once restored, they exhibit in their intercourse with strangers an excess of inquisitiveness often positively embarrassing. Sober, fairly honest, and of a disposition naturally cheerful, they have but few wants, and are consequently inclined to be sluggish and lazy.||

To general discretion of action they add a wise discernment in the common concerns of life, politeness and affability of manner, and considerable astuteness in matters of trade.

Above all, they are thoroughly humane and liberal in conduct. This last trait is confirmed by a long series of instances in which their "enlightened humanity" has prompted these Islanders to treat shipwrecked persons with marked kindness and hospitality, transporting them (under the Sultan's orders) in their own vessels to some port of Ceylon or the coast of India.¶

Christopher observes:—"Of the character and disposition of the natives we were impresssed on the whole with rather a favorable opinion. They are a quiet, peaceable race, hospitable and kind to strangers, though suspicious and distrustful of them. Unacquainted, indeed, with the practice of the higher virtues, but equally unfamiliar with vice in its darker forms, with desires and wants circumscribed and limited, and the means of satisfying them attainable without much labor, they have little incitement to increased

---

* Note (1). † Pyrard, p. 103. ‡ See Hunter's "Imp. Gaz. of India," Art. 'Laccadive Islands.'

§ Trans. Bombay Geo. Soc., 1836-8 (Reprint, 1844) p. 65.

|| "The inhabitants of the Máldive Islands are honest and pious people, sincere in good faith, and of a strong will."—Gray, quoting *Voyages d' Ibn Batoutah* par Def. et Sang. Tome IV., 114.

¶ Vide Appendix B.

THE MÁLDIVES.

INHABITANTS.

exertion for the purpose of augmenting their productions; and hence, in all probability, the little attention paid to the improvement of their resources, and the absence of all care regarding the amelioration of their condition. The apathy and indifference evinced by them on these subjects seem, however, to result in a great measure from feelings of contentment, though of a spurious kind."

Towards each other the natives are kind and friendly, for, though usually of an indolent habit and disinclined to work, they readily assist one another on emergencies; to their kindred they are very affectionate.* The upper classes are extremely hospitable and not wanting in sociability.

In their few manufactures they display much ingenuity and expertness, whilst as bold and skilful navigators they stand, perhaps, unrivalled. "In general," says Pyrard, "the Maldivans are very ingenious. They apply themselves with great industry and success to all sorts of manufactures, and also to letters and sciences; after this manner especially to astrology, which they hold in great esteem. They are a very wise, cautious people, and very sharp in their merchandize and way of living."†

Crimes of a heinous character are scarcely heard of on these Islands, and even theft and personal violence are of rare occurrence: murder has been seldom known.

"From a phrenological examination, Dr. Campbell concluded that this favorable view of their moral disposition is not incorrect, since the organs of destructiveness and combativeness were seldom distinguishable, whilst those of benevolence and veneration are strongly developed."‡ It is only natural to learn that cautiousness and secretiveness were observed to be the most developed of all the phrenological indications. "Dr. Campbell's observations are equally favourable to their intellectual powers, among which constructiveness and order appear most prominent."‡

One of the worst features in the character of the natives is their sensuality, which is little curbed by the very severe law for checking its indulgence and extension. This vice, added to habitual idleness, has undoubtedly weakened their general constitution.§

PHYSICAL TRAITS.

Physical traits.

The physical traits of the Máldivians vary greatly, but exhibit in the main the broad characteristics both of the A'ryan and Drávidian types, though the latter certainly preponderate.

On the one hand there is the A'ryan "oval contour of face," with large bright "freely-opened eyes" more than balanced on the other by the Drávidian "flatter face, with features less symmetrical, but perhaps more expressive, at least of individuality;" the wide, short, but not ill-shaped, nose; thick fleshy lips, and excess of jaws and mouth.‖ The general expression is pleasing, and free from any trace of sullenness. Very many (chiefly among the Northern Islanders) present undeniable traces of Arab or Máppilla descent, and closely approach the "Moors" of Ceylon.¶ A small proportion disclose in their physiognomy a decided admixture of the African type, due to the occasional importation of the Zanzibár slaves in former years.**

In the Máldivian form there is in general "little symmetry," poor physique, "much dumpiness and flesh." The average height of the men is about 5 feet 2 inches.††

---

* Trans. Bombay Geo. Soc., 1836-8 (Reprint, 1844), pp. 60, 66.

† Pyrard, quoted in Harris's Collection of Voyages, London, 1744, Vol. I., p. 705.

‡ Trans. Bom. Geo. Soc., p. 108.

§ Trans. Bom. Geo. Soc., p. 64. Pyrard too (pp. 141-2) strongly animadverts on the gross inmorality which then prevailed on the Islands.

‖ Brian Hodgson ("Essays") on the Physical Characteristics of the A'ryans and Tamilians.

¶ "When ships arrive, those on board take wives, and repudiate them on their departure; it is a kind of temporary marriage."—Gray, quoting *Voyages d' Ibn Batoutah*, Tome IV., 125.

** Trans. Bom. Geo. Soc., p. 58. For possible traces of Malay contact with the Máldives, see Note (2).

†† Trans. Bom. Geo. Soc., p. 58. An average supported by the measurement of 24 Máldivians from six different Atols made by the writer.

The men are commonly of a dark copper colour, but their skin is often marked by blotches of a lighter hue. At Málé some of the higher classes have a much fairer complexion, which may perhaps be attributed to descent from Persian stock.*

Without exception, the men, from the Sultan downwards, keep their heads, and usually their faces, shaved, though free to allow as much hair to grow on the latter as they like—a noteworthy departure from the custom of not three centuries back, which permitted the soldiers, officials, and those of gentle birth to wear their hair as long as the women, whilst forbidding all but church dignitaries and *Hájis* to grow beards according to fancy.†

The women are short, usually of a more olive colour than the men, much resembling in this respect the "fair-skinned Kandyans," with oval-shaped faces, regular features, and shapely figures. Clean and healthy in appearance, they are generally good-looking; some decidedly pretty. Their long hair, which they are at pains to render both thick and black by frequent washing and the liberal use of dyes and unguents, is tied high up on the back of the head.‡ Pyrard says that girls have their heads shaved once a week from infancy to their eighth year, leaving a small tuft on the forehead to distinguish them from the boys.

DRESS.

Dress.

The ordinary dress of the men consists of short drawers (M. *haruválu*), a cloth wrapped round the waist after the Siŋhalese fashion (M. *mundu*) and a plain handkerchief twisted over the head (M. *rumá*). On board their vessels and when in foreign ports, some don a thin shirt, generally white (M. *kuru libás*), and Turkish waistcoat (M. *saduriya*), which, with the peculiar coarse blue waist cloth edged with red, and the red handkerchief, mark a Máldivian at once among other races.

The upper orders and those who have been the *Hajj* wear besides the waist cloth (particularly on Fridays when attending Mosque) a kind of long dressing gown (M. *digu libás*), reaching to the ancles, somewhat similar to those worn by Muhammadan Priests in Ceylon.§ At Málé the soldiers are still required to appear in a distinctive "uniform" when on duty, viz., a waist *féliya*, with a peculiar handkerchief (M. *kachché; bolu féliya*), bound up in stiff angular shape.‖

No Máldivian not of the Priesthood now ventures to wear a turban (M. *fagudi*) in the Royal presence or Island, this headdress being retained by the Sultan exclusively. The *Fadiyáru*, or Kázi, and the lesser Priests wear the appropriate Muslim garb.

Like the Siŋhalese, the women wear a waist cloth, generally of native manufacture, coarse in texture, the ground of a rich chocolate colour, relieved by black and white stripes (M. *féliya*). The upper part of the body is covered by a loose-fitting red-coloured "jersey" reaching to the knees, short sleeved, and edged at the neck with silver tinsel lace (M. *libás*),¶ whilst round the high-worn *kondé* is twisted a handkerchief matching the *libás* in colour,** the *tout emsemble* forming a very becoming and picturesque costume. A

---

* Trans. Bom. Geo. Soc., p. 58. † Pyrard, pp. 81, 83.

‡ Pyrard, pp. 79, 80 :—"Quant aux femmes, elles sont belles, horsmis qu' elles sont de couleur oliuastre : et mesme il s'en trouve plusieurs ausi blanches qu' en Europe. Toutesfois elles ont les cheueux tous noirs : mais ils estiment cela beauté."

§ The dress of the men, as minutely described by Pyrard, must formerly have been richer and more elaborate, including the use of turbans, silk scarfs, gold and silver chains, and fancy knives.

‖ Cf. Pyrard, p. 123.

¶ The *libás* (Ar.) was only partially adopted in the 14th century. "Most of them wear only a cloth covering them from the navel to the ground: the rest of the body remains uncovered," writes Ibn Batúta, who was much exercised at the scandal, which, even as Kází, he was unable to abate.

** The head-kerchief is a comparatively modern innovation at Málé, and said to be still as much "honoured in the breach as in the observance" on the distant Southern Atols. Pyrard (pp. 80–1) speaks only of "une fausse perruque," which the women occasionally added to their natural *kondé*, and set off with flowers and jewels. Ibn Batúta, too :—"The women of these Islands do not cover the head: the Sovereign herself does not so." (Gray, quoting *Ibn Bat.* IV., 122.)

profusion of bangles, with necklace, earrings, and other ornaments, deck the person. The use of gold trinkets is no longer rigidly restricted to women of quality.

Girls, from the time they begin to walk until 9 or 10 years old, wear only a cloth reaching from the waist to below the knees. Boys are forced to put on waist cloths after circumcision at the age of seven. "Young children are covered with ornaments of different metals according to the wealth of their parents to distinguish them from those whose parents are poorer."*

MEALS.

Meals.

The Máldivians have nominally three meals a day—one shortly after rising, with coffee: another about six hours later, the midday meal: and the third after dark, just before retiring to rest;† but among the common folk at least it is rather the practice, as remarked by Pyrard, to observe "no set meal times, eating when their appetite provokes them."

The usual meal of the natives consists of rice (often only half-boiled) mixed with a few chopped chillies, a little fish, "fish sugar," and scraped cocoanut. This they consume in silence, even when eating in the company, and with a haste that savours of greediness. A draught of water closes the repast. Betel is universally chewed, and the *guḍa-guḍá* smoked constantly before and after meals.

For the supply of rice, their staple food, they have to depend entirely on foreign importation. Those who can afford luxuries indulge in such articles as tea, sugar, tobacco, biscuits, &c., the consumption of which has much increased since a few "Moors" and Pársí traders have opened boutiques at Málé.

The women wait on the men at meals and eat after them. Food is commonly dressed only by women-cooks (M. *badu-gé anhenun).*‡

HABITATIONS.

Habitations.

The dwellings of the poorer natives consist on some Atols of rows of huts adjoining one another on either side of the street. The walls are of cocoanut thatch or wattle-and-daub, with thatched roof. These are little better than the ordinary Tamiḷ cooly "lines" observable in Ceylon, low-roofed and dark, but not untidily kept. This is the class of habitations on Gáfaru Island, and common also at Málé. In the Suvádiva (Huvadú) Atol the inhabitants appear to live in similar huts, a number of which stand within *kraals* or enclosures.§

At Málé the upper orders possess houses with a yard or compound attached, substantially built of wood, the posts, beams and rafters of cocoanut or the tough *kuradi (? Pemphis acidula,)* with cross sticks of *duburi (Calophyllum inophyllum).* The walls, sometimes boarded, are generally of daub, or mats; cocoanut thatch cover the roof, and the floor is plastered.

In general about 28 feet long and 12 feet broad and 15 feet high to the top of the roof, they are dark and cheerless inside, having but one window at most. A partition near the middle divides the house into two rooms, of which the inner (M. *eteri-gé; mával-gé)* is reserved for the women, and considered private, whilst the outer room is open to all visitors. In this public room (M. *béru-gé)*‖ there are two ranges of seats 2 feet high by 4½ wide; the smaller one on the right of the entrance (M. *kuḍa arhi)* is held to be the more honorable; the other (M. *boḍu arhi),* carried across the house, is left for persons of less importance. The degree of respect intended to be shown to anyone is marked by the seat to which he is invited. The various weapons used at festival sports are ranged on a rough loft or shelf overhead. Most of these houses contain a few articles of furniture, the most

---

* Trans. Bom. Geo. Soc., 1836–8, p. 60. † *Ibid,* p. 61.

‡ The contemptuous term *sidí* (Pyrard *cisdy*), applied to men who descend to this menial service, retains its old force.

§ *V. s.,* Note (3), p. 19.

‖ The "*málem*" apartment (*Ibn. Bat.* IV., 118) in which "the master of the house sits with his friends."

prominent being invariably the swinging bed described by Pyrard.* The women's apartment, as well as the entrance door, is merely screened by a curtain.

Sultan's Palace.

Besides the Sultan's Palace, there would seem to be but one house at Málé built of stone or brick, faced with mortar—that of *Galolu-gé Hasan Díaí*, the wealthiest Máldivian merchant. It has a pillared front verandah and tiled roof, according to the modern design commonly followed by native architects in Ceylon.†

The Sultan's Palace is thus minutely described by Pyrard :—"The Royal Palace is of stone, one story high, and has a great many fine apartments, without the ornaments of regular architecture. It is surrounded with gardens, in which there are great fountains and cisterns of water, walled in and paved with large smooth stones, and guarded continually to hinder people from washing in them, as being solely reserved for the King and Queen's use. The Palace is divided into several courts, each of which has a well in the middle, paved with fair white stones, and in one of these courts the King has two magazines—one for ordnance and the other for ammunition. At the Palace gate there is a guard, with many pieces of ordnance and other arms. The portal is made like a square tower, and on festival days the musicians sing and play upon the top of it.‡ Passing on from the gate, you first come to a hall where the soldiers wait, then to another great hall where the noblemen and gentlemen attend; for none but the officers of the household, with the King and Queen's slaves or servants, are allowed to go further. The floor of these halls is raised three feet high from the ground, to avoid the ants, being neatly boarded with wood and covered with a sort of party-coloured mats which they make in these Islands. * * * * The walls are hung with silk tapestry as well as the ceiling, which has pretty fringes hanging about it. * * * * The chambers and inner apartments are hung with silk tapestry, and enriched with gold flowers and branches of several colours. * * * * Daylight is never seen in the Queen's chambers, or those of the ladies of quality; for their only light is lamps burning continually, and the place of the room where they usually retire is blocked up with four or five rows of tapestry."§

SANITATION.

Sanitation.

The Máldivians on their Atols are decidedly above the average among Oriental races in cleanliness. Not even on densely populated islands, such as Málé, are any unpleasant sights and smell encountered. "There is no filth, no pigs, and, except a little fishy odour here and there where fish is being salted and dried, all is sweet and wholesome."‖

Though much aided by nature in possessing a loose, sandy, porous soil, considerable credit is due to these Islanders for the sanitation that exists. Their compounds are kept constantly swept and clean, and the streets always present a tidy appearance. Personal cleanliness is no less attended to; men and women bathe regularly once or twice a day.

RELIGION.

Religion.

Muhammadanism has been the accepted religion of the Máldivians for at least six centuries past, and had not improbably obtained an earlier hold on the more Northern Atols. On the evidence supplied by Ibn Batúta, Mr. Gray fixes "the probable date of the conversion at A.D. 1200." The ever-growing commercial intercourse, however, between the Máldives and Arab traders, added to the influence of the Muslim merchants settled

* Pyrard, p. 157. Cf. Yule's Marco Polo, Vol. II., pp. 282, 289.

† Another proof of the "general deterioration" noticeable on the Máldives. The Indian Navy Surveyors saw the ruins of some madrepore houses (Trans. Bom. Geo. Soc., 1836–8, p. 103), and the statements of Ibn Batúta and Pyrard make it clear that such houses were common enough in former days. "They cut the stones, each two or three cubits long, and place them in piles; then they lay across these beams of the cocoanut tree, and afterwards raise the walls with boards." (Gray, quoting *Ibn Bat. IV.*, 118). And Pyrard, (p. 89) :—"The chief men and the wealthy have them built of stone which is taken from the sea under rocks and reefs, where it is to be had in any required length and thickness."

‡ Christopher says much the same. (Trans. Bom. Geo. Soc., p. 57.)

§ Pyrard, in Harris, Vol. I., pp. 713-14.

‖ Allan Hume, on the Lakkadive Islanders, in "Stray Feathers," Vol. IV., 1876, p. 441.

THE MÁLDIVES.

INHABITANTS.

along the coast of Malabar and Ceylon from the eighth and ninth century, may well have brought about a partial religious revolution amongst the scattered Islanders some time prior to its penetrating to the court at Málé.*

Tradition assigns to a Shaikh *Yúsuf Shams-ud-dín*, a native of *Tabríz*,† the honor of being the acknowledged successful apostle of Islám on the group, and knows his first kingly convert as "*Darumavanta Rasgefánu*"—doubtless the Sultan *Ahmad Shanúrázah*, of Ibn Batúta's narrative.‡

During the few years they held the Máldives in subjection in the sixteenth century, the Portuguese, in accordance with their bigoted policy, rigorously propagated the tenets of their faith amongst the Islanders; but the foreign yoke was soon thrown off, and Muhammadanism once re-established has remained unassailable to the present time.§

Like the Musalmáns of Southern India and Ceylon generally, the Máldivians are of the *Sunní* sect.‖ "In observing the fasts and ceremonies of their religion the Islanders are very particular;" but withal exhibit a freedom and laxity unrecognized by orthodox Muhammadans. Thus, the month of Ramazán (*M. Ródá*), kept throughout as a general holiday, is characterized as much by exuberant frivolity and licentiousness as by strict religious fervour.¶ Their general religious knowledge Christopher puts at a low standard, amounting to a bare acquaintance with "outward observances" and a loose knowledge of "a few Arabic sentences."**

Mosques.

"Their temples (Mosques) are built of good stone, well cemented, and have a thick wall. They stand in the middle of square walled inclosures, where they bury their dead, except those who desire a separate sepulchre. Their temples are square, and face the west, as pointing to Mohammed's tomb. They have three doors, each of which is faced by a broad well with steps, the bottom and sides of which are lined with polished and flat stones, the floor of the temple being covered with mats and tapestry, whereas the church-yard is nothing but sand."†† Their temples are kept scrupulously clean. "The roof or ceiling is of wood, admirably well polished, and the walls are wainscoted, both of them being firmly joined without nails, pegs, or any other visible artifice. Upon the walls of the temples are large tables of stone or of wood with Arabic inscriptions. They have a particular place for the King and his Court, and galleries for the guards and separate apartments for certain dignities, qualities, and ages, insomuch that any person who takes up an improper place is fined accordingly. They constantly burn lamps, for which end certain low trees are consecrated. Some of the islands have nine or ten temples, but that in which they solemnize a general festival is built and supported at the common charge, under the name of *Oucouru mesquite* [*Hukuru miskitu*,†† 'the Friday Mosque.']"

Demonolatry and Nature worship.

Side by side, however, with Muhammadanism there has continued to exist an older creed—not the less real because disowned—in demons and spirits, spells, charms, and the like. "Of demon-worship, bali-worship, and Siṇhalese superstitions generally," says Mr. Gray, "abundant illustration is afforded by both Pyrard and Christopher, in descriptions which have their counterpart in Knox's 'Ceylon,'"‡‡ and anyone thrown in contact with the modern Islanders (particularly those of the Southern Atols) will find demonolatry and nature worship as rife as of old, if pursued now-a-days somewhat less obtrusively. They believe in the existence of spirits and supernatural beings, who

---

* Note (3).

† Tabríz' tomb at Málé "is held in great veneration, and always kept in good repair."—Trans. Bom. Geo. Soc., 1836–8, p. 74.

‡ Note (4).

§ "Covetousness couched under the pretence of religion carried the Portuguese to conquer those remote countries; and the insatiable avarice of some expels and makes them esteemed less than rebels and pyrats."—Stephens' *Faria y Sousa*, Vol. II., p. 382. See Hough, "Christianity in India," Vol. I., Chap. VI.

‖ Note (5). ¶ See Pyrard, Chap. XI. ** Trans. Bom. Geo. Soc., 1836–8, p. 74.

†† Pyrard, quoted in Harris, Vol. II., p. 707. Cf. with the *Hukuru Miskitu*, the "*Metzid Adine*," at Ardebil (Mandelso's Travels, 1637, p. 239.)

‡‡ Journ. R. A. S., Vol. X., n. s., 1878, p. 179. Note (6).

exercise a disastrous influence on human affairs—in extraordinary phenomena, presaging calamity, and in the auspiciousness or otherwise of certain times and seasons for particular transactions.* To be well versed in astrology and "the black arts" (M. *fadita*) is no mean distinction; some persons even gain their livelihood by writing philters (M. *tavídu*) and other charms, worn as amulets, which are much relied on.†

Buddhism at the Máldives.

On present evidence it would be unsafe to assume that Buddhism extended to these Islands. The religious books of the Siŋhalese make no mention of any mission to the Máldives; nor does it appear unlikely that no organized attempt at conversion was ever made, considering their isolation, unimportance, and, as far as is known, independence of Ceylon rule. Mr. Gray, who seems to favour the idea of its existence at some period, is bound to admit that "the traces are curiously faint." At any rate, there is little to be gathered from the customs now prevalent among the Máldivians, and in their traditions lives only a vague belief that Muhammadanism supplanted a rank form of demon worship, untempered by Buddhistic or Bráhmanical influence.‡

But as Mr. Gray aptly remarks:—"Whatever further inquiry in that direction may prove, the picture presented by the modern religious state of the two branches of the Siŋhalese family is curious indeed. The one has held to the cosmopolitan principles, the atheistic creed, and the simple worship of the Buddhist faith; the other has adopted the exclusive monotheistic, and ceremonious faith of Muhammad. These religions have not, however, altered to any extent the characteristics of the race, and both have suffered the co-existence of the older worship of demons and of the elements—a common inheritance of both branches of the family, but an alien to both their creeds."§

EDUCATION.

Education.

Children of both sexes are required to read the Kurán, under the tuition of the minor priests, from the age of three or four. When considered to be sufficiently grounded in its precepts they receive no further instruction beyond being initiated into the ceremonials of religion.‖

Christopher is at fault in asserting that a knowledge of writing is left to be acquired anyhow. "Their studies," says Pyrard, "are to read and write and learn the Kurán. * * * * They write their lessons on small white tablets of wood, and when they have got these by heart they rub out what they wrote and whiten (the tablets) afresh." He adds that the letters are drawn on fine white sand spread over these boards.¶ It would otherwise be difficult to account for the fact that at the present day the majority of the men seem to possess a fair acquaintance with the ordinary Máldive character (M. *gabuli tána*) if they had received no instruction when young.

Some who have visited India and Ceylon speak a little Hindústání, Arabic, and Siŋhalese.

MARRIAGE.

Marriage.

Marriages are not contracted very early, but a plurality of wives is allowed according to Muhammadan license. Few, however, are able or disposed to support more than one wife. Notice of intended marriage is required to be given, for which a small fee of 1 *bodu lári* or 4 *kuda lári* (equal to about four cents Ceylon coinage) is charged. The bond is as lightly dissolved. Both parties need only declare before the *Katíbu* their wish to annul it. The woman is not forced to attend, provided two witnesses appear on her behalf. Among the lower orders many simply dismiss their wives without more ado. Naturally, intrigues are not uncommon, and it is said not to be held disgraceful for a widow to live unmarried with a paramour. Recognised prostitution is unknown.**

---

* Trans. Bom. Geo. Soc., 1836-8, p. 76.

† See Ceylon A. S. Journ., Vol. VII., Part II., 1881, pp. 119-124.

‡ Note (7).

§ Journ. R. A. S., Vol. X., n. s., 1878, p. 180.

‖ Trans. Bom. Geo. Soc., 1836–8, p. 60.

¶ Pyrard, pp. 134–5.

** Trans. Bom. Geo. Soc., 1836–8, pp. 59, 60.

THE MÁLDIVES.

INHABITANTS.

The following details are supplied by Pyrard:—" Upon a design of marriage they address themselves to the *Pandiare* [*Faḍiyáru*] or *Naybes* [*Náibu*] who, after being sufficiently informed that things really are as they are represented, takes the man by the hand and asks him if he is willing to take such a woman on the conditions proposed, and the woman always being absent, he likewise questions her parents as to their consent. If they all agree, he marries them, and calls the bystanders to witness their consent; then the whole company waits upon the woman home, and several other persons visit her. All the visitors being entertained with feasting, music, dancing, &c., the new-married man makes presents to the King and the great lords, and the bride pays the like compliments to the Queen and the other ladies; both make presents likewise to their relations.

" But when the King is married he does not give, but receives, presents from all his subjects, viz., cloths, garments, turbans, victuals, fruit, flowers, &c., and all these presents, which arise to a great value, belong to the new-married Queen.

" A man may have three wives if he can maintain them, but not more.† * * *

" The bridegroom receives no dowry with his wife, and is obliged not only to bear the charge of the nuptial solemnity, and to maintain her, but to settle upon her a jointure equal to what her mother and other ancestors had. They are so nice on this last condition, that if the priest apprehends the husband cannot afford such a jointure, he refuses to marry them, notwithstanding both parties require it; but, after all, the bride may renounce either whole or part of the jointure, after marriage, and, indeed, that is frequently practised.

" Brothers and sisters, first cousins, and those who by way of friendship and intimacy have used to call one another by the names of son or daughter, father or mother, brother or sister, these, I say, are prohibited to marry.

" The males may marry when they will, but a female orphan cannot marry till she is fifteen years of age; indeed, if her father be alive (for the mother has no power) he marries her at ten or eleven years of age, and that to the first suitor, whether old or young, provided his quality is in some measure suitable to hers; for they reckon it a great sin to keep the daughters unmarried.

" A man may turn away his wife, but unless she consents to the separation, she may demand her jointure, though, after all, that demand is seldom made, as being reckoned a mean action, and a sign that the woman fears that her merit will never procure her another husband. On the other hand, the woman cannot part from the husband without his consent. This sort of divorce, which is very frequent, must be attested by witness, or they cannot have the benefit of a second marriage. The divorced parties frequently repent of their separation, and marry again a second, third, or fourth time."‡

BURIAL.

Burial.

The Máldivians, following the universal Muhammadan custom, bury their dead;§ but the funeral ceremonies, as carefully recorded by Pyrard, would seem to depart considerably from the burial rites usually observed by Muslims.

" In the first place, the corpse is washed by persons of the same sex, who buy that office of the King, and are paid for their service; then they are wrapped up in cotton and covered with fine white cotton cloth (which goes afterwards to the priest), the right hand of the deceased person being laid upon his ear, and the left upon his thigh. This done, the corpse is laid upon the right side in a coffin of *candou* [*kadu*] wood, and carried to the burying place by six relations and friends, attended by the women washers, who cry and howl most hideously.

" Every man in his lifetime provides for himself a burying place and all the other necessaries; nay, they are so superstitious that they will rather starve than touch the money they have laid up for that purpose.

---

† Pyrard errs here. The limit is *four* wives, according to the ordained Muslim licence.

‡ Pyrard, quoted in Harris, Vol. II., p. 709.

§ Trans. Bom. Geo. Soc., 1836-8, p. 63.

"Besides the six principal mourners, the other relations and neighbours are present without invitation; and upon the march from the house of the deceased person to the grave, they scatter shells for the benefit of the poor,* to whom they likewise distribute sacks of rice and millet; at the same time they give to the priest pieces of gold and silver, the number of which is proportionable to the estate of the deceased person; and these pieces are distributed by the priest to those who have assisted in praying for the deceased person. The priests sing continually during the whole course of the ceremony, and in the procession a person of quality sprinkles the assistants with water made of sweet flowers.

"The grave is covered with a large piece of silk or cotton, which, on the interment, goes to priests of the temple. When the corpse is laid in the grave, they turn the face of the deceased person to the quarter that faces Mohammed's tomb, and then fill up the grave with fine white sand, sprinkling it with water.

"When the ceremony is over, the relations entertain all the company with victuals, and the three following Fridays they pray over the grave, where the priests sing, eat, and pray every day till the third Friday passes, after which a general feast is prepared for the relations, friends, and priests, who pretend that the soul of the deceased person is then conveyed to paradise. This feast is prepared every year, and on All Souls' Day they throw fresh white sand on the grave, and perfume it with burnt incense.

"The grave is surrounded with wooden pails, for they reckon it a great sin to walk over it. They never bury two corpses in the same place, for they have such a reverence for the bones of the dead, that even the priests dare not touch them.

"If a great lord dies, the priests sing for him a whole year, and are entertained every day with dishes of meat and betel; but if a King or Queen dies the ceremony is continued to the death of the next successor."†

"The graves of the Súltans have each a building erected over them, all of the same form, about 10 feet long, 7 broad, and 10 high, with a peaked roof, the sides being built of coral stone covered with ornamental carving, except where at intervals a smooth surface has been left for Arabic sentences. Over the entrance is hung a cloth marked with a few words written in large characters."‡

"In this country, the mourners make no alteration in their habit: only they go bareheaded to the grave, and continue so for a few days after the interment.

"Those who die fighting with persons of a contrary religion are buried upon the spot where they fall, without any ceremony; and, in regard that they are accounted holy and happy, neither the priests nor their friends pray for them.

"They never transport corpses from one island to another, and even the King himself is buried where he happens to die.

"If any person dies at sea, they wash the corpse, and put it into a coffin, which they place upon a float of candouittes wood. Within the coffin they put silver in proportion to his circumstances, and a written paper describing his religion and withal praying those who meet with the corpse to take the money and bury it handsomely."†

EMPLOYMENTS.

Employments.

"The labouring classes, exclusive of those engaged in pursuits connected with trade, follow various employments as a means of subsistence. The most common of these are fishing, gathering cocoanuts, drawing toddy, weaving cloth, and collecting the small cowries.

"The domestic duties are mostly attended to by the women." They beat out the cocoanut fibre and twist it into coir yarn, make mats, prepare breadfruit for keeping, extract oil from the nuts, spin cotton, and dye thread for the loom.§

* Christopher witnessed the "scramble, very much out of character with the occasion," for these cowries, during the funeral procession of the Sultan's grandmother at Málé.

† Pyrard, in Harris, Vol. II., p. 709.

‡ Trans. Bom. Geo. Soc., 1836-8, p. 63.

§ Trans. Bom. Geo. Soc., 1836-8, p. 61.

The liberty enjoyed by the women is remarkable. Though their apartments are considered strictly private, they are not kept from the view of strangers nor now debarred from openly walking abroad unveiled in the daytime.* In every respect their status would appear to compare favourably with that of Muhammadan women in India and Ceylon.

RECREATIONS.

Recreations.

It may be said of these Islanders with much truth that they 'take their pleasures sadly.' They appear to have few games or other forms of amusement, and even these are carried through mechanically and with little zest.

Fishing.

Pyrard mentions foot-ball as their sole diversion, adding that "the most universal and the most considerable exercise they have is that of fishing, which is so common an exercise all over the Maldives, that there is no such thing as a particular trade of that nature, for gentlemen and even their Kings pursue fishing as we do hunting in this part of the world. Every man there enjoys the natural liberty of fishing where and for what he pleases."†

Chess.

Chess (from the names of the pieces probably the Indian game) is commonly played by men and boys.‡

Sports.

On fête-days at Málé, sports (M. *kuli jahan)* are exhibited, under rules and restrictions to prevent injury to the performers. To teach the use of the weapons employed, masters (M. *eduru)* are appointed by the Sultan, who always attends these sports and remains till their close. The arena is simply a portion of one of the main streets, with thatched buildings on either side from which the Sultan and ladies of the harem may view the sports. All the male spectators stand round in a ring. The sports consist entirely of mimic hand-to-hand combats between successive sets of performers, two at a time, armed with sword (M. *kaḍi)* and targe (M. *aḍḍana),* lance (M. *daḍi-haliya)* or quarter-staff *(kuli jaha daḍi).* The players do little more than posture at each other *ad nauseam,* and show but little skill in managing their weapons. The Sultan and by-standers alike appear to evince no real interest in the proceedings, which are conducted from first to last in gravity and silence, and repeated for days together with wearisome monotony.§ It is not considered beneath the dignity of the principal men to take part in these games.

Fire-arms.

As curiously illustrating the absence of progress among the Máldivians, it is worthy of note that the use of fire-arms, which Christopher found just being acquired in 1835, is to this day little understood. The principal men are no less anxious now to be initiated into the mysteries of the "big-guns" (M. *boḍu baḍi),* but will not venture their lives by firing even an ordinary fowling-piece.‖ This timidity seems the more unaccountable considering the fact that the Islanders have had not unfrequently in past years to defend their Atols against the attacks of Malabar enemies, in which cannon and small arms played a part.

Music.

For music they show an undoubted fondness, said to amount among boys to a "prevailing passion." The tambourine (M. *tára)* is common in their houses, whilst tom-toms or drums (M. *beru),* trumpets (M. *tálafili),* and flagiolets (M. *dummárhi)* figure at festivals.

Many songs are current, particularly among the sailors.¶

---

* Two and a-half centuries have worked a revolution in this respect. "Quand les femmes vont par la ruë, soit de nuit ou de jour, *bien qu'il soit fort rare qu' elles sortent de jour, elles portent un voile sur la teste."* —(Pyrard, p. 124.) Even now Máldivian ladies of the upper classes do not walk, but pay their visits in closed palanquins.

† Pyrard, quoted in Harris, Vol. II., p. 711.

‡ Note (8).

§ Mr. Ellis describes a very similar performance by Sakalavas at Antananarivo in 1856, which seemed "grave work with them all." (Madagascar, pp. 399-401.)

‖ On the occasion of a recent visit to Málé (November, 1879) a most miscellaneous assortment of guns, long disused, was produced—from the lengthy Arab gun to an obsolete air gun and revolver of European make. Nor would the owners rest content until each and all had been discharged—with considerable misgiving—by the writer, who was subsequently sorely pressed to fire one of the rusty iron cannon on the ramparts.

¶ Christopher noticed Persian influence apparent in the musical taste of the Islanders.

SOCIAL DISTINCTIONS.

Social distinctions.

The reigning Sultan and Royal family naturally rank highest.

Only closest relations of the Sultan have the right to assume the title of *Mannipul;* whilst descendants of former Sultans, and, from the fourth generation, those of the dynasty in power, have a claim to that of *Dídí*, which implies more distinct connection with Royal blood. Ladies of this pure aristocracy are designated *Dídí*.

Besides position that springs of birth alone, there are adventitious ranks which accrue either through court favour or the medium of wealth. Such are all State Officers, among which that of *Kilagé-fánu* takes precedence, being confined, formerly at least, to the Regent acting in the absence of the Sultan.*

Many persons of respectable birth receive from the Sultan the titular rank of *Takuru-fánu.* Their wives are styled *Bíbí*, and their lineal descendants *Maniku* (fem. *Manike.*)†

The title of *Kalége-fánu* can be purchased for a few rupees—a small additional payment ensuring the attainment of the higher grade, *Himádi Kalége-fánu. Kamuloge-fánu* is the appropriate designation of their wives.‡

The bestowal of all ranks rests with the Sultan, and is notified by public proclamations. Persons thus aggrandized are allotted the rent of certain Islands—the names of which they usually adopt—and live at the Royal charges.

Nobility descends in the female line. "If a noble woman marries a plebeian, she retains her rank, and upon her account the children are reckoned noble; but a woman of the lowest form cannot ennoble herself by marrying a noble man."§

Masters and tindals of vessels frequently assume the appellation of *Nákhudá, Névi,* and *Málimi,*‖ as implying skill and experience in seamanship.

Caste.

Caste distinctions are still rigidly adhered to. Pyrard speaks of ten companies commanded by ten of the grandees of the country who serve the King in various civil capacities, as sailors, masons, &c. None but gentlemen could enter the first five, and from the remaining companies toddy-drawers and slaves were excluded.¶ At least seven of such guilds are retained at this day, and there is no lower caste than the toddy-drawer (M. *Rá-veri.*)**

Class exclusiveness has lost none of its power. Inferiors always receive those of purer blood or higher rank standing, and remain so in their presence unless invited to be seated. Seats are invariably occupied and vacated according to the rank of those present.†† Common people meeting a noble stand aside in a respectful attitude to allow him to pass. None will eat with those of the lower caste.

The term *Kalo* (fem. *Kamulo*) applies to the common people generally.‡‡

Slaves (M. *Alun*), if not unknown, are no longer sufficiently numerous to be considered a distinct class.

Single Muslim names, *e.g.*, *'Alí, Hasan, Fatimah,* are most common, though a few, such as *Don Maniku,* bear the impress of Portuguese contact so noticeable in the nomenclature of many Siṇhalese families on the seaboard of Ceylon.

---

* Pyrard, *Quilague:* Ibn Bat. (French edition) *Caluky.* Probably of Persian origin.

† Pyrard, *Tacourou.* Col. Yule (Marco Polo, Vol. II., p. 110) notes that that the title *Takfúr* was "applied by the Mahommedans to the Greek emperors of Byzantium and Trebizond.........Redhouse thinks it is a corruption of Τοῦ Κυρίου, but Defrémery says it is Armenian, *Tagavor* 'a king.'" Cf. S. *Tikiri*, ටිකිරි; and with *Maniku, Manike,* the S. *Mẹṇika,* මැණිකා. A few persons (*e.g.*, the present Faḍiyáru or Kázi) are by courtesy styled *Maniku-fánu,* as more respectful.

‡ Pyrard, *Calogue, Camulogue.* Christopher says that the sum of "1,000 larins [copper *kuḍa lári*], or about Rs. 350, will entitle a man to be called '*Kelege*'; no money can purchase higher." (Trans. Bom. Geo. Soc., 1836–8, p. 314.)

§ Pyrard, in Harris, Vol. II., p. 713.

‖ *Nákhudá* (Hind.); *Málimi,* Ar. *Mu'allim; Névi,* cf. S. *nẹviyá,* නැවියා.

¶ Pyrard, in Harris, Vol. II., p. 713. ** Note (9).

†† Trans. Bom. Geo. Soc., 1836–8, p. 59.

‡‡ Pyrard, *Callo; Camulo.* Christopher (*Ibid.*) "'Kalo' is applied to the names of all who have no rank."

THE MÁLDIVES.

INHABITANTS.

GOVERNMENT.

The form of Government is despotic, but rendered mild by the peaceable nature of the people, and the influence of public opinion.

Sultan.

The supreme ruler is a *Sultan** whose title and rank are hereditary. He resides at Málé, the seat of Government. To the inherent veneration with which superiors are regarded, and the wise provision or happy accident which has made Málé the sole centre of Government and trade for the whole group, may probably be attributed the immense influence exercised by the Sultan over his widely-spread subjects. Rarely, indeed, is his authority disputed even by his own relations.†

The Sultan is the fountain head of justice, but is not above the laws: to him reverts the property of all Government officers at their death:‡ and with him rests the privilege of extending clemency to offenders, though it is seldom used without the advice of his Council.†

Every means is resorted to in order to produce an impression of state and dignity connected with the Sultan's person and authority. All communications with him must be made through his Councillors, and audience is seldom granted even to Europeans. He appears abroad only on public occasions. On Fridays he attends Mosque on foot, accompanied by all the principal officials and escorted by a large body-guard, returning with the same retinue. His dress is suited to his rank, but is noticeable for its want of display both in gaudy colours and profusion of jewellery.

"The customs and etiquette observed in the *durbár* are remarkable for their simplicity. The courtiers and officers take their stations according to their respective ranks. No salutation is expected."§ No one may presume to sit or wear any covering above the waist in the royal presence, except by permission.

The administration of the country is conducted on a basis of constitutional freedom hardly to be expected of a Muslim *régime*, and with a systematic completeness highly creditable to a people so situated. A contented acquiescence of centuries furnishes the best proof of its adaptability to their wants and inclinations.

Two distinct, yet cohesive, branches of Government are recognized. These may be broadly termed the ecclesiastical and judicial and the political and fiscal.

Faḍiyáru.

As "head of the church" and "chief magistrate" the *Faḍiyáru* or Kází‖ receives from all classes alike respect and veneration but little less than is accorded to their Sultan. This reverence for the Faḍiyáru "indicates the sincerity of the Islanders in their belief in the Mahomedan tenets. His decisions, as magistrate, are always received with deference, and the natives in general show that they entertain a high sense of the importance of his duties, particularly that of interpreter of the Koran, he being the only person amongst them who has a competent knowledge of the Arabic, for a purpose considered so necessary."¶

Náibu.

Both "in his sacerdotal capacity" and as "the expounder and administrator of the laws," the Faḍiyáru is aided by *Náibu* and *Katíbu,*** as deputies.

For each Atol he appoints one or two Náibu, who "govern the inferior priests, and are entrusted with the administration of justice and the management of religious concerns" within the limits of their respective Atols. Once a year, or oftener if need be, the Náibu go on circuit through their Atols "for the sake of justice as well as the promoting of religion." At such times they do not fail to "gather their dues and receive presents from an infinity of persons, so that the circuits furnish by this means the best part of their income."††

Katíbu.

On all Islands containing 40 male inhabitants, a Katíbu is stationed with deputed religious and magisterial functions. Marriages are solemnized before him. These Katíbu

---

* Note (11).

† Trans. Bom. Geo. Soc., 1836-8, pp. 70, 77.

‡ Note (10).

§ Trans. Bom. Geo. Soc., 1836-8, p. 67.

‖ Christopher writes *Fandiarhee:* Pyrard, *Pandiare:* Ibn Bat., *Fandayarkâloû.* Cf. T. *Páṇḍiyan.*

¶ Trans. Bom. Geo. Soc., 1836-8, p. 70.

** *Katíb; Náib; Muezzin*—Ar.

†† Pyrard in Harris, Vol. II., p. 712.

are not stipendiary officers of Government, but supported by the Islanders, and are subordinate to their respective Náibu.*

Mudímu.

To every Mosque is attached at least one *Mudímu*,† or minor priest. It is his duty to see that all is decent and in order; to lead the prayers, if required; to proclaim aloud the time for the performance of worship; and to take charge of the tombs of holy men.*

At Málé, the Faḍiyáru is assisted by four Náibu and two Katíbu. These Náibu, according to Christopher, "are usually employed in transcribing passages from the Koran relating chiefly to observances and ceremonies, with an explanation in the Maldivian language, for distribution in the different Attols." Further, as Augurs of the State, they are appealed to to declare auspicious times for momentous undertakings.*

Pyrard says the Faḍiyáru also makes a circuit once a year through the Island of Málé, "condemning all to be whipped that cannot say their creed and prayers in the Arabic tongue and construe them into the Maldivan."‡

Legal procedure.

Justice is dispensed in the house of the Faḍiyáru or Náibu, "and sometimes, in cases of moment, in the King's Palace."‡

"The mode of trial is equally summary and simple. On a complaint being made, the defendant is cited to appear before the Fandiarhee or his deputy" by the *Déváni*,§ or process servers (six in number), acting by virtue of a special letter from the Náibu. An accused person can even be at once arrested in the commission or upon strong suspicion of a criminal or illegal act. "If he lives out of the Naybe's jurisdiction, he is summoned by letters from the Pandiare, which enjoin him to come from any part of the realm to the Island of Malé. The Pandiare's writ is served publicly upon the defendant by the Catibe or the superior of the Island, and if he does not appear at the place appointed, he is not only excommunicated and excluded from eating and drinking with his neighbours or coming to church, but seized by a party of soldiers." "The testimony of one witness in support of an accusation is held sufficient to establish its truth." When the complainant can produce no witness, the accused, to clear himself, must make oath as to his innocence; should he decline this test, he is adjudged to be guilty. If appearances or probability be in favour of the truth of the complaint, the accused will not necessarily escape punishment by taking the oath.‖

"Indictments, depositions, or sentences are never put in writing, being all very short; nay, in civil matters, the allegations are never written, unless it be in a suit for land of inheritance, or cocoa trees, which are reckoned immoveable: then indeed the judges give letters sealed with ink (wax they do not use) for an evidence of the person's right, to be transmitted to posterity. If either plaintiff or defendant suspects the partiality of the Naybe, they have recourse to the King, who orders the cause to be tried before impartial judges."‖

Sentences are executed by the Déváni, who, for their general services, receive a small monthly allowance of rice, and one-twelfth share of all awards and proceeds of sale.

Máldive law.

The Máldivians have a written as well as an unwritten law, the former being based on the Muhammadan code, whilst the latter is founded in the established and well-known customs of the country.‖

Penalties.

The penalties inflicted at this day bear a marked favourable contrast with those in force a few centuries back. Mutilation in case of theft has long given place to scourging—the ordinary punishment in all offences short of murder. Murderers are dealt with at Málé, whence they are banished, after being publicly disgraced and flogged, to some distant and sometimes uninhabited island.

A curious custom, still surviving, permits an insolvent debtor to work off his debt as his creditor's servant. "If he thinks himself ill used, he may turn himself over to another master, provided he lays down the money due to the former." These bondmen are called *Femuséri*.¶

---

* Trans. Bom. Geo. Soc., 1836–8, pp. 70, 71.

† *Katib; Náib; Muezzin*—Ar.

‡ Pyrard, in Harris, Vol. I., p. 712.

§ Pyrard, *Deuonits*. Cf. Pers. *Divanbeki* 'judges.'

‖ Trans. Bom. Geo. Soc., 1836–8, p. 77; and Pyrard, in Harris, Vol. I., p. 712–3.

¶ Pyrard, *Pemoussere*. See Gray, J. R. A. S., Vol. X., N. S., 1878, pp. 204–5; and *Voyages d' Ibn Bat. IV.*, 124.

THE MÁLDIVES.

INHABITANTS.

Viziers.

Christopher mentions that severe regulations exist regarding the respect due to married women, and gives some details of the penalty exacted in cases of adultery.*

The management of all State and revenue matters is entrusted by the Sultan, subject to his approval, to Viziers (M. *Vazíru*) or Councillors (formerly called *Muskuli.*)† "He very frequently consults with them—a custom which tends much to cherish a reciprocal confidence. Although the Viziers have the privilege of offering advice, they possess no authority to control the Sultan, but the influence they acquire from their situations often enables them indirectly to restrain him from arbitrary exertions of power, or from adopting measures injurious to the public interests, by exciting the people to remonstrate in a body."‡

Until comparatively recently this branch of the administration was vested in the hands of six Viziers, a Treasurer, and a Harbour-Master, whose titles and duties had remained substantially the same for centuries past.

The six Viziers were styled respectively :—

1st—*Dorhiméná.*	4th—*Fámudéri.*
2nd—*Hakurá.*	5th—*Máfaï.*
3rd—*Veláná.*	6th—*Dáhará.*

Of their functions and status (*circa* 1835) Christopher writes :—"The Viziers are executive magistrates in the different quarters of the town where they respectively reside, exercising authority also over all the soldiers belonging to their respective quarters. When an offender has been found guilty by the Fandiarhee, it is the duty of the Vizier to whose quarter he belongs to see the sentence enforced. The Viziers superintend public works and undertakings, such as building up the wall that protects the boats from the swell, and, in fact, the execution of all orders issued by the Sultan. They are appointed by the Sultan, and are removable at pleasure. On their installation they receive from the Sultan a staff of office, which they carry when attending on his person, on public occasions, and in his processions to the Mosque, &c. The nomination is proclaimed in all the streets of Málé by the public crier, who blows a trumpet to attract attention. We were informed that an oath of allegiance was administered to them and other public officers."‡

Christopher found that, with the exception of the Dorhiméná and Veláná Viziers, who had the respective supervision of military and naval matters, the rest had apparently no particular duties allotted them.

As each incumbent of the first five Vizierships died, no successor appears to have been appointed, and the titles thus gradually became extinct. That of the sixth Vizier alone survives in the person of the son of the former Dáhará.§

At the present day the Sultan has only three Chief Ministers, viz. :—

1. The *Hadégiri.*
2. The *Dáhará.*
3. The *Míru Baharu.*

Hadégiri.

1. The *Hadégiri* or *Bodu Badéri*‖ is, as his name implies, Chief Treasurer of the realm. He seems to rank above the other two Ministers and to possess greater influence in the community. A staff of accountants and clerks are employed to assist him in the revenue duties at Málé.

"The Hindeggeree is vested with authority to enforce the payment of revenue when a complaint is made to him by the Attol-wari."¶ In case of default in the transmission

---

* See Trans. Bom. Geo. Soc., 1836–8, pp. 77–8.

† Christopher, *Muskull* 'elder' ; Pyrard, *Mouscoulits, Mouscouly auare.* Cf. S. *Ẹpá* (Mahávaŋso.)

‡ Trans. Bom. Geo. Soc., 1836–8, pp. 69, 71.

§ Note (12).

‖ Christopher, *Hindeggeree ;* Pyrard, *Endequery.* Ibn Bat. calls the *Hendidjéry*, 'Preacher,' assigning the duties of Chief of the Treasury and Receiver General of Revenue respectively to the *Fâmeldâry* and *Mâfâcaloû* Viziers. Cf. S. *Bhánḍágáriká* (Mah. *Bhánḍágáriko Amachcho* 'Lord High Treasurer.')

¶ Trans. Bom. Geo. Soc., 1836–8, p. 71.

of the established dues, when no explanation is tendered, the Atoḷu-veri is held personally responsible, and called to account for his remissness.

Dáhará.

2. The *Dáhará* has no specific department of public business to supervise. But for a certain voice in the military and municipal affairs, his office would be a titular sinecure.

Míru Baharu.

3. The *Míru Baharu* (in the Arabic form *Emir-el-Bahr*)* is the Port Doctor and Master Attendant of Málé. He visits all vessels that arrive and refuses permission to land until it has been ascertained to his satisfaction that there is no sickness on board. It lies with him at discretion to put in force the strictest quarantine.

Generally speaking, the entire management and control of all public business not falling within the province of the Hadégiri, and distributed a few years back among the six Viziers, devolve now on the Míru Baharu and the Dáhará.

Atoḷu-veri.

For the collection of the revenue from the different Atols one or two agents, called *Atoḷu-veri* or *Váru-veri*,† are appointed by the Sultan on the recommendation of the Hadégiri.

They do not necessarily live in the respective Atols assigned to them. The majority remain at Málé and employ sub-agents. Each Atol has a storehouse (M. *váru-gé*), where the Government revenue is temporarily warehoused until required to be transmitted to Málé. The emoluments of this office must be considerable, as it is held by relations of the Sultan and Chief Ministers, and frequently by the Ministers themselves. Its tenure lasts for life, or during the Sultan's pleasure, and at the decease of an Atoḷu-veri his estate is held liable for any balance due, or alleged to be due, for his division.

Rarhu-veri.

In respect to the collection of the revenues, each island has its own headman, *Rarhu-veri* or *Veri-miha*, generally a Katíbu, who stands in the same relation to the Atoḷu-veri as the latter does to the Hadégiri.‡

The revenue of the different Atols (usually paid in native produce and manufacture) is collected into the Treasury (M. *boḍu baḍéri-gé*) at Málé, whence it is shipped in the Sultan's and private vessels on Government account to different ports of India and Ceylon.

REVENUE.

Revenue.

It is impossible to form any estimate of the total revenue received annually by the Government at Málé. On no subject are the Islanders more chary of affording information. It cannot, however, be inconsiderable. "As for the King's revenue," says Pyrard, "he has many islands which are Crown lands, besides a fifth part of all the grain and fruits of the country, and a tax on dried fish, shells called *bolly* [*boli*, cowries], and cords of cocoas, which he lays upon them according to their circumstances; for he has no taxes paid him in money, abating what is paid as a purchase for titles and offices, or for licenses to wear fine apparel. He obliges his people to make him every year as much cotton cloth as clothes his soldiers, for he gives them clothes as well as pay."§ Each Atol is bound to pay yearly a certain portion of its produce, said to be levied as a poll-tax upon every male and female over twelve years of age, at the following rates:—1 *koṭṭa* of cowries, 12 cadjans (*M. faṇ*), and 1 *tula* (28 lbs.) of coir for every woman and girl; and for each man and boy the same, with the addition of 50 dried fish, 100 cocoanuts, and 50 *adubá* of jaggery. A payment of cloth and mats is also exacted from Atols where it is manufactured. Native money is now occasionally accepted in lieu of produce.

Besides a claim to all wrecks, the Sultan further asserts a right of pre-emption at low rates on all cargoes imported from foreign ports.

The burden of taxation must be light, as it appears never to be demurred to. The people at Málé pay no taxes.

* In Pyrard's day there were two "*Mir vaires*" subordinate to the "*Velannas.*"

† Christopher, *Attol-wari*; Pyrard, *Varuery*. ‡ Christopher, *Rarhu-wari*.

§ Pyrard, in Harris, Vol. I., p. 714.

THE MÁLDIVES.

INHABITANTS.

Military force.

MILITARY FORCE.

There can never have been a warlike spirit prevalent among a race so peaceful by nature. "They make no war," says Ibn Batúta, "and their weapons are prayers."* Long periods of peace, broken very rarely by rumours of war or actual conflict with enemies other than roving Indian pirates, added to their constitutional timidity, has reduced the military efficiency of the Máldivians to a mere shadow.

The sole military force consists of a non-descript militia *(Hagu-bé-kalun)*† at Málé, divided into six companies numbering nominally 100 men each, but with an actual strength at the present day of probably not less than 1,200 all told. These companies were formerly under the command of the six Viziers as Captains *(Bodu-bé-kalun.)*

"The soldiers bear no arms, and are under no sort of discipline beyond that which results from the habit of assembling, without much order or arrangement, when called together." Their duties, according to Christopher, are so anomalous that they often serve as sailors on board the public boats.‡

A body of 40 men *(Kudi-bé-kalun)*§ is required to mount guard in rotation at the Sultan's palace, and is in charge of an officer called *Má Badéri Takurú-fánu.* These men have certain privileges, and are distinguished from the Hagubé-kalun by their head-kerchief.

A small body guard *(Degedetere-bé-kalun)* bearing muskets, escorts the Sultan when ever he appears in public.

The Government sailors *(Kalási-kalun)*‖ number from 200 to 300, and are separately commanded by eight officers.

Soldiers and sailors alike receive a fortnightly allowance of 12 measures *(náli)* of rice per man, and once a year additional pay in cloth and money.

Language.

LANGUAGE.

Little light has been thrown hitherto on the Máldive language. The grammar has still to be written; whilst the only vocabularies extant—those of Pyrard (1602–7)¶ and Christopher (1836–8)**—are very incomplete.

The language spoken by these Islanders is substantially the same throughout the group—including Maliku (Minakaï)—though dialectal variations of the Málé standard occur at Minakaï, and particularly in the Southern Atols, which have been less affected by foreign intercourse.

It can easily be understood that at Málé—the emporium of trade for the whole group—the language must have incorporated into itself many foreign words and lost much of its original purity. "There are other languages," says Pyrard, "such as those of Cambaye, Guzerati, of Malalaca, and the Portuguese, which some learn for the sake of trade, and by reason of the communication they have with those peoples."†† The modern vernacular has in this way become specially interlarded with Hindústání phrases.

---

* Lee's Travels of Ibn Batúta, 1829, p. 176.

† Herft (Ceylon Miscellany, Vol. I., 1855, p. 128), *Hangoobacolom;* Christopher, *Hanggube;* Pyrard, *Engou.* Mr. Gray compares S. *anga*, අඟ, in *chaturanga*, 'army.'

‡ Trans. Bom. Geo. Soc., 1836–8, p. 72.

§ Herft, *Hodobicaloom;* Christopher, *Kudibe.*

‖ Pyrard, *Callasir.* Hind., *Khalásí.*

¶ *Dictionaire de quelques mots de la Langue des Maldiues interpretez en François,* Supplement to *Voyage de F. Pyrard,* Paris, 1619.

** "Vocabulary of the Maldivian language."—J. R. A. S., Vol. VI., o. s., pp. 42-76.

†† Gray, J. R. A. S., Vol. X., N. S., 1878, pp. 181–2. The Portuguese language especially ruled in correspondence between European and natives in India and Ceylon during the 17th and early part of the 18th centuries. The Danish Missionaries to Malabar, writing in 1709, speak of its "going almost through all parts of the East." (Account of Danish Mission to Malabar, Part II., p. 14, London, 1718). The majority of Rája Siŋha's letters to the Dutch (between 1635–40 *circa*) were written in Portuguese, and there are extant at least three letters from the Máldive Sultan, Ibráhím Iskandar, in the same language. *V. s.*, p. 31.

Recently Mr. Gray has done something towards showing the connection between the Máldive and Siṇhalese languages by a partial comparison of vocabularies.* It is likely that further investigation will establish the position that the Máldivian should be classed among the A'ryan group of languages, by proving it very closely allied to Siṇhalese (under its older form of Eḷu)† both in grammatical structure and phonetic character.

In the Southern Atols the dialect approaches Siṇhalese most nearly.‡

Since the Muhammadan supremacy, *Arabic* has been the language of religion on the Islands, but not generally that of foreign official correspondence until within the last half century.§

Besides the Arabic (old and new style), the characters found on tombstones and Mosque tanks are of two kinds, generally carved in intaglio.

Dives akuru.

A knowledge of the oldest called *Divehi akuru* or *Dives akuru*, 'the letters of the Island (kingdom)'—probably used by the original settlers—is confined at the present day to the Faḍiyáru and a few others at Málé, though it is more widespread in the Southern Atols. Orders to these Atols are not now, as they seem to have been in Christopher's time, made out in this old character. It is written from left to right and is syllabic. The letters bear some resemblance to old Siṇhalese, as Mr. Gray has shown, but would seem rather to be modifications of the old Vaṭṭeḷuttu character once used throughout the South Tamil and Malayáḷam districts of India.‖

In the *Dives akuru* alphabet (which has never been published in full) there are twenty-five letters (not counting duplicates) capable of some hundreds of vowel mutations.

Gabuli tána.

The modern character, called *Gabuli-tána,*¶ is that usually employed. It is said to have been introduced when the Máldivians recovered their independence after the temporary subjection to the Portuguese, and has certainly been in use for more than two and a-half centuries.

The alphabet contains eighteen letters peculiar to itself, besides a few derived from Arabic and Persian, and is written from right to left, as opposed to the *Dives akuru.* "It will be difficult," says Mr. Gray, "to find another instance of so radical a change." The first nine letters are merely the Arabic numerals from 1 to 9: the last nine probably simplifications of the corresponding letters in the old alphabet. Vowels are not inherent, but are supplied by diacritical strokes common to the Arabic. Unlike the *Dives akuru*, these letters do not admit of being joined in writing. "It is customary to intersperse sentences with salutations, &c., in the Arabic character."**

There are varieties of *tána* writing, such as the *Harka tána* and *Defo' tána,* but these are awkward and rarely employed.

Much confusion in the sound of letters and difficulty in determining the correct orthography of words arises from the absence of any acknowledged written standard, and the consequent vagaries of each writer.

With the exception of short expositions of the Kurán, called *tartib,*†† in lithographed manuscript, and treaties on navigation and astrology—the property of ship captains—no

---

* "The Maldive Islands: with a vocabulary taken from François Pyrard de Laval, 1602-1607," J. R. A. S., Vol. X., N.S., Art. VII., 1878. See, too, "Contributions to Siṇhalese Grammar," by Dr. E. Müller (Ceylon Sessional Papers, 1880). Prof. E. Kuhn contributed in 1879 an article bearing on the subject to the *Munich Sitzungsberichte der Philos-Philol. Hist. Classe der K. Akademie der Wissenschaften,* Vol. II., Pt. III., pp. 399-434, of which Mr. D. Ferguson is preparing a translation for the Indian Antiquary.

† Note (13).

‡ See Ceylon A. S. Journ., Vol. VII., Part II., No. 24, 1881, pp. 119-24. "In the Atoll of *Souadou* and towards the south they speak a language hard to understand, rough and barbarous, but still it is the common (Maldive) language." (Gray, *loc. cit,* quoting Pyrard.)

§ With rare exceptions the whole series of the annual letters from the Sultans to the Dutch Governors in Ceylon during the 18th century was written in the Máldive language and modern character *(gabuli tána)*, and the practice continued until *circa* 1830, since which time Arabic has been regularly employed.

‖ First pointed out by Dr. A. C. Burnell in the Ind. Ant., Vol. I., 1872, p. 229.

¶ *Gabuli* 'accepted;' cf. Ar. *kabúl: tána;* cf. Jav. *tanu* 'writing.'

** J. R. A. S., Vol. VI., o.s., 1836, p. 43.

†† Note (14).

THE MÁLDIVES.

INHABITANTS.

other books exist. Not a few songs and charms are committed to writing for private use on loose leaflets of paper, which has to a great extent superseded the use of *pandanus* (M. *Má-karhikeyo)* leaves.

Notes.

NOTES.

(1)

Population.

POPULATION.—Lieutenant Christopher, in 1836, (J. R. A. S., Vol. VI., O.S., p. 43) "estimated that there were full 20,000 persons on those Islands," but added, "their numbers are evidently diminishing rapidly, although very few, if any, of the people are known to reside permanently in a foreign land." As far as concerns the alleged progressive diminution of population, this statement would appear to be refuted by the following comparative table (unfortunately, not quite complete) of the number of inhabited Islands throughout the group, shown in the Admiralty Charts corrected up to 1866 (Gray, J. R. A. S., Vol. X., N.S., 1878, p. 197), as tested very recently by a close personal examination of Islanders from different Atols :—

Atols.	1836 (Admiralty Charts.)	1882.
Tiladummatí	24	?
Miladummaḍulu ...	32	?
Fádiffoḷu	2	4
Máḷosmaḍulu... ...	30	? 32
Mále	8	13
Ari	13	18
Felidu	5	5
Mulaku	8	10
Nilandu	13	14
Koḷumaḍulu	11	13
Haddummatí	12	13
Suvádiva (Huvadú) ...	17	21
Aḍḍú...	7	7
	182	

It is said that a census of the Islands was last taken during the reign of S. M'uín-ud-dín, but no particulars are forthcoming.

(2)

There would seem to be but slight traces of Malayan influence on the Máldive group.

Among prevalent superstitious ceremonies, the Máldive custom of launching a small bark loaded with perfumes and flowers, and turning it adrift at the mercy of wind and waves as an offering to the Spirit of the Winds, Dr. Leyden* compares to the very similar offering to the god of evil made by the Biajús, a race of Malay sea gypsies in the Indian Archipelago.

Prinsep (Journ. Bengal A. S., Vol. V., 1836, p. 793) considered the Máldive orthography of Arabic to partake of "the Malay style ;" and a small proportion of Malayan words, though of little importance, is undoubtedly to be found in the language of these Islanders, amounting only to 1·9 (Yule) per cent. in the Máldive vocabulary (275 words) given by Pyrard. This admixture may be casual, and have been brought about, as Crawfurd points out in the case of Malagasy, by chance visits of "those strong fleets of rovers that, in all known time, have ranged the seas of the [Malayan] Archipelago. I suppose them, while either in quest of booty or adventure, to be driven into the South-Eastern monsoon or trade wind by a tempest. Unable to regain the shores of the Archipelago, they would from necessity, and after some struggle, put before the wind and make for the first land. * * * * They would settle, amalgamate with the inhabitants, and convey some instruction to them along with a portion of their languages."†

---

* "On the Language and Literature of the Indo-Chinese Nations." Mr. Gray (J. R. A. S., Vol. X., N.S., p. 203), quotes Surgeon-Major Davie, 'Medical History of the Laroot Field Force.'

† Crawfurd, "Dictionary of the E. Indian Islands," 1856, p. 232.

Two Malayan invasions of Ceylon are recorded during the reign of Paṇḍita Parákrama Báhu III., (*circa* A.D. 1267), and to this day the west face of the Fádiffolu Atol is known to the Máldivians as "*Jáva kara*"—*i. e.*, 'the Malay Coast'—although the islands on that edge have for centuries remained uninhabited.

(3)

Date of Muhammadan Conversion.

Date of the Muhammadan Conversion.—In his paper on the Máldives (J. R. A. S., Vol. X., n.s., 1878, Art. VIII., p. 177,) Mr. Gray notes: "Ibn Batuta, while residing at the Maldives, married, about 1340 A.D., the daughter of a Vizier who was grandson of the Sultan Daoud, who was the grandson of Chenourāzah, the first king who embraced the Muhammadan faith. (Ibn Bat., Paris, 1858, Vol. IV., p. 154.) The probable date of the conversion is, therefore, 1200 A.D. Ibn Batuta saw the record engraven in wood in the chief mosque."

If restricted to the first *Royal* convert on the group, the approximate date here assumed can hardly be gainsaid. "They have a tradition," writes Christopher, "that about 400 years ago [A.D. 1435 *circa*], the Muhammadan religion was introduced among them by a man whose name was Tabriz, or whose country was so called. The probability is that the latter was the case. * * * Tabriz, they say, came from Persia; and they state that shortly after his death some of his countrymen, who came in search of him, remained, and, when they died, were buried on the S. E. point of the Island."*

Further confirmation would be afforded were it possible to identify the famous Muhammadan saint of the biographies Shaikh Jalál-ud-dín Tabrízí who died in A.H. 642 or A.D. 1244 and was buried according to the A'ín-i-Akbarí at "Bandar Dín Mahall" (held by some authorities to be the Máldives) with "Tabriz," as known to the Máldivians under the name of Yúsuf Shams-ud-dín, or even with one of his companions.†

Crawfurd properly remarks, however, in commenting on the introduction of Muhammadanism among the islanders of the Malay Archipelago, that "the dates and times quoted for the conversion of the different people refer to that of their rulers, and not of the people generally; many converts had in every case been made long before the periods quoted, and many had still to be made."‡

It was probably so at the Máldives. The wave of Muslim proselytism might not reach Málé for more than a century—the spiritual conquest of the group dating from the conversion of the sovereign at Málé, *circa* A.D. 1200,§ though the Southern Islanders may well have repelled the faith for some time longer.

As in the Eastern Archipelago, the progress of conversion would be likely to be gradual. "The missionaries who effected the conversion were not, for the most part, genuine Arabs, but the mixed descendants of Arab and Persian traders from the Persian and Arabian gulfs—parties who, by their intimate acquaintance with the manners and languages of the Islanders, were far more effectual instruments. In the course of several ages Arabian and Persian merchants and Mahomedan merchants from Gujrat and other ports of India had settled in various parts of the Archipelago. Unaccompanied by their families, they intermarried with the native inhabitants, and from this union sprang the apostles of Islam."‡

So Pyrard :—"They received Mahometanism through the Moors and Arabs who, while trading over all the Continents and islands of India, brought also their law, which has since remained in most of those parts."‖

(4)

Legend of the Muslim Conversion.

Legend of the Muslim Conversion.—The story of the Muhammadan conversion, given by Ibn Batúta, runs as follows :—

"When the people of the islands were idolators, there appeared to them every month an evil spirit, who came from the sea, resembling a ship filled with lamps. It was the custom of the natives, when they beheld him, to adorn a young virgin and to conduct her to a *boudkhânah*, or temple of idols, built on the shore, and having a window by which she could be seen. They left her for the night, and when they returned in the morning they found her violated and dead. So

* Trans. Bombay Geo. Soc., 1836-8, p. 74.

† Journ. Bengal A. S., Vol. XLII., Pt. I., 1873, p. 260.

‡ Crawfurd, "Dictionary of the E. Indian Islands," p. 236-7.

§ Sir W. Robinson puts the date of conversion of the Lakkadive Islanders A.D. 1250 *circa*.

‖ Gray, J. R. A. S., Vol. X., n.s., p. 177.

THE MÁLDIVES.

INHABITANTS.

Notes.

every month they cast lots, and he on whom the lot fell gave up his daughter. In course of time arrived a Maghrébin, named Abou'l Berecât, the Berber, who knew by heart the gloroius Korān. He lodged in the house of an old woman at Mahal. One day he found her family assembled, and the women weeping as at a funeral. He asked but could not be made to understand the cause, until an interpreter came, who told him that the lot had fallen upon the old woman, and that she had one only daughter. Abou'l Berecât then said to the old woman, 'I will go to-night in thy daughter's stead': he was then entirely beardless. So, at night, after his ablutions, he was led to the idol temple. There he set himself to recite the Korān, and in a while beheld the demon. He continued his recitation, and the demon, as soon as he came within hearing of the Korān, plunged into the sea. So, when it was dawn, the people, who came as was their custom to remove and burn the corpse, found the Maghrébin still reciting the Korān. He was conducted to the King named Chenourāzah, who was astonished to hear what had happened. The Maghrébin then proposed to him to embrace the true faith, and pressed him to receive it. But Chenourāzah said: 'Stay with us till next month: and if you do again as you have now done, and escape the evil genie, I will be converted.' The stranger remained, and God disposed the heart of the King to receive the true faith. He became Mussulman before the end of the month, with his wives, children, and court. At the beginning of the following month the Maghrébin was conducted to the idol temple; but the demon came not, and he recited the Korān till the morning, when the Sultan and his subjects arrived, and found him so employed. They then broke the idols and razed the temple to the ground. The people of the island embraced the faith, and sent messengers who converted the other islanders also. The Maghrébin remained among them and enjoyed their high esteem, and it was the doctrine of his sect, viz., that of the Imām Mālik, which the natives professed. Even at present they respect the Maghrébines for his sake. He built a mosque which is known by his name. I have read the following inscription graven in wood on the enclosed pulpit of the grand mosque: '*The Sultan Ahmed Chenourāzah has received the true faith at the hands of Abou'l Berecât, the Berber, the Maghrébin.*' "*

Vestiges of this romantic legend have been handed down by tradition current among the Islanders to this day. But with more probability they assign to *Yúsuf Shams-ud-din*, of *Tabríz*, the honour which Ibn Batúta not unnaturally would claim for a Maghrébin, and the votaries of Hazrat Mírá Sáhib for the later Nágúr saint (A.D. 1504–1570.)†

"Throughout the world," observes Mr. Conway, "are found legends of beautiful virgins sacrificed to demons or deities." That connected with the *Bahiráva-kanda*—a hill overlooking Kandy—bears a close resemblance to the Máldive tradition,‡ and Mr. Conway quotes a somewhat similar legend current in Japan concerning the fiend Shuden-dozi.§

(5)

Sunní Sect.

SUNNI' SECT.—Muhammadans in general are divided into two great sects.

1.—The *Sunnís*, or Traditionists; so called because they acknowledge the authority of the *Sunna*, or collection of moral traditions of the sayings and actions of their Prophet, as concurrent with and supplementary to the Kurán. The Sunna directs the observance of several things omitted in the Kurán, and in name as well as design answers to the Mishna of the Jews.

The Sunnís are sub-divided into four chief sects (which derive their names from their respective founders), viz., *Hanífis, Sháfa'ías, Málikis*, and *Hambalis*. These sects, though all are considered sound in fundamentals, differ in some points of law and religion, and follow the interpretation of the Kurán and the traditions of the four great doctors Abú Hanífa, Málik, Al Shafa'í, and Ibn Hambal.

The Arabians and Muslims of Southern India, Ceylon, and the Lakkadive and Máldive Islands generally, follow the teachings of Al Sháfa'í.

2.—The *Shía'hs*, or partisans of the house of 'Alí, adhere to their own traditions, and reject the authority of the Sunna. According to the Shía'h doctrine the sovereign *Imámat*, or temporal and spiritual headship over the faithful, was by divine right vested in 'Alí and in his descendants through Hasan and Husain, the children of Fátimah, the daughter of the Prophet; and thus the Persian Shía'hs add to the formula of belief the confession, "Alí is the Kaliph of God."

* Gray (J. R. A. S., Vol. X., N. S., pp. 180-1), quoting Ibn Bat, French edition, Tome IV.

† Ceylon A. S. Journ., Vol. VII., Pt. II., No. 24, 1881, pp. 135-136.

‡ Ceylon A. S. Journ., 1865-6, pp. 30-1.

§ "Demonology and Devil-lore," Vol. II. pp., 405-8.

Between these two sects (*Sunnís* and *Shía'hs*) exists the most inveterate enmity. Though the difference arose at first on a political occasion, it has notwithstanding been so well improved by additional circumstances and the spirit of contradiction, that each party anathematizes the other as abominable heretics and further from the truth than either the Christians or the Jews.*

(6)

Superstitions.

SUPERSTITIONS.—" Where the mass of the people is sunk in ignorance, as is the case here with only a few exceptions, it is not surprising to find the most absurd and superstitious fancies exerting a powerful and pernicious influence. In describing their superstitions, it may not be irrelevant to premise that, in the absence of other and better sources of information, an account of these may throw some light on the nature of the religion of the islanders which preceded the one which they now profess.

" One of the most remarkable of their customs is the offering made to the sea when a boat is to be launched [M. *salavátu*]. On such occasions a small vessel, three or four feet long, being decked out with flags, and having samples of the various fruits of the island, is set adrift ; should it be a boat newly built, other ceremonies are observed, accompanied with feasting, music, &c. The miniature vessel is decorated with flowers, and her gunwales are hung with fruits, for which, as soon as she enters the water, there is a general scramble."†

" When they set out upon a voyage they avoid touching or meeting any body, for if any unlucky accident befalls them, they impute it to the person that touched them. When they go a-fishing they must not salute any, or bid them good-morrow ; from sunset on Thursday till three or four o'clock next morning they suffer nothing to be carried out of their house, but receive all that is brought in."‡

" Before a voyage is undertaken an offering is made to some saint for success, and in danger or distress the mariners trust chiefly in the efficacy of vows or offerings to the tomb of some personage (dead or living) of eminent piety. We are informed of large sums given as votive offerings, made during boisterous weather, to an old priest resident at Calcutta. All moneys paid at Malé in fulfilment of such vows go to the priest.§ It is also a common practice for persons labouring under sickness, or any other sufferings, to dedicate certain sums as means of ensuring relief. An amulet obtained from a reputed saint is prized very highly as a preventive of calamity, and those who possess such a thing constantly wear it."†

Mr. Gray has translated some remarks of Pyrard regarding other superstitious practices of these Islanders:—" '*Siare* [M. *Ziyára*] ; a spot dedicated to the *King of the Winds* in a secluded corner of each island, where those who have escaped from danger (at sea), come to make offering daily of little boats and ships fashioned on purpose, and filled with perfumes, guns, flowers, and odoriferous woods. They set the perfumes on fire, and cast into the sea the little boats, which float till they are burned ; and this, say they, in order that the *King of the Winds* may accept them.' We have here the remains of pre-Buddhistic worship of the elements, which grew into a propitiation of the god or devil at whose hands they feared harm. This worship seems to have survived Buddhism, and to have lived with Islam, just as the Dewalc-worship lived with Buddhism in Ceylon, or as the mysterious grove-worship existed along with Hebrew monotheism." Again : " 'Also when they find difficulty in launching their ships and galleys, they kill some cocks and hens, and throw them into the sea in front of the ship or boat.' A cock is a favourite offering to the Ceylon devils."‖

" They likewise pay a superstitious deference to the imaginary *King of the Sea*, and dare not spit to the windward of the ship, nor look behind them."‡

" 'They believe that evil is caused by the devil troubling them, and that he is the sole author of death and sickness. They invoke him accordingly, offering flowers and preparing a banquet of all sorts of meats and drinks, which they place in a secret spot and leave to be wasted, unless perchance some of the poor come and take them. With the same design, they kill some cocks and hens, turning towards the sepulchre of Mahomet, and then and there lay them down and leave them, praying the devils to accept the offerings and to take himself off and leave the patient at ease. This sorcery they call *cauery*' (Sans. *kawi* 'incantation.')"‖

---

* See Sale, 'Koran' ; Stobbart, 'Islam' ; and, for a forcible skit on the "differences" between the Sunnís and Shía'hs, Moore, 'Two-penny Post-bag' (Abdallah to Mohassan). † Trans. Bom. Geo. Soc., 1836–8, p. 75.

‡ Pyrard, quoted in Harris, Vol. I., pp. 710–11. M. Garcin de Tassy has shown that the god of the sea reverenced by the Máldive Islanders is identical with the mysterious saint *Khája Khizr*, in whose honour, as the discoverer of the water of life and patron of the waters, the festival of the *Bíra* is held during the month of Bhádún, (August—September).—Sell., 'Faith of Islam,' pp. 260-1 ; and see Mandelso, 'Travels,' 1637, p. 336.

§ Cf. Ceylon A. S. Journ., Vol. VII., Pt. II., No. 24, 1881, p. 126. ‖ J. R. A. S., Vol. X., N.S., 1878, pp. 202–3.

THE MÁLDIVES.

INHABITANTS.

Notes.

Buddhism on the Máldives.

(7)

Buddhism on the Máldives.—Mr. Christopher (Trans. Bom. Geo. Soc., 1836-8, pp. 313-4) adduces the following evidence in favour of the pre-existence of the Buddhist cult on the Máldive group :—

(i.) The posture employed in burial alleged to be similar to that of the recumbent Buddha, viz., the body laid in the coffin on its right side, the right ear resting on the right hand, and the left arm placed along the thigh.

(ii.) The assertion of a Buddhist priest, "considered a clever man, and well read in Singalese books," that there were formerly on the Máldives "two noted temples of Buddh."

(iii.) The *Bó* tree *(Ficus religiosa)* said to be "still suffered to stand alone in the vicinity of mosques, when all other shrubbery is cleared away for the burial ground."

(iv.) "The dread the Maldivians manifest of taking animal life."

The points raised will be found to be materially weakened on examination :—

(i.) Christopher here evidently follows Pyrard (p. 117) whose exact words are * * * "luy mettant la main droitte sur l'oreille, et la gauche tout au long de la cuisse, et le posent * * * couché sur le costé droict *iusques à ce que le corps soit porté en terre;*" but further on (p. 119) "Quand ils mettent le corps dedans [la fosse], ils luy tournent la face vers le costé du sepulchre de Mahomet," &c.—in fact the usual Muslim burial with the important exception of the *position of the arms.* Can Pyrard have been mistaken ? In Ceylon Muhammadan burials the body is inclined on the right side with the face looking towards Medina, the head slightly raised and supported on sand, and the arms placidly folded in front. This is said to be also the practice now in vogue at the Máldives.

(ii.) In the absence of corroborative testimony, the accuracy of this nameless priest's statement may fairly be impugned. It is quite possible that he may have identified the Máldives *(Mála-diva)* with *Puvañgu-divayina,* or some other undetermined island quoted in the *Vihára-asna,* a list of Ceylon Buddhist shrines ; indeed, it is very probable, for, adds Christopher, "he named the islands on which they were situated, but I could not recognize them as perpetuated to the present day" The religious and historical books of the Siṇhalese yet discovered are altogether silent regarding any Buddhist mission to the Máldives, or the existence of Buddhist temples on the Islands.

(iii.) Only two *Bó* trees [M. *Bói gas*] are known to be growing at the present day on the group—one upon the uninhabited island of *Keḍerá* in Suvádiva (Huvadú) Atol, and the other at *Málé,* near the palace, but not within the walled enclosure or burial ground of any mosque. Pyrard says nothing to support the belief that the Máldivians held the *Pipul* in greater regard than other trees, and they do not in any way respect it now.

(iv.) Christopher again follows Pyrard (p. 129): "Ie prenois plaisir à voir que pour l'ordinaire pour tuer vne poule, il falloit courir par toute vne isle pour trouuer vn homme qui sceust tuer, encore pourueu qu' il le voulust faire : dautant qu' ils reculent tant qu' ils peuuent à faire ce mestier-là." This reluctance to turn butchers, instead of a survival of Buddhistic orthodoxy, may perhaps as reasonably be attributed to the superstitious requirements enjoined on the select few qualified to kill animals. "Quand il faut tuer quelque animal pour leur viure, il y a bien du mystere. Ils leur coupent la gorge en se tournans du costé du sepulchre de Mahomet, et disent leurs prieres, et tout aussitost ils les quittent, ou ils les iettent sans y toucher iusques à ce qu' ils soient morts entierement. Que si quelqu' vn y touchoit auparauant, ils ietteroient cette chair, et ils n'en mangeroient point. Ce n' est pas tout, il faut que ce ne soit que par vn certain endroit seulement qu' on leur coupe la gorge, autrement personne n'en mangeroit. De plus, tout le monde ne s' entend pas à cela ; ce sont principalement des Prestres ou des Moudins qui le sçauent ; ou bien ceux qui l' entreprennent doiuent estre anciens et non pas ieunes, et il faut qu' ils ayent eu des enfans."

In this connection should not be omitted Mr. Gray's comparison (J. R. A. S., Vol. X., N.S., p. 179), of the Máldive festival "*poḍcacan* (Pyrard) celebrated at the full moon of April or May" with "the '*depóya*' (full moon) of Wesak, when the Singalese commemorate the attainment of Nirwána by Gautama"; but, as Mr. Gray himself adds, "the Maldivans attribute the origin of the festival to the first introduction of rice to the islands, which would connect it rather with the *Alut Sāl*, or 'new rice,' festival of Ceylon (held in January) than with the thoroughly Buddhistic holiday of May."

Whilst, therefore, the evidence available is both insufficient, and of a nature too vague, to warrant any definite conclusion, it is far from improbable that a close scrutiny of names of islands, of non-Muhammadan customs and festivals, and, above all, an archæological survey, will make it abundantly clear that Buddhist missionaries, in the spirit of the Aṣoka edicts, departing 'to intermingle among all unbelievers, teaching better things,' carried their doctrine across the sea even to the despised and little known Máldives.

[Since the above note was penned important evidence has come to hand in favour of the contention of "an intervening Buddhism" on the Islands :—

(*a*) The strikingly Buddhistic title "*Darumavanta*" (S. ධර්මවන්ත, *Dharmmavanta* 'Religious,' 'Just') applied by the Máldivians to their first Sovereign converted to Muhammadanism.

(*b*) Similarly, the undeniable significance of such island names as *Muñña-furhi* (? S. *Munipura*, 'Buddha's city') in Haddumatí Atol, *Huḷudeli* (S. සලදළ, *saladaḷa* 'Bó tree' isle) in Nilandu Atol, *Vihama-furhi* and *Vihamanà-furhi* ('the island of the delightful Wiháres,' Gray) in Ari and Mále Atols.

(*c*) According to the reliable assertion of resident natives, on the island of Fua Mulaku (lat. 0° 7′ S.) exist the jungle-covered ruins of a *tope* or *dágaba*, and amid them the stone image of a Buddha in the *sthána-mudrá* or standing position. This *tope* is described as resembling the solid bell-shaped *dágabas*, rising from platforms, usual in Ceylon.

Such ruins the Islanders of the Southern Atols term *astabu* (Aḍḍú Atol), *havitta* (Fua Mulaku), and *vére* (Atols further north), in which it is easy to recognise the Sanskṛit *stúpa*, *chaitya*, and *vihára*.

"It may be that during long centuries no life was imparted to Maldive Buddhism from Ceylon, and that the religion of 'the Blessed One' at last *flickered to extinction*, while the barbarous rites and superstitions of the Dewales and the groves remained connected in the native mind with those purely temporal ills from which in their daily life men sought deliverance."]*

(8)

Chess.

CHESS.—Sir W. Jones assigns the invention of chess to the Hindús ('Asiatic Researches,' Vol. 7, 1803), and Major Forbes ('Eleven years in Ceylon,' Vol. II., p. 265), mentions the Hindú belief that it was originated by Rávaṇá's Queen, Wandódarí, during the tedious mythical seige of Ṣrí-Laṅká-pura.

The Sanskṛit name for the game is *Choturaṅga, i.e.*, 'the four members of an army,' which. according to Amarakósha, are *hasti* (elephants), *asva* (horses), *ratha* (chariots), and *pádátan* ('foot soldiers.') The same names are employed in India at this day.

Pieces.

English Game.	Sanskrit.	Máldive.
King	*Rájá*	*Boḍu.*
Queen	*Mantri*	*Mantiri.*
Bishop	{ *Hasti* / *Pílu* }	*Boḍu-bo.*
Knight	*Asva*	*As.*
Castle or Rook ...	{ *Ratha* / *Roka* }	*Riya.*
Pawn	{ *Padáti* / *Padica* }	{ *Máná* / *Sipái.* }
Chess	*Chaturaṅga* (cf. S. *sivuraṅga keli*, සිවුරඟ කෙළි)	*Rázuvá kuli.* (cf. S. *Rájavil keli*, රජවිල් කෙළි.)

Máldive chess-men are of wood, roughly carved into the simplest of forms, in accordance with the Muslim prohibition against the making an image of anything that has life.

---

* Gray, J. R. A. S., Vol. X., N.S., 1878, p. 180.

THE MÁLDIVES.

INHABITANTS.

Notes.

Social Distinctions.

(9)

SOCIAL DISTINCTIONS.—Compare Mr. E. G. Thomas' account (Madras Journ. Lit. and Science, 1859–60) of the different class appellations borne by the inhabitants of Máliku (Minakaĭ.) The divisions are :—

(1) *Malikans*
(2) *Malummies* (*Yáekurá*)
(3) *Klasies* (*Kalo*)
(4) *Maylacherries*

1. "The *Malikans* (about 116 in number) form the aristocracy of the Island. Three of them have considerable landed property there, and own all the trading vessels which go to Bengal, &c. Though now consisting of several families, they are all connected, being sprung from Kambakoth Kombaramy, who lived 200 years ago. They have by no means the over-weening influence exercised over their countrymen by the aristocracy of the Laccadive Islands. This is consequent on the different relative position of the parties. The Beebee of Cannanore has endeavoured more or less to identify their interests with her own, by supporting their wishes occasionally with reference to the conduct of their sailors, and by usually employing one of them as her Agent or Konnakar on the Islands.

2. "The *Malummies* are the pilots and mates of the vessels. This is no hereditary title, but is conferred by their neighbours for ability. Any man in Monakoy may obtain this rank, and is not then excluded from the society of the Malikans who will even intermarry with them. They number abont 180.

3. "The *Klasies* (1,107 in number) form the bulk of the population, and, though in general poor, are exceedingly independent of the other classes. They possess no sea-going boats or vessels of their own, nothing fit to use far outside the lagoon ; but they work the larger vessels and the *mass* [fishing] boats of the Malikans, as it is impossible for the merchants without their aid to carry on their trade : and as the Klasies are not landed tenants-at-will as in the Laccadives, but, with very few exceptions, small landed proprietors themselves, and only going to sea for regular wages given for work done at the time, they enjoy a very comfortable independent position, and both on land and at sea yield by no means implicit obedience to either Beebee or Malikans. "Besides those who are employed in the Beebee's and Malikans' vessels, many of them take service in English ships, and are absent for many years together. During this period they get high wages, but usually spend it all before they return to Menakoy.

4. "Those who follow the occupation of the *Maylacherries*, or tree climbers, are about 583 in number. They climb the trees of the ryots and the Beebee for hire, and extract the juice from which sugar is made."*

(10)

The Sultans of the Máldives.

THE SULTANS OF THE MÁLDIVES.—The rule of succession governing in the Malabar States generally, and notably in Travancore and Cochin, according to the usages of the Nairs in favour of descent in the female line does not appear to have extended to the Máldive Islands. On the death of a Sultan the Sovereignty usually passes to one of the sons. History—so much at least as has come to light—affords but three instances of a female succeeding to the throne—the first in the ninth century, the second four centuries later, (Khadíjah, *circa* A.D. 1344), and the last after the lapse of a similar period (A'miná, A.D. 1754).

The Máldive Sultans have assumed the fulsome cognomen *Iskandar*,—applied by Arab and Persian writers to Alexander the Great ("Iskandar Al Rúmí"),—perhaps by virtue of supposed descent from the wide-ruling Iskandar Dhu'lkarnein (*i.e.*, 'the two-horned'), a Persian king of the first race, the contemporary of Abraham, and alleged tenth descendant from Noah, through Japhet and Elisha.

Other eulogistic epithets (clearly of Sanskṛit origin) attached to the Sultans' names in written communications are explained elsewhere.†

The ordinary Máldive term for the Sovereign is *Rasge-fánu*, but the Arabic title *Sulṭán* is used to accompany his Muslim name after Muhammadan custom.‡ The Sultans' wives are called *Rasge-fánu Abi-kabalun*, and their children *Goma-fulun* or *Gon-fulun*.

Eligibility for future Sovereignty is betokened by the elevation of the umbrella over some member of the Royal family. This honour was conferred upon a younger brother of the Sultan during the residence of Mr. Christopher at Málé. "On this occasion there were great rejoicings in the

---

* Report on the management during Fusli, 1268, of the Five Laccadive Islands. † Vide Note (13) *infra*.

‡ A'miná is styled in her Minister's letters to the Dutch *Raṇi-kilage-fánu*.

town. Guns were fired, and the public were entertained in the evenings with games, at the conclusion of which they were treated to a grand feast. On this day the young Prince was for the first time seen in public. The ceremony partakes of a religious character, inasmuch as the heir-apparent is required to proceed in procession to the mosque, and to the tombs of the principal saints to repeat the Fatha. The umbrella [M. *hai-koḷu ;* S. සත්, *sat.*] being one of the insignia of Sovereignty, none but the Sultan can have it carried over him."* Among other insignia borne by his attendants are a fan of peacock's feathers (M. *samara-koḷu ;* S. සෙමෙර, *semera)*, a brass betel-box (M. *adafi forhi koḷa*), and ornamented slippers (M. *faivaṇ-koḷu).*

(11)

Sultan's Claim to the Property of Deceased Máldivians.

SULTAN'S CLAIM TO THE PROPERTY OF DECEASED MÁLDIVIANS.—This is confirmed by a statement in one of Sultan M. M'uin-ud-dín's letters of 1819 regarding the property of a certain Sayyid or Muhammadan Priest, towards whom the Sultan appears to have acted with much consideration and liberality.

"Strangers who take their refuge in this Island, and who, for want of money, may crave the assistance of Government, are always supported and kindly treated by us. But it is customary with Our Government on this Island when money is issued from the Public Treasury to individuals to enable them to carry on trade, at the death of such persons to take to Government alone all such property as they may leave behind, whether too little or too large *(sic);* so money is never issued but to those who consent to the above conditions. Nevertheless in this case of the Sayyid I have not taken one rupee from his estate. I have written these circumstances to Your Excellency thinking that it would be proper that Your Excellency should be acquainted with the same."†

Previously, in 1804, the Sultan having received intelligence that a suit had been commenced in Ceylon about the estate of a Máldivian named Don Kalége-fánu, requested that His Excellency the Governor would, "after investigation of the case, cause all the goods [of the deceased] and the money for the goods he disposed of there," to be delivered over to the hands of the Ambassador "as all of the same did not belong to his relations but to the Sultan's Court." *(sic.)*‡

Upon another claim to a house in Ceylon made by the same Sultan in 1830, it was considered advisable to point out that Máldivian law had no extra-territorial effect in civil proceedings *in rem.* "There are Courts of Law established on the Island," wrote Sir E. Barnes, "which are open to all persons; and Your Highness may order your Agents to have recourse to the Courts for the recovery of any property Your Highness may have to claim; and the case will be decided according to law and justice: but it is not customary for Government to interfere in such cases wherein the rights of property of the inhabitants are concerned, and which may be decided by law by the Courts of Justice appointed for that purpose."§

See also Lord Torrington's reply (1850) regarding 'Alí Dídí.‖

(12)

Government.

GOVERNMENT.—The constitution of the Máldive Government has ever continued to retain the main features of the ancient Indian polity, based on the Institutes of Manu, and followed "throughout the history of Ceylon. At the head the King [*Mahá Rája*], bound by no law, but never altering the law; his despotism only restrained by his own sense of justice or fear: at his Court one or more ministers, [*Meti, Mantri*], among whom the departments of State were sometimes divided, but to anyone of whom usually an appeal lay from every inferior officer, and who [as the *Amátya-mandalé* or Council of State] advised the King, or administered in his name, on all affairs: over each province a Chief [*Yuva-rája*], bound to pay into the Treasury not the exact revenue he received, but a lump sum, and intermediate appeal judge in all cases arising in his district: under him, again, inferior officers, some of whom were clerks and accountants with specified duties, others petty territorial headmen over villages or small districts, with judicial as well as administrative power."¶

A comparison of the modern designations of the Máldive Sultan's Ministers of State, and their respective functions, with those recorded by Pyrard as ruling at the commencement of

* Trans. Bom. Geo. Soc., 1836-8, p. 66.
† Sultan's letter, A. H. 1235; (translation dated November 16th, 1819.)
‡ Sultan's letter, (translation) dated November 2nd, 1804.
§ Governor's reply, dated December 18th, 1830.
‖ Governor's reply, dated October 4th, 1850.
¶ Rhys Davids, J. R. A. S., Vol. VII., Pt. II., N.S., Art. XVII., p. 370.

THE MÁLDIVES.

INHABITANTS.

Notes.

the 17th century, and by Ibn Batúta two and a-half centuries earlier, discloses that, whilst a redistribution of duties may have occurred from time to time, the official titles at least have suffered but slight change.

Of these the majority bear intrinsic evidence of ancient A'ryan origin.

(*a*) ***Hadégiri***, in whom are combined now-a-days the offices of Chief of the Treasury and Receiver-General of Revenue (Chris., *Hindeggeree;* Pyrard, *Endequery*, "a Lord Privy Councillor, always in attendance upon the King;" but Ibn Bat. *Hendîdjéry*, 'Preacher'). Cf. *Bháṇḍágáriko amachcho*, the Lord High Treasurer of the old Siṇhalese Court (Turnour's Mahávaṇso, p. 231, 3).

(*b*) ***Dorhiméná***, (Chris., *Durimind*, 1st Vizier, "Chief or General of the Army;" Pyrard, *Dorimenaz*, *Torimesnas*, "Commander-in-Chief of the Army;") possibly the *Dvára-náyaka* (Mah., p. 260, 10), but cf. T. துரை, *turai* :

(*c*) ***Fámudéri*** (Chris., *Famederi*, 4th Vizier; Pyrard, *Pammedery calogue*, one of the great lords; Ibn Bat., *Fâmeldâry* "Receiver-General of Revenue." Cf. S. පාමොක්, දෙට; *pámok, deṭa*, and the *Amachcha Pámukha* (Mah., p. 69.)

(*d*) ***Máfaï*** (Chris., *Mafae*, 5th Vizier; Pyrard, *Manpas*, "Chancellor, Keeper of the King's Privy Seal;" Ibn Bat., *Mâfâcaloû*, "Receiver-General of Revenue.") Cf. S. මහා, *mahá*, and පති, *pati*, in *Senápati*, *Chamupati* (Mah. *passim*).

(*e*) ***Dáhará*** (Chris., *Dahara*, 6th Vizier; Pyrard, *Darade Tacourou*, "Count or Duke." Cf. the *Dovárika* (Mah., p. 117, 11.)

Ibn Batúta makes no mention of the *Dorhiméná*, *Hakurá* (Chris., *Hakura;* Pyrard, *Acouraz*) and *Veláná* (Chris., *Wilono Shadander;* Pyrard, *Velannas* "First Lord of the Admiralty and President of the Board of Trade") Viziers; but styles "the Minister of Police" *Fitnâyec*, and the "Admiral" *Mânâyec*. Cf. S. මහා, *mahá*, නායක, *náyaka*.

(13)

Without attempting in the compass of a Note to enter into a lengthened comparison of Siṇhalese and Máldive vocabularies, already partially essayed by Mr. Gray (J. R. A. S., Vol. X., Art. VIII.), it may strengthen the position assumed regarding the affinity of the two languages (whilst serving of interest on other grounds) to insert here a fac-simile of one of the annual letters of the Máldive Sultans of the last century, with a transcript in Roman characters and an English translation.

It will be at once seen that the proportion of words clearly traceable to Siṇhalese or Sanskṛit sources is large, amounting to at least 65 per cent.

TRANSCRIPT.*

Ḥuwa' l ghaní.

As-Sultán Hasan Núr-ud-dín

Suvastí sirímata mahá sirí bari kusa furadá :
: na sirí kula sada ira siáka sástura audána Ka :
: ttiri *As-Sulṭán Hasan Núr-ud-dín Iskandar* Kattiri Bowana
Mahá Radun. Koḷubu Gorunu Dóre-ve kiyá Rasge-fána' mita'
lakka hás farhuṇ *salám*. Maniku-fánumeṇge Koḷubu-gai ihu u :
: luṇvi Ras-Ras-kalunnái, mi Ḍivehi Rájjé-gai ihu uḷuṇ :
vi Ras-Ras-kalunnái ra*hmat*rikaṇ beheṭṭevi fadaiṇ-me, Mani :
: ku-fánái Timaṇ Maniku-fánu hif-fuḷu-gai *rahmat* bahaṭṭavaigeṇ hunne :
: víme. Maniku-fánumeṇ kibaiṇ edi-tibímáve. Mi Divehi Rájjeiṇ oḍi :
: ye' dóñe' behigeṇ gos Maniku-fána' *khabar*i-vé tanaku tibi na :
: ma, e bayaku geṇdavai, e míhuṇge haihúnu-kaṇ bellavumái. Mi Divehi
Rájjea' '*adá*vátteriaku Maniku-fána' egijje nama, e bayaka'
Maniku-fánumeṇ nu-russevumeve. Maniku-fánumennái arafődigeṇ-
nuvá kuḍa hadiyá-kaḷa-kái *Ahmad* Kuḍa Baḍéri Kéví tiá fonuvvímu. Mi a :
: ḷá dennevi kame' kuravvai; mi aḷuṇ kibain *taksír* vias *mu'áf*
: kuravvai. Avvalu músumu-gai furuvá kama' edi-vaḍaigeṇ hunne :
: víme. 1210 *sanat*.

---

* The Máldive character (*gabuḷi-tána*) is transliterated as far as possible according to the system recommended by Sir William Jones and Professor Wilson, and adopted by the Ceylon Government (Minute of November 16th, 1869), for the Siṇhalese and Tamiḷ languages.

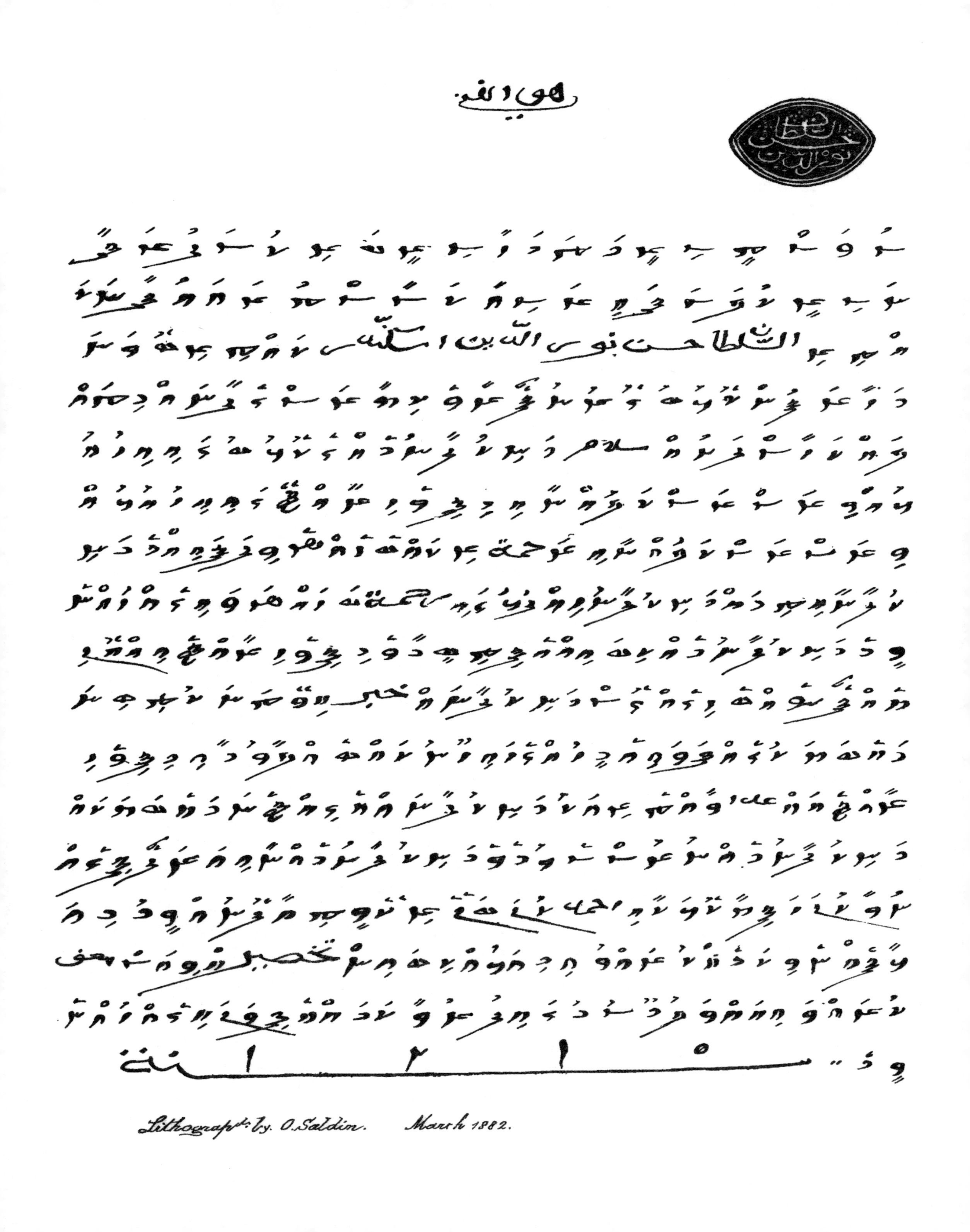

هو الله

Lithograph by O. Saldin. March 1882.

Translation.
He (God) is the richest !

Seal of Sultan Hasan Núr-ud-dín.

Hail ! Sultan Hasan Núr-ud-dín Iskandar, Mighty Monarch of the Universe, a Kshatriya, endowed with beauty, possessed of great wealth, who imparts wisdom, (born) of illustrious race, resembling the sun and moon, conversant with arts and sciences, of unsullied (fame), to the Ruler namely, the Governor of Colombo, many million salutations ! As the former Rulers at Colombo—Your Excellency's predecessors—and the former Rulers of this Island Kingdom (Máldives) preserved mutual friendship, Your Excellency and Ourselves have borne (reciprocal) friendship in our hearts. May this (amity) continue on Your Excellency's part ! Should any Máldive vessel *(odi* or *dóni)* be driven ashore at any place with which (Your Excellency) is acquainted (We request that Your Excellency will kindly, send for those (shipwrecked) persons, and enquire into their wants. Should Your Excellency be aware of any persons ill-disposed towards this Island Kingdom, (be pleased to) show them no countenance. We send for Your Excellency's acceptance—all unworthy though it be—a small present by the hands of (Our Ambassador) Ahmad Kuḍa Baḍéri Kéví. (We beg Your Excellency will kindly) issue directions, that his requests be attended to. Should he commit any fault, (We hope that Your Excellency will) pardon it. (We trust that Your Excellency will) allow him to return in the favourable monsoon. A.H. 1210 (A.D. 1795.)*

Explanatory Notes.†

Suvastí * * * * *Mahá Radun.* Adopting the above translation, the Sultan's title may be rendered into Siṇhalese as follows :— සැප වේවා ; ශ්‍රීමත්වූ ; මහත් ශ්‍රී ධරන්නාවූ; ප්‍රඥා ප්‍රදානකරන්නාවූ ; (කල්‍යාණ දායකවූ) ; ශ්‍රී වංශ ඇති ; හිරසඳ බඳුවූ ; ප්‍රත්‍යක්ෂ ශාස්ත්‍ර ධාරිවූ ; ශුභ්‍ර (කීර්ති) ඇති ; ක්ෂත්‍රිය වංශ ඇති ; ලෝකයේ මහා රජ: *Sẹpa vévá ; ṣrímatvú ; maha ṣrí dharannávú ; prajñá pradána karannávú ; (kalyáṇa dáyakavú) ṣrí vaṇsa ẹti ; hira sanda banduvú ; pratyaksha ṣastra dhárivu ; ṣubhra (kírti) ẹti ; kshatriya vaṇsa ẹti ; lókayé mahá rája.*‡

Mahá siri-bari = S. මහා ශ්‍රීභාරි, *mahá ṣrí-bhári*, 'possessed of (a great weight of immense glory" (or) 'wealth.' Cf. *inte ralia* inscriptions at Ẹlavẹva Pansala and Ẹtavíragollẹva (Goldschmidt, C. A. S. Journ., 1879, p. 34.) In some letters *diri* takes the place of *bari : diri* may equal S. ධෛර්‍ය්‍ය ඇති, *dhairyya ẹti*, 'courageous' (*S. D.*) ; but, as reasonably also, S. දුල, *dula*, 'glittering,' 'splendid,' by metathesis දිලි, *dili*, thence දිරි, diri.

Kusa furadána = S. කුශ ප්‍රධාන, *kuṣa pradhána*. The meaning 'wisdom' = S. ප්‍රඥාව, *prajñáva (D.)*, or 'goodness' = S. කල්‍යාණ, *kalyáṇa*, has been assigned to *kusa*. The compound will also bear the sense, 'lord of the waters' = S. ජලප්‍රධානවූ, *jala pradhánavû*, *(S.)*, and 'Chief of Kusa,' *i.e.*, one of the great *dwípas* or divisions of the universe, *(S.)*, some letters reading *kusha* (S. කුෂ, *kusha.*)

Sada ira :—The order of Sanskṛit compounds is here followed, *hira sanda* becoming *sanda ira*, and by abbreviation *sada ira*.

Siáka sástura ;—*Siáka*, a doubtful word. Subhúti proposes to read *siyána* (Hindí) 'clever' or 'wicked,' and renders the compound by *(a)* S. දක්ෂ අනුශාසකවූ, *daksha anuṣásakavú*, 'skilful teacher' or 'commander,' or *(b)* S. ධූර්තජනයාට සතුරුවූ, *dhûrta janayáṭa satruvú* 'enemy of wicked men.' Dhammáloka, deriving *siáka* from Sans. *sáyaka*, 'bow,' would make it *(c)* = S. ධනුර්ධරවූ, *dhanurdhravú*, 'skilled with the bow.' Guṇasékara suggests :—*(d)* = *Shiáka satura (satru)* 'enemy of the Shía'hs (heretics,)' *(e)* = 'subduer of (his) passions,' *i.e.*, S. සිය, *siya*, 'own ;' අක, *aka* (Sans. *aksha*, 'organs of sense.') *(f)* = S. සිය, *siya*. අක. *aka*, 'eye ;' S. ප්‍රත්‍යක්ෂ, *pratyaksha*, 'experienced,' coupling it with *ṣástura*, S. ශාස්ත්‍රවූ, *ṣástruvú*, 'experienced teacher.'

---

* In Bennett's "Ceylon and its Capabilities" (London, 1843), opposite to p. 252 may be seen a fairly correct copy in lithograph of Sultan M. Mu'ín-ud-dín's letter to the Galle Commandant in 1825 ; and at p. lxiv. of the Appendix the rough official translation. Lieut.-Colonel Campbell (" Excursions, &c., in Ceylon," Vol. I., pp. 199, 200) also gives a like translation (dated January 3rd, 1821) of a letter from the same Sultan, received by him when in command of the detachment at the Southern port. For another specimen of Máldive writing, see the private letter at the end of Christopher's Maldivian Vocabulary, (J. R. A. S., o.s., Vol. VI.)

† A complete glossary is held over for the Ceylon A. S. Journal.

‡ Towards the elucidation of these complimentary epithets valuable aid has been generously afforded by the learned scholars Waskaḍuwé Subhúti Unnánsé (*S.*), Dhammáloka Unnansé of Ratmalána (*D.*), and B. Guṇasékara, Government Translator (*G.*).

The last translation has been followed.

Audána :—appearing almost invariably in immediate connection with *kiriti* (S. කීර්ති *kirtit*, 'fame,')—may perhaps be traced to Sans. *avadáta*, 'white' 'unsullied' (*G.*)

Bowana :—Older letters give the true form *buvana* (S. භුවන, *bhuvana*, 'the universe.')

The list of magniloquent epithets—'great swelling words of vanity'—employed by the Sultans in their annual letters to the Ceylon Governors has strangely waxed and waned, so to speak, since the commencement of the 18th century.

Sultan Imád-ud-dín Muzaffar (A.D. 1711 ?—1721) was content to affix to his name, *Rannavalóka Mahá Radun*. By 1750 Máldivian official bombast had reached the height, beginning *Suvasti, &c.*, and attained its zenith some twenty or thirty years later. Reaction then ensued, and in letters subsequent to 1805 (?) the Sultan's Arabic titles have been followed merely by the words, *Kula Sundura Kattiri Bówana Mahá Radun*—expressions which Christopher considered "unexplainable at the present day."* The fuller string of epithets is still prefixed to orders and communications issued by the Sultan to his subjects.

Rasge-fánu :—*V. s.*, p. 76, Note (10). In early letters of last century sometimes written *Radunge-fánu*, or *Rasge-fánanse*. *Fánu*, *fananse*, = S. වහන්සේ, *vahansé*, honorific affix, by consonantal change through *vanansé*.

Maniku-fánu-men :—*V. s.*, p. 63.† Euphemistic plural-singular.

Fadaiṇ-me :—'as,' 'in the manner,' = S. පරිදි, පරිද්දෙන්, *paridi*, *paridden*, by rejection of liquid medial consonant ; *me* = S. ම, *ma*, intensive suffix.

Hif-fuḷu-gai :—'in mind,' loc. = *hit* (S. හිතේ, *hité*) + *fuḷu* (honorific) + *gai* (*gátun*, 'near'), by euphonic assimilation.

Behigeṇ gos : = S. බැහිගන ගොස්, *behígana* (බහිනවා, *bahinavá* 'to descend') *gos* ; Pyrard, *behigue*, a term applied to being driven by the current.

Arafódigeṇ-nuvá :—'in all humbleness,' 'unworthy though (the giver and the present) be.' Alternative forms in older letters, *ara hódi*, *arai hodí*, *aranu hóde*, *arainu hóde*. Cf. Pyrard, *vedon a Rouespou*, the present paid to a delegate of the Sultan. Christopher, *vedun*, 'present.'

Baḍeri :—*V. s.*, p. 66 ‖ 'Hadégiri.' Originally confined to the Treasurer or Keeper of the Royal Stores (S. භාණ්ඩාගාරික, *Bháṇḍágáriká*), the title, as in the Kandyan districts of Ceylon, gradually acquired a wider use, though still restricted to persons of high birth.

Kéví :—? *Névi*, *q. v.*, p. 63 ‖ *supra*.

Aḷá, *aḷuṇ* :—Cf. T. ஆள், *áḷ*, 'person.' *Aḷu-gaḍu*, *aḷu-gaḍu-men*, the ordinary designation employed by the Sultans and Máldivian nobles when writing of themselves in the first person. *Gaḍu*, *koḷu*, *fuḷu*, (*e.g.*, *hadíyá-koḷu*, *hif-fuḷu*), honorific suffixes, generally implying connection with Royalty.

Avvalu * * * * *hunnevíme* :—A periphrasis for the simpler expression, occasionally found, *daturu* (H. *játrá*) *avas-kurravvai*, "(kindly) hasten (his return) voyage." *Vaḍaigen*.—Cf. the Siŋhalese complimentary use of වඩිනවා, *vaḍinavá*, as applied to Buddhist priests.

Some ruling vowel and consonantal changes from Siŋhalese into Máldivian may be noticed :—

Vowel Changes.

Siŋhalese	*a*,	becomes Máldive	*e*,	(S. *danvanavá*, *balavanavá* ; M. *dennevi*, *bellavumai*)
			i,	(S. *tamun* ; M. *timan*)
			o,	(S. *evanavá* ; M. *fonuvvímu*)
			u,	(S. *ihaṭa*, *karanavá* ; M. *ihu*, *kurravvai*)
"	*i*,	"	*u*,	(S. *innavá* ; M. *hunnevíme*)
"	*u*,	"	*a*,	(S. *tamun* ; M. *timan*)
			o,	(S. *bhuvana* ; M. *bovana*)
"	*e*,	"	*i*,	(S. *mé*, *tibenavá* ; M. *mi*, *tibí*)
"	*o*,	"	*u*,	(S. *no-(rusanavá)* ; M. *nu-(russevumeve)*
"	*ę*,	"	*e*,	(S. *hęngenavá*, *tęna* ; M. *egijje*, *tana-ku*.

* Even in the official translations (English) these words appear simply transcribed as part of the Sultan's name The Dutch translators entirely ignored them.

Consonant Changes.

Siṇhalese	*t*,	becomes Máldive	*r*,	(S. *piṭatvenavá ; M. furuvá)*
,,	*d*,	,,	*h*,	(S. *dás ;* M. *hás)*
,,	*n*,	,,	*ḷ*,	(S. *unna, uluṇ)*
,,	*p*,	,,	*f*,	(S. *prudhána ;* M. *furadána)*
,,	*v*,	,,	*ʃ*,	(S. *evanavá, vara ;* M. *fonuvvímu, farhun)*

Many words, purely foreign or of probable foreign origin, occur :—

Arabic :—*Iskandar ; salám ; rahmat ; khabar ; adá ; hadiyá ; takṣír ; mu'áf ; musimu ; sanat.*

Tamiḻ :—*Dóre* (துரை, *turai*) ; *mita* (மிச்சம், *michcham*) ; *Ras* (cf. T. form அரசன், *arasaṉ*) ; *oḍi* (இடம், *óḍam*) ; *dóñe* (தோணி, *tóṇi*) ; *koḷu*, (? கொழு, *kolu*) ; *aḷá*, *aḷun* (ஆள், *áḷ*).

Malay :—*Edi* (? *ada*, 'be.')

Dutch (English).—*Gorunu* (Governor.)

Truly "a party coloured dress
of patch'd and py-ball'd languages."

(14)

TARTIB.—Copies of these commentaries on the Kurán are now freely exposed for sale in the boutiques at Málé, at from Rs. 1 to Rs. 1½ each—a faint, but possibly hopeful, sign of mental awakening too long delayed.

In 1835-36 Captain Moresby thought that the natives did not "appear indifferent to improvement, for all (particularly the chief) evinced a strong desire to become acquainted with our language and with our knowledge."*

This is unfortunately contradicted by facts. Governor Mackenzie offered, in 1838, to educate, free of cost, two Máldive boys chosen by the Sultan and sent over to Ceylon for the purpose. "Having understood," the Governor writes, "that it is the wish of Your Royal Highness as well as that of many of your subjects to be taught the English language, I am prepared to give them the opportunity of acquiring that language without any cost to themselves, and I invite two of Your Royal Highness' subjects, not exceeding 16 years of age, whom you may be pleased to select and send to Colombo. I would also propose that those youths should be accompanied by some members of their own family, who will be kindly received on a temporary visit. They will have the means of seeing where the scholars are to be settled, and of being satisfied as to the place and situation where the two youths will reside while they remain in Ceylon to learn the English language."†

The Sultan's answer of the ensuing year, though couched in language studiously polite, destroyed any hopes which might have been entertained that the time was ripe for this experiment. "Your Excellency has been pleased to desire us to send from our dominions two youths below 16 years of age to your Island for the purpose of being educated in your language, without any expenses to us, either, for their education or boarding, and, moreover, that two of our people may be sent thither, to see if these youths are well settled and confortably kept there. This proposal, we are aware, emanated from Your Excellency with a view of promoting and perpetuating the good understanding existing between us, but we regret that our religious principles do not allow us to avail ourselves of the benefit of the kind offer thus made by Your Excellency, because our religious tenets prohibit our children being so instructed in their youth.' ‡

This reply was at the time accepted as "decisive against education and conversion of the Maldivians," for the subject was not again broached.

Happily, the course of events in the interval of forty years had led, though by an indirect channel, to a partial realization of the enlightened objects contemplated by the Right Honourable J. A. Stewart Mackenzie.

A chance law-suit brought over to Ceylon, in 1850, the Sultan's cousin, 'Alí Dídí, son of the late astute Prime Minister Ahmad Dídí (*V. s.*, p. 37.) Settling ultimately at Galle, where he died a few years back in affluent circumstances, he gradually established, as the recognised Máldivian agent, a brisk through trade between the Islands and Indian rice ports.

---

* Trans. Bom. Geo. Soc., 1836-8, p. 108.

† Governor's letter, dated November 26th, 1838.

‡ Sultan's reply, dated Sháwwál, A. H. 1255.

THE MÁLDIVES.
INHABITANTS.
Notes.

His son (Ibráhím Dídí) and nephews ('Alí and Isma'íl Dídí), as they grew up together, in addition to acquiring a fair knowledge of the English language, imbibed involuntarily just impressions of European breadth and freedom of thought, which, with advancing years, have taken deep root.

Háji Ibráhím Dídí is now the most trusted adviser of his Sovereign, and in all matters of moment is summoned to the aid of the Council at Málé. He and his cousins may yet live to exert a salutary influence on the future destiny of the Máldivian race, by weening the minds of the ruling aristocracy from the narrow exclusiveness and "Cimmerian darkness of ignorance" in which they have persistently been enveloped.*

---

* For a sweeping condemnation of the English policy in India regarding Muhammadan education, see the trenchant remarks of Dr. W. W. Hunter, B.C.S., in his "Indian Musalmáns," Chap. IV.: 'The wrongs of the Muhammadans under British rule.'

VI.—PRODUCTIONS AND MANUFACTURES.

THE Máldive Islands present a field of botanical and zoological research, almost unexplored, but hardly likely to yield much fresh store of plant and animal life, judging by results obtained on the more Northern and very similarly situated group.

A short cruise among the Lakkadives sufficed to establish that "they have no distinctive Fauna or Flora : no mammals, except the common Indian *Mus rufescens*, that even in the neighbourhood of Calcutta infests cocoanut trees : no land birds, except a very few of the commonest Indian species : no non-Indian plants, the flora consisting mostly of species common on the sea-coasts of India, and more or less diffused over China, Java, and the Straits, extending in many cases to the Malayan Archipelago, Australia, and the South-Sea Islands, and in several to the tropics generally : that the majority of the species of plants possess, according to native ideas, medicinal properties, and are, therefore, just those most likely to have been introduced by human agencies ; and that, as a matter of fact, it is in the largest island, where the population is greatest and the communication with the mainland has been on the largest scale, that the number of species is greatest.*

VEGETATION.†

Vegetation.

At a little distance most islands appear "a mass of vegetation down to the waters' edge, dense with cocoanuts above and screw pines below." The undergrowth, in which the rich green fleshy-leaved *scævola* everywhere stands out prominent, runs riot in entangled luxuriance of growth, impenetrable in places.

Cocoanut.

The fine coraline sand of these low-lying sea-girt Atols is peculiarly suited to the growth of the cocoanut palm *(Cocos nucifera)*, which thrives with a vigour and luxuriance unequalled, save, perhaps, on the Polynesian groups.

At least three distinct species are found, bearing fruit ranging in size from the huge gourd-like nut (M. *ubukaḍá kárhi)* to the tiny nut not much larger than an orange (M. *furedde oḍi kárhi)* so valued for its copperah.

To the Islanders, the economic value of the cocoanut is incalculable. "It is far the best and most wonderful manna imaginable ; inasmuch as this single tree can provide every necessary of life for man, supplying him with wine, honey, sugar, milk and butter in abundance. Moreover, the kernel or almond may be eaten as bread with viands of all kinds ; besides which, the wood (of the tree) and its leaves, with the husk and shells (of the fruit), serve for the manufacture of the greater part of their furniture and utensils."‡

Timber Trees.

Few indigenous trees are fit for timber. In boat-building resort is had almost exclusively to the cocoanut. The tall straight *varu* and *mas kadu* (M.)—the softest and lightest of their woods—are not sufficiently durable for this purpose, but the latter is used for rafts (M. *kadu-fati.)*

The *duburi* (S. *domba, Calophyllum inophyllum)* is well adapted for the minor wood-work of their houses, as wall sticks, &c., and is valuable also on account of the gum resin which exudes from the tree when wounded, and for the medicinal oil obtainable from its seed.

Of large trees the most noticeable are the *los* (the *bois mapou* of the Chagos), *kadu*, and *hirundu* (S. *súriya, Thespesia populnea)*. The banyan (M. *nika, Ficus indica)* is hardly less rare than the bread-fruit (M. *bamba-keyo, Artocarpus incisa)* and jack (M. *sak-keyo, A. integrifolia.)*

A dark and extremely tough wood which the Islanders much rely upon is the *kuradi (? Pemphis acidula)*. This tiny-leafed tree—or rather shrub, for it rarely exceeds 15 to 20 feet in height—grows on nearly all the islands. Its wood is selected for implement-handles, wall-plates, cross-beams and pieces in houses and boats—in fact, wherever strength and durability are needed.

---

* Allan Hume, in "Stray Feathers," Vol. IV., 1876, p. 459. † Note (1).

‡ Pyrard, p. 85, who later (*Traitté des animaux et des arbres et fruits des Indes*, pp. 22-33), devotes a special chapter to this "wonderful tree."

THE MALDIVES.

PRODUCTIONS AND MANUFACTURES.

Pandanus.

From the scarcity of good timber a high value is set on teak and other hard woods, occasionally obtained from wrecks. Some timber is annually imported.

The natives make some use of the fruit of the *Pandanus*, but would seem to be otherwise ignorant of, or indifferent to, the many serviceable purposes to which this despised tree is capable of being turned.* The leaves even are no longer used as a writing material.

Fruit.

At Málé and other populous islands, a variety of exotic fruit trees are found, which have been introduced gradually from the continent. Such are the lime *(Citrus limetta)*, biling *(Averrhoa bilimbi)*, and almond *(Terminalia catappa)*, with bananas, oranges, pomegranates *(Punica granatum)*, rose apple *(Jambosa vulgaris)* shaddocks *(Citrus decumana)*, custard-apple *(Anona squamosa)*, guava *(Psidium pyriferum)*, and pine-apple. The areka palm *(Areca catechu)* is rare, necessitating the importation of the nut, on which the Islanders set great store for mastification with the leaves of the betel-creeper *(Chavica betle, Miq.)*

Vegetables.

Among esculent vegetables cultivated are chillies, pumpkins, brinjals *(Solanum melongena)*, and several yams, notably a large bulbous root, "round and large as the two fists," in shape and appearance much resembling an ordinary potato, called *hittala* (? S. *hiritala, Dioscorea oppositifolia)*, which, after being grated down and steeped in water for some time, is dried, and forms a very palatable flour.† "The castor-oil plant *(Ricinus communis)* is very common, and appears to be indigenous, but the seed is not collected either for domestic use or exportation." A little cotton (M. *kafa*, S. *kapu*, *Gossypium Indicum)* is grown, chiefly in Miladummaḍulu Atol.

Fine grain.

Rice will not thrive, but two kinds of millet are raised on the Southern Atols—*Setaria Italica* (M. *urǎ*, S. *tana hál)* and *Panicum miliaceum* (M. *kudibai*, S. *menêri)*,‡ and some nacheri or *kurakkan (Cynosurus corocanus*, M. *bimbi)* at the North of the group.

Flowers.

Pyrard says the Islanders are passionately fond of flowers, which bloom perennially in great variety, using them commonly as chaplets, garlands, &c. He particularises the *innapa* [*hiná-faĭ*]—used as in Persia for dyeing the hands, feet, and nails red—the *onnimaus* [*uni-má*], a white sweet-scented flower, that falls after twenty-four hours, and the *iroudemaus* [*irude-má*], the *śúriya-kántá* or 'sun-flower' of the Siṇhalese. Roses (M. *fini-fen-má)* are not unknown at Málé, but are cultivated with difficulty.

ZOOLOGY.§

Zoology.

The zoology of the Islands is only redeemed from complete insignificance by a fair show of sea-birds, terns, gulls, &c. (all known species), and an extensive ichthyology, yet unworked.

Animals.

Domestic animals are everywhere scarce. Except a few cattle kept for the use of the Sultan at Málé, the only ruminant reared is the goat.‖ Cats are not common, and the dog and pig, as unclean animals, are naturally absent.¶ The mongoose (M. *mugarhi; Herpestes griseus)* is rare.

---

* See Cooper, "Coral Lands," Vol. II., pp. 220-37, London, 1880.

† Trans. Bom. Geo. Soc., 1836-8, p. 80. Pyrard, *itelpoul*. Ibn. Bat, Tome IV.

‡ "All the Máldive Islands are destitute of grain, except that in the Province of *Souweïd* [*Suvádiva*] there is a cereal like the *anly* which is brought thence to *Mahal*."—Gray, quoting *Ibn Bat.*, Tome IV., 112.

§ Note (2).

‖ Horses have been rarely imported into the Islands, and are retained for the exclusive use of the Sovereign. Ibn Batúta (A. D. 1344) scandalised the natives by venturing, even as Kází, to ride one of the only two—a stallion and a mare—then kept in the Royal stables. Sultan Ibráhím Iskandar obtained a horse from Ceylon in 1724 (D. R. Miscell.), and more than a century later (A.D. 1840) Ahmad Dídí induced the Ceylon Government to present his son with a horse, saddle and bridle. In November, 1879, there were but two horses at Málé, "wretched wry-legged weeds, not fit to ride," and apparently, with a caged leopard, &c., merely forming a motley menagerie.

¶ De chiens il n'y en a point, et dauantage ils ont en horreur. Pendant que j'y estois les Portugais de Cochin en enuoyerent deux au Roy par rareté, qui les fit incontinent noyer.—Pyrard, p. 88.

THE MÁLDIVES.

PRODUCTIONS AND MANUFACTURES.

Animals.

The "flying-fox" (M. *vávulá, Pteropus Edwardsii)* is very plentiful, and only second in destructiveness to the cocoanut-rat (M. *bodu midá, Mus rufescens.)* As in the Lakkadives, these rats are a source of great annoyance and loss to the natives. "Living up in the crowns of the cocoanut-palms they incontinently drop the nuts on the heads of passers by and otherwise seriously diminish the outturn of the trees,"* by eating into the nut, or by drinking the toddy. Minor pests are ants and mosquitoes.† To escape the ravages of the former, granaries have to be built on piles some distance into the lagoons.‡

With the exception of the ubiquitous scavenger crow—nowhere more persistently obtrusive than at the Máldives—and the half-wild domestic fowl, the only land bird is the Indian koil, *Eudyamys honorata* (M. *kaḷu* and *diḍi kovili.)* Pigeons and parrots are occasionally met with, but are migratory.

Birds.

Of the ordinary sea-birds, turnstones *(Strepsilas interpres)*, noddies *(Anous stolidus)*, and terns *(Sterninae)* are numberless, and herons *(Ardeidae)* very common in the shallows. A variety of teal come over from the continent in large flocks at certain seasons.§

Reptiles.

Lizards, "blood-suckers" and *geckoos*, frequent gardens and houses, as on the coast, but noxious reptiles are confined to the sea. The 'water-serpents,' *Hydrophis Spiralis* (M. *fen-harufá)* and *Pelamis bicolor* (M. *máridá)* are much dreaded by the natives. The only land snake known is the harmless *Lycodon aulicus* (M. *nannagati)*.

Turtle.

These Islands would seem to be a special habitat of the turtle; from the largest —the logger-head (M. *musimbi, Couanea olivacea)*—or *velá*, the shell of which is sometimes of sufficient size to roof a hovel, and accommodate ten or more persons seated‖—to the smaller edible (M. *kahabu, Chelonia virgata,)*¶ and hawksbill turtle *(Caretta imbricata)*, which supplies the tortoise-shell of commerce. Many small islands were entirely covered by them formerly, and the supply has always exceeded the greatest demand. "They commonly take turtle while it is floating at the surface, and also when it lands."** On Sultan's Island the small fresh-water tortoise (M. *kanza kahabu, Emys trijuga)* is found in tanks.

Fish.

It has been claimed for the Máldives that no place in the world can vie with them in the abundance and diversity of the fish caught in the encircling seas.†† Within the Atol lagoons coral-fish of every hue may be descried. The *bêche-de-mer (Holothurion)* is found, but the collection of this sea-slug does not form an industry as in the Polynesian groups.

The much dreaded shark, large (M. *miyaru*, the *tuberão* of the Portuguese) and small (M. *femunu)*, is only too plentiful. "The natives catch the largest sharks with a hook. While the fish remains within the Attol in 20 and 30 fathoms depth of water, they pay out a long scope of line, and the shark when unable to descend deeper darts onwards horizontally, dragging the boat after him, but if a large fish is hooked and it dashes outside of the islands into deep water, they immediately cut the line asunder for fear of accidents."‡‡

The sword-fish (M. *hibaru, Xiphias gladius)* is common, "and sometimes attains 18 feet in length." Porpoises (M. *kó-mas)* yield some oil,‡‡ and the dried skins of the larger Rays, when well stretched, still serve to cover drums and tambourines.§§

---

* Allan Hume, "Stray Feathers," Vol. IV., p. 433. The Lakkadive Islanders organize fortnightly rat-hunts *(koot)* to keep down their number.

† "There was a vast number of mosquitoes or gnats that made the blood run where they stung." Stephen's Faria-y-Sousa, Vol., III., Ch. XI., p. 397, of the shipwreck of D. George de Almeyda on the Máldives in 1631. Cf. Mr. Thomas (Madras Journ. Lit. and Science, 1859-60) of Minakaï.

‡ Pyrard, p. 87.

§ Trans. Bom. Geo. Soc., 1836—8, p. 79.

‖ So Pyrard *(Traitté*, &c., p. 5), and cf. Tennent's Natural History, p. 293.

¶ The Máldivians, according to Pyrard, resort to "the cruel expedient" of suspending turtles alive over fires to obtain their shell. Cf. Tennent, *loc. cit.*

** Trans. Bom. Geo. Sec. 1836—8, p. 79.

†† Pyrard *(Traitté*, &c., p. 7.)

‡‡ Trans. Bom. Geo. Soc., 1836—8, p. 79.

§§ Pyrard, *loc. cit.*, p. 8.

THE MÁLDIVES.

PRODUCTIONS AND MANUFACTURES.

Bonito fishery.

As fishing is "the most constant exercise" of these Islanders—the *bonito* fishery in particular having mainly supplied them with the means of subsistence for centuries—Pyrard's detailed description of the various times and modes of fishing adopted at the Máldives will not be out of place :—

"The fish which are taken in the deep sea about six or seven leagues off the bars of the *Attollons* are large and of seven or eight sorts, such as bonitos, albacores, guilt-heads, &c., which are all much of the same taste, and have no more scales than a mackrel. The instruments with which they catch them are a line of a fathom and an half of great cotton thread tied to a cane, together with a hook that in form resembles the letter *h.* The bait is not fastened upon the hook, but thrown about into the sea ; for they drag after their boat a quantity of small fish like our roaches, which are very numerous among the banks and sands, and which are preserved alive in purse-nets of cocoa-thread ; and when they come to the deep sea they cast there little fishes about, and throw in their line. Upon which the great fishes perceiving an unwonted quantity of little fish crowd upon them in shoals, greedily swallow the whitened hook, taking it for one of the little fish. The fish that swallows the hook falls off as soon as the line is brought into the boat, and so the line is thrown in again. At this rate they will fill their boat with fish in three or four hours' time,* and (which is very strange) the boat is all along under sail. The fish thus taken are all black, from whence they are called *cobolly masse* [*kaḷu-bili-mas*] *i.e.*, 'the black fish.'†

Other modes of fishing.

"They have another way of fishing in the night time upon the banks that surround the *Attollons*. At every full and every new moon they convey themselves to the banks upon hurdles [or rafts, *kadu-fati*], and the fishing lasts three days every time. 'Tis performed by lines of hard coarse cotton thread, some of which are fifty or sixty fathom long, and are blackened over with the bark of a tree that serves instead of pitch, in order to preserve it from corruption. At the end of this line they have a hook with a bait fastened upon it, after the same manner as is usual among us. By this means they catch a prodigious quantity of large red fish, such as I never saw elsewhere, which eats most deliciously and is by them called the *King of the Sea.* In fine, they have such plenty of several sorts of fish, and different ways of taking them unknown to us, that 'tis impossible to distinguish them ; for, besides the lines abovementioned, they have all sorts of nets of cotton, twine, wheels and other instruments for fishing. Upon the flats near the shore they catch small fish like pilchards with casting nets.

"At the two equinoxes they have a general fishing, which is very remarkable. At these two periods of the year, as the tides flow beyond their wonted bounds, so they ebb more than usual and discover several rocks and flats, which at other times continue under water. Upon this occasion the Maldivians pitch upon several dry corners, which they encompass with stones raised like a wall to a great height, being forty paces in circumference, with a door or entrance left that is three paces wide. This done, thirty or forty of them stretch out, all round the flats, a large wide circle of the great cocoa cords at each fathom of which they tie a piece of cocoa shell dried, and that supplies the place of cork, making the line float. Now the fish inclosed within the circle are so scared with the shadow of the floating line as if it had a net underneath it, that instead of making their escape by swimming, they fly from it, and by the gradual contraction of the line are brought into the inclosure, the entry of which is thereupon stopped with all expedition with faggots of the boughs and leaves of cocoa compacted together of the bigness of a man ; after all the sea runs out and leaves the fish on the dry land. This fishery, which continues fifteen days together, produces commonly ten or twelve thousand fish."‡

Crustacea.

Crustacea are widely represented, including most species of cray-fish from the larger *Palinuri*, and crabs—Painted, Hermits, Paddlers, Occypodes, &c.—in numbers sufficient to "cover whole islands."

---

* "The quantity thus taken in a day by one boat sometimes amounts to 1,000" (Trans. Bom. Geo. Soc., 1876—8, p. 79) ; 600 or 700 is considered a fair take.

† See Note (3) on 'Fish-curing at the Máldives.' ‡ Pyrard, quoted in Harris, Vol. I., pp. 711, 712.

Mr. Allan Hume found the Lakkadives "a perfect paradise for crabs," none new, but in variety astounding. "There were massive built, sturdy, purple chocolate rascals *(Eriplia scrabicula* and *levimana)* that ensconced themselves in holes of rocks in which they fitted to such a nicety that it was most difficult to dislodge them. Small long-legged silvery fellows *(Occypode cordimana)* that scampered along the land at the rate of ten miles an hour, and just when you thought you had them, vanished into a hole. Then there were some strange enormous-clawed, cream-coloured, and grey-mottled, knobby fellows, grubbing about in shallow water *(Calappa tuberculata)* which, when they opened out their huge arms, seemed to be dividing their bodies into three parts. Then, under every stone we turned, were dumpy brownish-red individuals, with black tips to very stout claws *(Leptodius sanguineus)*, the hardest biters of the lot. Hundreds of orange-red or Hermit crabs *(Cenobita Olivieri)* lurked under branches of all the low-growing littoral shrubs. Of course, the variegated *Grapsi* swarmed in myriads on every part of the reef, and on the coral blocks at the outermost face of the island."*

Mollusca.

Throughout these groups *Mollusca* abound in rich profusion. "The shallows were full of shells—huge massive Cones, enormous Tiger-claw shells *(Pteroceras lambis)* with their beautiful wide-spreading glossy pink lips: cowries of many species, amongst them some very large tiger shells *(Cyprea tigris)*, deep-red King Conks *(Cassis rufa)*, *Olives Cerithium, Murex, Mitra, Nassa, Natica, Nerita, Trochus, Volvorina.**

"The sea beach was strewed with large bunches of a delicate snow-white pointed coraline *(Isis hippuris)*, that looked as if it would have formed an appropriate moss for the Arctic regions."

Cowries.

The small money cowry (M. *boli, Cypraea moneta)* is found in myriads at the Máldives.

Twice a month, when the tides suit, men and women wade into the sea waist deep and detach them from the stones under which they cling.† One man will sometimes gather as many as 12,000 in a day. The shells are then buried until all traces of putrefaction have disappeared; after which they are generally put up for the market in three-cornered bundles of cocoanut leaf-plat known as *koṭṭas*, weighing 25 lbs. each.

Ambergris and Sea-cocoanut.

Two minor products, obtained by the Islanders from the sea, require notice. These are ambergris (M. *goma, mávaharu)*, and the so-called 'sea-cocoanut' (M. *táva-kárhi, Lodoicea Seychellarum)*—rated at so high a value in the estimation of the Máldive Sultans as to be retained as part of their royalties.

Ambergris—the kind known to the natives of the continent and Ceylon as *mín* or 'fish' amber—was formerly found in large quantities, and occasionally exported.

The curious double-cocoanut, now proved to be confined to the Seychelles, but long believed to grow beneath the sea near these Islands, and hence called *Coco-de-mer* or *Coco des Maldives*, is rarely washed ashore at the present day.

Both these casual products have ever been held in the greatest request by natives throughout the East on account of their real, or supposed, valuable medicinal properties.‡

MANUFACTURES.

Manufactures.

The chief manufactures in which the Máldivians display much skill, and have attained considerable success, are those of coir, mats, and cloth.

Coir.

The coir (M. *rónu)* of these Islands, as that of the Lakkadives, has been noted for centuries for its light colour, fineness, and comparative strength, as contrasted with Ceylon and Indian coir, and fetches a much higher price in the market. The Portuguese drew most of the rope required for their fleets in Indian seas from the Máldives. The best quality is made in Tiladummatí Atol.

---

* Stray Feathers, Vol. IV., pp. 435-6. "From our cruise we brought back over 100 species of univalves, of which at least 12 were new; and a still large number, I think, of bivalves."

† The practice of collecting cowries, by placing cocoanut boughs in the sea, as described in the Travels of the Two Muhammadans, and later by Barros (Asia, Dec. III., Liv. III., Cap. IV., p. 312), and Captain A. Hamilton, Account of the East Indies, 1727, (Pinkerton, Vol. 8, p. 389), would seem to be obsolete.

‡ Note (4).

THE MÁLDIVES.

PRODUCTIONS AND MANUFACTURES.

Mats.

The well-known Máldive mats [M. *tuḍu kuna*] are made only in Suvádiva (Huvadú) Atol, from a rush (M. *háu*) which thrives best there. In delicacy of pattern, in happy combination of the only three colours adopted—black, yellow-brown and white—and in permanency of dye, these fine mats surpass anything in the same line the world over, and have justly obtained unqualified commendation. The best quality are worked up on Gaddú Island, the ordinary mats at Havara-Tinadú, and a small kind on Gemaná-furhi.

Cloth.

Two or three qualities of cotton cloth are woven, chiefly in Máḷosmaḍulu (Edafurhi island), Aḍḍú, and Suvádiva Atols, though occasionally made elsewhere for private use.

A peculiarity in this article consists in the uniform tasteful colouring of the waist and head cloths, sometimes plain red, or blue edged with red an inch wide, but more commonly of a rich chocolate colour relieved by a black stripe between two of white on either side, and finished at the ends by a narrow yellow silk border and a neat fringe.

The dyes employed are excellent, particularly the red and chocolate, which are extracted from a root (M. *ahi, Morinda citrifolia.)* The black dye is obtained by boiling gall-nuts and rusty iron together in cocoanut water.

The price of cloths of native manufacture is much higher than that of the various coloured ones imported from India, in consequence of the demand induced by all persons being expected on public occasions to wear the former.

The natives also spin a large quantity of foreign cotton. "The spinning-machine (M. *tatun)* is simply a large and small-wheel of light frame work."

Lacquer and fancy metal work.

In painting fancy articles, such as favourite boats, lances, wooden dishes (M. *kurandi)*, axe-handles, &c., they have reached a degree of perfection both in brilliancy and gradation of colour and beauty of design, which it would be difficult to surpass, throwing in the shade the by no means contemptible efforts of the Kandyans in similar lacquer work. The best specimens are procurable at Tuládú in Máḷosmaḍulu Atol.

The art of working in metals, though still imperfectly understood, needs but developing.

As it is, ordinary Máldive waist-knives (M. *vali)* chastely inlaid with silver and mother-of-pearl, leave nothing to be desired in portability and serviceableness, whilst for shape and handsome finish the larger silver-mounted knife-dagger with ivory handle (M. *fiyohi,)* worn exclusively by grandees and soldiers, is unique.

Knife-handles are carved from *kuradi* wood, black coral (M. *endiri)* and whales' teeth (M. *boḍu-mas daĭ)*; and some small cleverly-designed betel boxes are fashioned in brass.

Jewellers (M. *aikan-kura míhun)* are now to be found on most Atols, but were formerly limited to two islands in Nilandu Atol—Ribudu and Huḷudali—whence they made their rounds periodically to the other Atols, taking their tools, &c., with them, and remaining at each island as long as they got employment.

Other artizans still follow this practice of visiting Atols "where there are no workmen in the same line."*

Scientific instruments.

Among ingenious—if to European notions crude and antiquated—instruments, constructed on scientific principles hardly to be expected of a people so cut off from the world, the quadrant (M. *digu-fila*), astrolabe (M. *ré-fila)* and bellows (M. *giruba)*, merit special praise.

Architecture.

There is little, if any, attempt at ornamental architecture discoverable on the group. The Mosques, even at Málé, are poor, cadjan-roofed edifices ; nor does the Sultan's palace redeem the general mediocrity.

Stone carving.

In the art of carving on stone, however, whether in intaglio or basso-relievo, the Máldivians exhibit skill of a high order. Nearly two centuries back the excellence of their chiselling called forth deserved eulogy. "At the island of Hammandou, which lies

---

* In Pyrard's time, "each different trade was confined to a distinct cluster of islands, as the weavers in one, the goldsmiths in another, the locksmiths, mat-makers, potters, turners, joiners, on other several clusters."—Pyrard, p. 86, quoted in Asiatic Annual Register, 1802.

Máldive boats.

in 7°," says Captain Alexander Hamilton, "I saw carving on some tombstones, as ingeniously cut with a variety of figures as ever I saw in Europe or Asia."*

Máldive sailing boats are remarkably well-built. The trading vessels, indeed—*furedde* ('foreign') *oḍi*—100 to 200 tons burthen, which venture as far as Calcutta, "from their build and rig, are totally unfit to work to windward, or to make moderate progress, unless the wind is even abaft the beam ;" but smaller trading boats [M. *baḍu* or *Oḷudú* and *daturu oḍi*] of about 50 tons are very fair sailers, with a fine entrance and good bearings ; the smaller fishing boats [M. *mas oḍi*], in particular—often not exceeding 2½ to 3 tons burthen—have superior swift sailing qualities.

The boats are generally sewn together, but few nails being used, and have a single mast and square sail of matted work. "Small sails of cloth are occasionally set on a temporary light mast or hoisted on a shifting back-stay taken to the taffrail."†

From stern to stern these boats are built and equipped with materials furnished by the cocoanut palm, and not unfrequently provisioned and laden with products from the same tree.‡

"In going from island to island within the Atols the natives often use rafts [M. *kadu-fati*]."

NOTES.

Notes.

(1)

Flora of the Máldives.

FLORA OF THE MÁLDIVES.—No regular botanical exploration of these Islands has been, as far as is known, yet carried out. There is, however, every reason to believe that a close examination of the flora will prove it to be similar in nearly all respects to that of the Lakkadive group, already dealt with by the late Mr. Hall (Report, November, 1871)§, and casually by Mr. Allan Hume (Stray Feathers, Vol IV., 1876).

Mr. Hume writes :—

"Two large shrubs are very abundant and are common to the shores of India, Ceylon, the Archipelago, Australia, and South Sea Islands. The one a *Scaevola* (*S. Konigii*, Vahl.) with masses of large glossy apple-green somewhat fleshy leaves surrounding irregular panicles of white flowers, the other, a great coarse wild heliotrope (*Tournefortia argentea*, L.) with an infinite number of close-set whorls of oval leaves. with an universal glaucous blue tint. Of course the sandy shores, as elsewhere in all tropical countries, were covered by the bright green-leaved, purplish-lilac flowered, trailing sand convolvulus (L. *Pes-capræ*), and inside this were everywhere huge patches of that remarkable rigid-leaved grass (*Spinifex squarrosus*) peculiar to the shores of India, which is often called the sea-pink [? M. *biliṇ hui*] ; not that it is anything of the kind, but only that its densely crowded masses of stiff glaucous blue leaves remind one irresistibly at a short distance of a bed of pink plants after they have done flowering. A large sedge (*Cyperus arenarius*, Retz.) grew here and there in profusion, and masses of a beautiful white moon creeper (*Calonyction comospermum*, Bojer) were in places densely draped over clumps of the large bushes already mentioned, converting them into an impenetrable thicket. Everywhere the shore Quassia (*Suriana maritima*, L.), common on all tropical coasts, a stunted woody shrub, with multitudes of tiny leaves, occupied the external and most exposed positions.

---

* Pinkerton, Vol. 8, p. 390. † Trans. Bom. Geo. Soc., 1836—8, p. 82.

‡ "Their hulls, masts, sails, rigging, anchors, cables, provisions, and firing are all from this useful tree. It also affords them oil for their kitchen and lamps, sugar and candied sweetmeats, and pretty strong cloth"—(Captain A. Hamilton, Pinkerton, Vol. 8, p. 388)—a statement almost literally true at this day.

"The Ambassador informed me that the same process adopted in Ceylon for propagating trees by annular incision obtained at the Maldives for increasing the bulk of cocoanut trees intended for boat-building purposes. Hence, perhaps, the superiority of their cocoanut wood for building vessels over that of Ceylon, which, unless it be over fifty years old at least, is scarcely fit for anything except fuel, fences and aqueducts."—(Bennett, Ceylon, &c., p. 358.)

§ Unfortunately not available in Ceylon.

THE MÁLDIVES.

PRODUCTIONS AND MANUFACTURES.

Notes.

" The only other plants on the island [Bitra Par] were a sort of dandelion (*Microrhynchus sarmentosus*, D. C.), a miserable everlasting (*Achyranthes bidentata*, Blume) infamous for the reckless prodigality with which it expends its seed on all passing legs, another covered with a little white woolly caterpillar-like inflorescence (*Aerva lanata*, Juss.), and a tropically-universally diffused nyctago (*Boerhavia diffusa*, L.).

" This completes the scanty flora of the island—all plants of the commonest description and the widest distribution."

Of Cardamum (Kadamat) Island.—"The common southern milk plant (*Calotropis gigantea*) was noticed here for the first time [M. *ruva*]. There were also mallow-worts, the small trailing *Sida humilis*, (Müll), and the *Abutilon Indicum*, (G. Don) ; quantities of wild indigo—whole fields of it, if I may use the expression—only broken by patches of a scarlet-flowered ixora (*I. bandhuca*, Roxb.), large clumps of a broad-leaved shrub, not unlike the common dāk (*Butea frondosa*), for which I think previous visitors have mistaken it, but which is really *Guettarda speciosa*, L.

" A great part of the jungle is composed of a dwarf tree, a verbena (*Premna integrifolia*, L.) closely allied, though very different in appearance, to the gigantic Teak. A tall, fine, loose-flowering grass (*Apluda aristata*, L.) fills all the outskirts of the jungle. A few other insignificant herbs (*Wedelia biflora*, D. C., and *Euphorbia pilulifera*, L.), complete the list of wild plants which we first met with here, and to which have to be added almost all those found on Bitra-Par and Kiltan."

Amini resembles Málé in possessing a goodly number and variety of fruit trees. "Here there are some 700 bread-fruit trees, numbers of lime bushes, a good number of betel-nut palms, plantains and pomegranates. Castor-oil plants, papaya [M. *falo*] and horse-raddish [M. *muragá*] trees are common. I saw also several banyan, some tamarind, some aonla (*Embica officinalis*), and a number of poon [M. *duburi*] trees (*Calophyllum inophyllum*, L.), so valuable for masts and cross-pieces of small vessels, like those in use in these Islands. A good many vegetables are also grown here—yams, sweet-potatoes, arooees (*Collocasia antiquorum*) and others.

" With the comparatively large trade of this island, it is not surprising that many more wild plants are found here than in the other islands. We procured every species here that I have already enumerated (except the sedge found on Bitra-Par), and, besides, saw many plants of the Datura or Stramonium [M. *kaḷu oreni*], of the winter cherry (*Physalis Peruviana*, L.), of a large Cowitch with bunches of deep blackish-purple flowers (*Mucuma capitata*, W. and A.) looking like Hamburgh grapes, of the lovely blue-flowered creeper so common in Indian gardens—(*Clitorea ternatea*), of two yellow-blossomed Acanthads (*Barteria prionitis* L., and *ciliata*, Roxb.), and many other inconspicuous herbs, including the broad-leaved, jointed (*Panicum compositum*, L.), and common three-toed (*Dactyloclenium Ægyptiacum*, Weld) grass."

At Bingaroo the undergrowth was also very dense. "Enormous patches of a great sedge (*C. pallidus*, Heyne) common in Burmah, the Malay Peninsula, and Borneo, and now in full flower, were very conspicuous. We observed most of the plants already recorded, but they grow here with a luxuriance which contrasted strongly with the generally-stunted growth of the same species on Bitra-Par. The rosemary-like shore Quassia (*Suriana maritima*, L.) was here in great densely-packed bushes, dotted with small orange-yellow flowers. Interiorly the place was an almost impenetrable thicket, full of grass of many species not obtained elsewhere, *Panicum verticillatum*, L.—[*Cynodon dactylon* ?]—a species of *Hemarthria*, *Morinda bracteata* (Roxb.), and others not in flower and not identifiable.

" Masses of *Cæsalpinia bonducella*, Flem., with its all-pervading sharp double recurved thorns, recalling the "Bide-a-wee" thickets of the Cape, in many places barred all progress."

To which should be added the following plants verified by Dr. King :—*Cleome viscosa*, L. ; *Cardiospernum Halicacabum*, L. ; *Crotolaria verucosa*, L. ; *Vernonia cinerea*, Less ; [M. *valikofá*] ; *Ageratum conyzoides*, L. ; *Plumbago Zeylonica*, L. ; *Tylòphora asthmatica*, W. and A. ; *Peristrophe bicalyculata*, Nees ; *Rungia pectinata*, Nees ; *Leucas aspera*, Spreng ; *Euphorbia atolo*, Forst ; *Phyllanthus Madraspatensis*, Müll : and from the Máldives, identified by Mr. W. Ferguson, F.L.S., *Gloriosa superba* [M. *vihala goḍi* or *vuyula tári*] ; *Cassia sophera* [M. *digu tiyára* or *téra*] ; *C. auriculata* [M. *rana' ura*] ; *Adenanthera pavonica* ; and the 'four o'clock' *sendrikka*, *Mirabilis jalappa*. [M. *asaru-má*].

(2)

The general nature and extent of Máldivian ornithology may be gathered from the list of birds—some five and thirty varieties in all—observed by Mr. Allan Hume during his cruise among the Lakkadives in 1874.—("Stray Feathers," Vol. 4, pp. 460-83.)

Birds.

English.	Classical.	Máldive.
The Common Peregrine ...	*Falco peregrinus*, Gmel. ...	—
The Kestrel ...	*Cerchneis alaudarius*, Briss. ...	—
	Cuncuma leucogaster, Gmel. ...	—
The Indian Pariah Kite ...	*Milvus govinda*, Sykes. ...	—
The Black-winged Kite ...	*Elanus melanopterus*, Daud. ...	—
Indian Koil ...	*Eudynamis honorata*, L. ...	*Kaḷu kovili, Ḍiḍi kovili.*
The White-eyed Tit ...	*Zosterops palpebrosus*, Tem. ...	
The Common Crow ...	*Corvus splendens*, Vieill. ...	*Káḷu.*
Asiatic Golden Plover ...	*Charadrius fulvus*, Gmel. ...	—
The Large Sand Plover ...	*Ægialitis Geoffroyi*, Wagler. ...	—
The Mongolian Sand Plover...	*Ægialitis Mongolicus*, Pall. ...	—
The Kentish Plover ...	*Ægialitis Cantianus*, Lath. ...	—
The Turnstone ...	*Strepsilas interpres*, L. ...	*Rappa, ratafai.*
The Crab Plover ...	*Dromas ardeola*, Payk. ...	*Toravá.*
The Whimbrel ...	*Numenius pheopus*, L. ...	*Buḷitibu.*
The Eastern Curlew ...	*Numenius lineatus*, Cuv. ...	—
	Tringa crassirostris, Tem. and Schl...	—
The Sanderling ...	*Calidis arenaria*, L. ...	—
The Common Sand-piper ...	*Tringoides hypoleucos*, L. ...	*Itoḷi.*
The Green Shank ...	*Totanus canescens*, Gmel. ...	—
The Common Heron ...	*Ardea cinerea*, L. ...	*Má-kaná.*
The Blue Heron ...	*Demiegretta gularis*, Bosc. ...	—
The Indian Pond Heron ...	*Ardeola grayi*, Sykes ...	*Ráboli.*
The Green Bittern ...	*Butorides Javanicus*, Horsf. ...	—
	Sterna albigena, Licht. ...	—
	Sternula minuta, L. (? *S. Sinensis*, Gmel.) ...	*Kiri dúni, villa.* —
The Large Crested Tern ...	*Sterna Bergii*, Licht. ...	—
	Sterna Bengalensis, Less. ...	—
The Brown-winged (Panayan) Tern ...	*Sterna anosthætus*, Scop.. ...	—
The Sooty Tern ...	*Sterna fuliginosa*, Gmel. ...	*Vári, váli.*
The Common Noddy ...	*Anous stolidus*, L. ...	*Kaḷu dúni, máragá.*
	Phaeton ætherius, L. (? *P. Indicus*)	—
	Sula fiber, L. ...	—
The Yellow-eyed Gannet ...	*Sula piscatrix*, L. (? *S. Cyanops*) ...	*Kaḍu-heda.*

For the Máldives the following may be also added, provisionally.

English.	Classical.	Máldive.
The Common Stilt ...	*Himantopus candidus*, Bonnat. ...	*Kokkágoḷi.*
The Grey Plover ...	*Squatarola Helvetica*, L. ..	*Durhin.*
The Caspian Tern ...	*Sterna caspia*, Pall. ...	*Boḍu-gau-dúni.*
The Lesser Crested Tern ...	*Sterna media*, Horsf. ...	*Má-koḷalá.*
The Antartic Skua ...	*Stercorarius antarcticus*, Less. ...	*Kukulu-má-dúni.*
The Indian Whistling Teal ...	*Dendrocygna Javanica*, Horsf. ...	*Ranvan réra.*
The Common Teal ...	*Anas creeca*, L.	*Háfati réra.*
	Spatula clypeata, L. ..	*Kaḷu réra.*
The Large White Egret ...	*Herodius alba*, L. ...	*Langaná-dúni.*
The Little Egret ...	*Herodius garzetta*, L. ...	*Iruvá-hudu.*
The Common Night Heron ...	*Nycticorax griseus*, L. ...	*Kará-ráboli, kaḷu-ráboli.*
The Brown Gannet ...	*Sula leucogastra*, Bodd. ...	*Kanifuḷu, galahiri.*
The Lesser Frigate Bird ...	*Fregata minor*, L. ...	*Má-horá.*

THE MÁLDIVES.

PRODUCTIONS AND MANUFACTURES.

Notes.

Systematic examination and description of the icthyology and conchology of this archipelago,—the widest and most promising branch of its zoology,—must be left to future investigators. For the present, a scanty list of sea fish and shells, identified with more or less certainty, is inserted, as of possible interest.

Fish.

English.	Classical.	Máldive.
White Shark ...	*Squalus carcharias*, L. ...	*Miyaru.*
Hammer-head Shark ...	*Squalus zygæna*, L. ...	*Budi miyaru.*
Elliot's Shark ...	*Carcharias Ellioti* ...	*Femunu.*
Saw-fish	*S. pristis*, L.	*Farutoḷi* (Chris).
Sword-fish	*Xiphias gladius*, L. ...	*Hibaru* (Chris).
	Histiophorus immaculatus ...	*Fan-hibaru.*
Sear fish	*Cybium guttatum*	*Toḷi.*
Bonito	*Scomber Pelamis*	*Kaḷu-bili-mas.*
Leopard mackerel ...	*Cybium interruptun* ...	*Kanneli.*
Dolphin	*Coryphaena hippurus*, L. ...	*Fiyala.*
Tamarind-fish ...	*Lates calcarifer*	*Faloḷu.*
Spotted Sea-Perch ...	*Serranus guttatus*	*? Kaḷu-boḍu.*
Block's Sea-Perch ...	*Priacanthus Blockii* ...	*Bereli.*
Humped Wrasse ...	*Cheilinus undulatus* ...	*Má-hibaḷu-mas.*
Russell's Parrot-Wrasse ...	*Pseudoscarus rivulatus* ...	*Oḷu-mas.*
Long-nosed Sea Beam ...	*Lothrinus rostratus* ...	*Failu.*
The Rangoo ...	*Lutianus* (g.)	*Ráveri, akerá.*
Coffer-fish	*Ostracion* (g.)	*Gon, gonu.*
Porcupine-fish ...	*Dioclon hystrix*	*Karikolu* (Chris).
Globe-fish ...	*Tetrodon* (g.)	*Fófi.*
Surgeon-fish ...	*Naseus unicornis*	*Tubá, tubi.*
Mangoe-fish ...	*Polynemus plebeius* ...	*Kéla-mas.*
Flying-fish	*Exocoetus evolans*	*Fulagi, huḷun-mahá.*
	Muraena (g.)	*Ven.*

Shells.

Classical.	Máldive.
Nautilus Pompilius, L. ...	*Nai-boli.*
Cassis, L.	*Feṇ-kakká-boli.*
Cassis cornutus, L.... ...	*Kuḍa-kokká-boli.*
Cassida rufa, L.	*Rabboli.*
Terebra maculata, L. ...	—
Conus aulicus, L.	—
C. Mallaccanus	—
C. betulinus, L.	—
Dolium perdrix	*Baḍu-kokká.*
Melo Indicus	*Kokká.*
Olivæ, (g.)	*Digu-boli.*
Turritella duplicata ...	*Fuheheri.*
Ampularia	*Fiṅhaki.*
Neritina dubia	*Haduwarigolá.*
Cypræa reticulata, Martyn ...	
C. mauritiana, L.	*Boḍu-boli.*
C. lynx, L.	—
C. moneta, L.	—
C. talpa, L.	—
C. carneola, L.	—
C. caurica, L.	—
C. helvola, L.	—
C. interrupta, Gray ...	—
C. asellus	*Kafahi-boli.*
Mazza rapa, (chank) ...	*Saṇgi.*

THE MÁLDIVES.

PRODUCTIONS AND MANUFACTURES.

Notes.

(3)

FISH-CURING AT THE MÁLDIVES.—The fish caught in the seas encircling the Atols of the Máldive archipelago are classed by the natives broadly into two chief kinds :—

1. *Faru mas.* This term includes what the Siŋhalese call ගල්මාළු, *gal máḷu*, and bears the same literal meaning, viz., 'rock fish'; such are the Sinhalese *tambuwá, síláwá, koppará.*

But among the Máldivians *faru mas* would seem to comprehend also the larger kinds, such as 'saw fish' (M. *farutoḷi)*, 'sword-fish' (M. *hibaru)*, 'sear-fish' (M. *toḷi*, S. *tórá*) and 'sharks' (M. *miyaru*, S. *mórá.)* These fish are of a soft, oily nature, unadapted for curing, only edible when fresh, and never salted for the foreign market.*

2. The real 'Máldive fish' (M. *kaḷu-bili-mas.*† vulgarly *komboli* or *kommala mas*, S. *umbala kaḍa*) of the Ceylon and Indian markets are chiefly *bonito* (S. *balayá, Scomber Pelamis*, L.) though two or three more species are similarly cured, *e.g.*, M. *goḍá* (? S. *ẹtawallá*), M. *kanneli* (? S. *kelawallá*), M. *rágoḍi* (S *rágoḍuwá.*) The flesh of these fish is tough, dark, and not very palatable, and—especially *kelawallá* and *balayá*—spoken of by the Siŋhalese as *giniyam*, 'heating.' At one season of the year a large number of these *balayó*, or bonitos, are caught off the south-west coast of this Island, and from the fishery the village of *Balapiṭiya* ('the hamlet of the *balayá*') on the sea-board, twenty-three miles north of Point-de-Galle, has derived its name.‡

The details of the *kaḷu-bili-mas* curing industry—the staple export of the Islands—are extremely simple.

After the fish are brought on shore a portion is sold whilst fresh, and the remainder treated as follows:—The entrails (M. *gohoru*, S. *boku*) and the lower part of the belly (M. *baḍu*, S. *baḍa-wata*) are extracted, the head and tail cut off and thrown away, the fish split up, and the spine bone removed. The two slices are then usually divided in one of two ways :—

(i.) If into two pieces (*i.e.*, four pieces in all) they are known generally as *Himiti-mas*, each individual piece as *gaḍu*, and all four together as *mahé* or *emmas* ('one fish').

Fig. I.

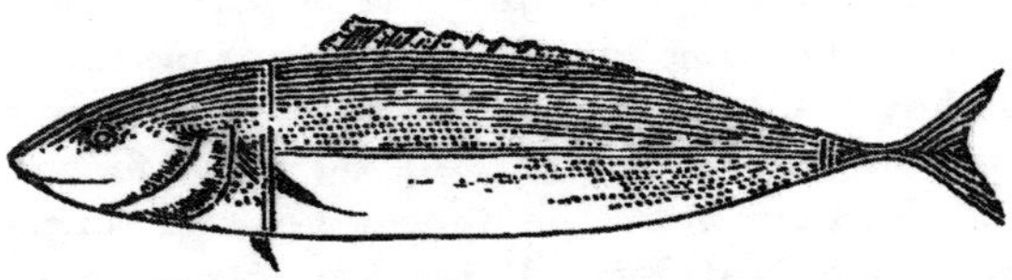

This plan of cutting the bonito is said to have originated in the island of Himiti (Nilandu Atol), and is followed also by the Islanders of Koḷumaḍulu and Haddumatí Atols.

(ii.) If the two slices are divided into four strips with a transverse cut across the front of the fish, thus,—

Fig. II.

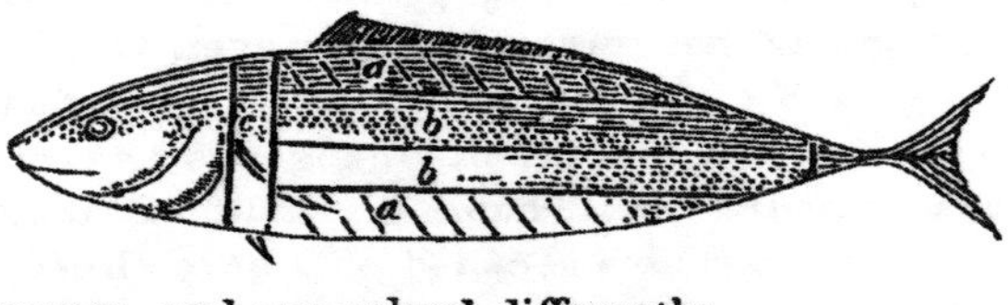

the pieces have separate names, and are valued differently—

a a the pieces along the back and belly, called *gaḍu mas* ;

b b those along the middle of the side, called *medu mas* ;

c that between the head and the ends of *a a b b*, called *kirá mas.*

Gaḍu mas, so called because they are supposed to be the best pieces§ ; *medu* (S. *mẹda*) *mas*, because they are from the centre ; *kirá mas*, because these pieces are weighed (M. *kiraŋ*, S. *kiranavá*,

---

* Christopher, however, (J. R. A. S., Vol. VI.) has *faru mas* 'salted and dried fish.'

† See *Ind. Ant.*, Vol. VIII., p. 321, "Notes and Queries," where Mr. D. Ferguson, on the authority of Mudaliyár L. De Zoysa, would set old Pyrard right, by deriving '*cobily mash*' from the Sinhalese *kẹbili* (pl. of *kẹbella*) 'pieces,' and *mas* 'fish.' *Kaḷu-bili* = *kaḷu* 'black', *bili* (S. *balayá*) 'bonito.'

‡ These seas are frequented by *Bonitoes* or good fishes, which are wholesome food, though the flesh is dry. They are of the same figure and bigness as carps, but somewhat thicker. They swim in shoals close together, and always follow the ships. These also devour a great quantity of flying-fish, which you find many times undigested in their bellies."—*A Collection of Voyages of the Dutch East-India Company*, translated into English (p. 132, London, 1703).

§ *Gaḍu. koḷu*, affixes employed when speaking of anything connected with the Sultan ; *e.g.*, *haï-koḷu*, 'the State umbrella ;' *vedun-gaḍu*, the large sweatmeat presented annually to the Ceylon Governor. *V. s.*, p. 80.

'to weigh')—not counted—in selling. This is the practice in Mulaku, Felidu, Ari, Mále, and, it is said, all Atols further north.

But in Huvadú and Fua Mulaku Island, and sometimes in Aḍḍú Atol, these fish are cut up, as in Fig III., and called by the name of the respective Atol or Island ;

Fig. III.

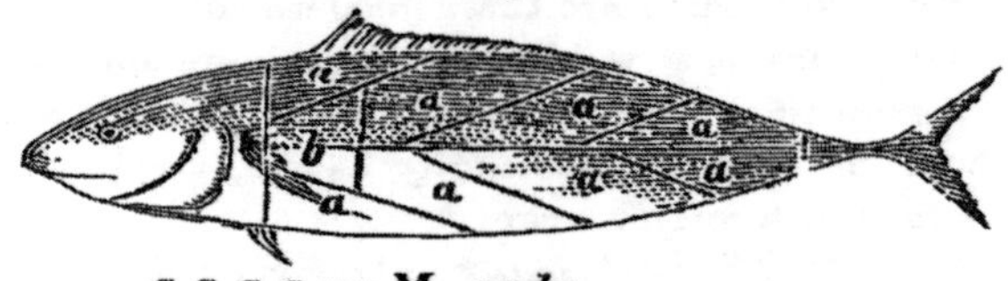

a a a a = M. *gaḍu*,
b = M. *kirá* or *uguru*,

and in Aḍḍú Atol as shown in Fig IV.

Fig. IV.

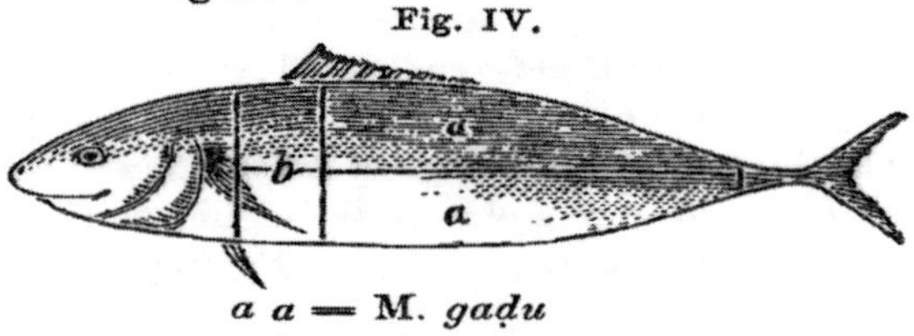

a a = M. *gaḍu*
b = M. *kirá*.

The march of civilization has introduced modern weights (cwts. qrs. and lbs.) into the Máldives, but until recently the different pieces of Máldive fish had a relative value to one another. Thus :—4 pieces *medu mas* = 2 *gaḍu mas* (of the same fish); 8 *gaḍu mas* = 7 pieces *Hipiti-mas*, —*kirá mas*, as above said, being valued against their weight of *gadu mas*, &c.

When the fish have been divided into the desired number of pieces, these are washed with salt water, then thrown into a caldron (or chatty) of boiling salt water and allowed to remain for a few minutes only, to prevent the flesh becoming too soft. It is said to be important that the water should be boiling from the first. On being taken out they are placed on the wattle loft or shelf (M. *mehi*, S. *mẹssa*) above the fire. There they are left three or four days till well blackened and dried, after which, if necessary, they are exposed to the sun to be finished.

Thus dried they are, as is well known, of the appearance and consistency of blocks of wood.

Fish-curing is carried on at the Máldives all the year round, but chiefly in the dry season from January to July. The same process obtains throughout the group, and it is worthy of note that it has remained unchanged since Pyrard's day (A.D. 1602—1607.) "The fish," says he, "which is caught in this manner, is called in their language by the general term '*cobolly masse*' because they are all *black*. They cook them in salt water, and then dry them by the fire on *clayes* so thoroughly that when dry they keep for a very long time. It is in this commodity they carry on so extensive a traffic, not only among themselves, but they even supply the rest of India, where this article is in great request." (p. 138). And again (p. 141): "The fish which are found on the banks or lagoons of the Atols are called in the Máldive language '*phare masse*' [M. *faru mas*,] that is to say, 'rock fish'; because '*phare*'* is a 'bank' or 'shelf of rock,' '*masse*' is 'fish.' The other kind which is caught in the high (open) sea is called, as I have already said, '*combolly masse*,' that is to say 'black fish.' It is in this that they have so large a trade, and with which they supply all the coasts of the Continent. It is cooked in salt water and dried, for it is not otherwise salted ; although sometimes they salt some of it, yet it remains always in the brine† until wanted. But it is not this that they export or send away. As there is no salt made at the Máldives, that of which they make use comes from the coast of Malabar, and it would not suffice for so large a quantity of fish as is daily caught for the supply of the inhabitants as well as for trade. For, in truth, I believe there is no place throughout India, nor elsewhere, where the fishery is richer and more plentiful."

Two and-a-half centuries earlier Ibn Batúta (A. D. 1344) also wrote of this fishery :—"The food of the natives consists of a fish like the *lyroûn*, which they call *koulb al mâs*. Its flesh is red ; it has no grease, but its smell resembles that of mutton. When caught at the fishery, each

---

* S. *para*. in ගල්පර, *galpara* 'reef.'

† *I.e.*, "the fish blood" and "salt fish" occasionally imported into Ceylon, called by the Máldivians *rhi-hakuru* (lit. 'fish sugar'.) This consists of the broth in which the bonito has been boiled, to which old scraps are added from time to time, the whole after two or three days being again boiled down to a gelatinous syrup containing more solid lumps.

fish is cut up into four pieces, and then slightly cooked. It is then placed in baskets of coco leaves and suspended in the smoke. It is eaten when perfectly dry. From this country it is exported to India, China, and Yaman. It is called *koulb al más*." (Gray, quoting *Voyages d'Ibn Batoutah*, Tome IV., 112).

(4)

AMBERGRIS.—"After having been long doubted, scientific opinion seems to have come back to the opinion that ambergris is an excretion from the whale. 'Ambergris is a morbid secretion in the intestines of the cachalot, deriving its origin either from the stomach or biliary ducts; and allied in its nature to gall-stones, ... whilst the masses found floating on the sea are those that have been voided by the whale, or liberated from the dead animal by the process of putrefaction. (Bennett, "Whaling Voyage Round the Globe," 1840, II., 326)."*

"It has a fragrant and peculiar odour when heated or rubbed; and when good it is solid, opaque, of a bright grey colour, which is darkest externally, and intermixed with yellow or reddish streaks. It is used in perfumery chiefly. *Localities:* Madagascar, Surinam, Java, Zanzibár, and the Arabian Gulf." †

The true origin of this substance much exercised the minds of older writers.

Arab travellers seem to have considered it a plant, or mushroom, produced at the bottom of the sea, whence it was detached and washed ashore by the violence of the waves. (Travels of the Two Muhammadans.) "The best ambergris," says Mas'udi, "is found on the islands and coasts of the Sea of Zinj (Eastern Africa); it is round, of a pale blue, and sometimes as big as an ostrich egg............... These are morsels which have been swallowed by the fish called *Awál*."*

Barbosa, notes of the Máldives:—"There is also a large quantity of ambergris *(ambre)* in great pieces, part of which is white, another grey, and a third black;" adding that the "Moors" considered it to be the dung of the sea-birds *(esterquo dauves)* which throng the reefs, and that the white kind *(ponambar)*, was held the most valuable, the grey next, and last the black-coloured *(minambar)*, which was swallowed and afterwards vomited by whales.‡

"As for ambergrise," wrote Tavernier as late as 1670, "there is no person in the world that knows either what it is, or where, or how it is produc'd. But the fairest probability is, that it must be only in the Eastern sea: though some parcels have been found upon the coast of England and in some other parts of Europe. The greatest quantity is found upon the coast of Melinda, especially in the mouths of a river call'd Rio de Sena. The Governor of Mozambique gets in the three years of his Government above 300,000 *pardos* of ambergrise, every *pardo* containing 27 *sous* of our money."§

Kaempfer devoted a special section in the Appendix to his "History of Japan"‖ to 'some observations concerning ambergrease.' "Authors differ widely in their opinions, concerning both its origin and production, nor do they so much as agree, what kind of substance it properly is. Some take it to be a bituminous substance, others a sort of earth or clay, others a sea-sponge, others an excrement of the whale, others the dung of the birds. Many more could be mentioned, if I did not avoid being tedious. * * * * It is found chiefly in the intestines of a whale, which is caught frequently upon the Japanese coasts, and is by the natives called *Fiakfiro*, that is, 'the hundred-fathom fish,' because of the length of its intestines, which is suppos'd to equal that number of fathoms. It is found, as I observ'd, in the intestines of this whale, mix'd with chalky limy excrements, almost as hard as stone, and it is from the hardness of these excrements they conjecture, upon dissecting, whether or no they are like to meet with ambergrease. The natives have given a very despicable name to this precious commodity, a name, however, becoming the meanness of its origin for they call it *Kusurano-fu*, that is, 'the excrement of whales.'¶ The ambergrease, as it is torn off by the waves from the bottom of the sea and thrown upon the coasts, before it is swallowed by the whales, is a deform'd, flat, slimy substance, and withal of a very disagreeable, ungrateful smell. People that find it thus floating on the surface of the water, or lying upon the coasts, take several small pieces, squeeze and press them close together into the

* Yule, Marco Polo, Vol. II., 342. † Faulkner, Dictionary of Commercial Terms, Bombay, 1856.

‡ Noticias para a Historia et Geographia das Nações Ultramarinas, Tom. II., p. 352.

§ Tavernier's "Travels in the East Indies" (English translation, 1678, London), Bk. II., Pt. II., p. 152.

‖ Kaempfer's "History of Japan" (English translation by J. G. Schenchzar, London, 1726.) Vol. I., pp. 111-112; II., Appendix pp. 46-51.

¶ Compare M. *goma* = ? S. ගොම, *góma*, 'cow-dung.'

THE MÁLDIVES.

PRODUCTIONS AND MANUFACTURES.

Notes.

form of a round ball, which, as it grows dry, becomes also more solid and weighty. Others mix and knead it with meal or flour of rice-husks, by which means they not only increase the quantity, but heighten and better the colour. However, the ambergrease thus adulterated is easily known, for if you take any quantity and burn it there will remain a coal, proportionable to the quantity of the stuff mixed with it. It is observ'd, besides, that the worms get quickly into this spurious sort of ambergrease. Others adulterate it by mixing it with a certain powder'd rosin of a very agreeable scent, but this cheat also is easily discover'd, for upou burniug a piece of it, the mixture of rosin will evidently appear by the very colour, smell and quality of the smoke. The Chinese have another way of trying whether it be genuine; it will dissolve and diffuse equally, which the adulterated sort doth not. The natives use it no otherwise but as an ingredient of other well scented spices, in order, as they say, to fix their volatile smell. In the main they value it but little, and 'tis owing entirely to the Dutch and Chinese, who would buy it up at any rate, that they have now learnt to prize it. And yet everybody is at liberty to take it up where he finds it and to sell it as his own property."*

Large pieces are occasionally obtained. Tavernier mentions two which weighed respectively 33 lbs. and 42 lbs.; but Kaempfer knew of a lump found in Japan seas weighing upwards of 100 cattis, or 130 lbs. Dutch weight, and of a yet larger tortoise-shaped piece (to be seen at Amsterdam), that the King of Tidor sold to the Dutch East India Company in 1693 for 11,000 Rix-dollars, or about £2,000. It weighed 185 lbs. (Dutch).

SEA-COCOANUT.—" There is also a kind of nut, occasionally washed on shore, which is as large as a man's head, and like two huge melons joined together. They [the Máldivians] call it *Tauarcarré* [*táva-kárhi*], and believe that it is produced by trees growing beneath the sea. The Portuguese named it *Cocos des Maldiues*: it is of great use in pharmacy and fetches a high price."†

"This fruit being uncommon, its form particular, and its origin unknown, all contributed to assign to it extraordinary properties and to give rise to fable concerning its existence .... The tree which produces the Sea Coco, rising in many parts of the isle upon the borders of the sea, the greatest part of the fruit falls into the water; where floating it is carried by the wind and currents to the Maldivian Isles, the only part of the world where this fruit had been found before the discovery of the Isle of Praslin [Seychelles], from whence the Europeans called this coco 'the Maldiviau Coco,' and the Maldivians *Travacarné*, that is, 'treasure.' It was afterwards called 'Solomon's Coco,' to give it a name corresponding to the marvellous, which was annexed to its origin. The tree being unknown that produced it, it was believed to be the produce of a plant that grew at the bottom of the sea, which came off when it was ripe, and by its lightness floated on the waves. There was nothing wantiug to complete the fable but to ascribe very great and extraordinary virtues to this fruit, and this was done accordingly. It was given out, and believed, and is still believed, not only in the Indies, but through all Asia, that the almond of the Sea Coco has all the properties which we attribute to *Theriaca Mithridate*, and which perhaps we exaggerate; (viz.,) that its outward covering is a certain antidote to all kinds of poison.‡ The grandees of Indostan still purchase this fruit at a very high price: they make cups and shell, which they adorn with gold and diamonds; and never drink out of any other, being persuaded that poison, which they are much afraid of because they often employ it themselves against others, let it be ever so active, cannot hurt them if their liquor is but purified in these salutary goblets. The king of the Maldivian Isles avails himself of this general error. His predecessors assumed, and he reserves to himself, the exclusive right to a fruit, which being carried upou waves, and driven ashore by the wind, ought to belong to whoever picks it up, but the Sea Coco, when it shall be found not to be so rare and extraordiuary a production, will doubtless soon lose its value and virtues, and the Maldivian Monarch the tribute, which has beeu paid him by ignorance and error.§

---

* Not so at the Máldives, where it was a criminal offence for private individuals to appropriate ambergris. Car il appartient au Roy, et nul n' oseroit, le retenir qu' il n' eust le poing couppé. (Pyrard, p. 163.)

† Pyrard, p. 163.

‡ Faria-y-Sousa (English edn. Vol. I., p. 229) says it is "a greater antidote against poison than bezoar stone." "Here [Colombo, in 1777] is seen likewise a *Borassus* or Sea-Cocoa brought from the Maldive Islands, which had been set in earth, had grown up, and was now in the third year of its growth, having only three leaves. The nut had lain eight months in the ground before it put forth the first leaf. ..... They take of it [the kernel] half or even a whole drachm. It is deemed a sovereign remedy against the flux, epilepsy, and apoplexy. The inhabitants of the Maldives call it *Tavarcare.*"—Thumberg, "Travels," 3rd ed. Vol. IV., pp. 133, 159. "So much as 4,000 florins were offered by the Emperor Rodolf II. for a single specimen."—Tennent, quoting Malte Brun, Vol. IV., p. 240.

§ Sonnerat's "Voyage to the Spice Islands" (English translation, pp. 2–6, London, 1781.) A description of the tree and fruit follows. Tennent (Vol. II., p. 126.) refers to Sir W. Hooker's full account in the Botanical Magazine, Vol. XII.

VII.—TRADE AND COMMERCE.

The early export trade of the Máldives consisted in cowries, coir, cocoanuts, and ambergris, and as regards the first two commodities had become so considerable by the 11th century as to warrant traders of the day dividing the group into 'Cowry Islands' *(Dyvah-kouzah)*, and 'Coir Islands' *(Dyvah-kanbar)*.* Early trade.

By the 14th century dried fish and cloth were included amongst the exports. 14th century.

"Ships export from the Islands the fish of which I have spoken, cocoanuts, fabrics, the *ouiliyân*, [M. *féliya*] and turbans : these last are of cotton. They export also vessels of copper which are very common there, cowries, and *kanbar ;* such is the name of the fibre which envelopes the cocoanut. The natives make it undergo a preparation in pits dug near the shore : then they beat it with picks, after which the women work it into rope. They make of it cord for joining the boards of their ships, and such cordage is exported to China, India and Yemen ; *Kanbar* rope is worth more than hemp : with this cord the (boards of) ships are joined in India and Yemen ; for the Indian sea is full of rocks, and if a ship joined with iron bolts strikes a rock it is broken up, but when it is fastened with this cord it has elasticity, and does not break."†

On their appearance in the East the Portuguese found the Máldives visited by trading and pilgrim vessels, passing to and fro between Arabia and the Persian Gulf, and the Malabar coast, Bengal and China. "Moor" merchants virtually ruled the Islands from Cannanore, exacting tribute of coir and other produce from the native King, and employing resident sub-agents, who rented the public duties and were invested by the King with administrative powers in order to enable them to levy their taxes.‡ 16th century.

The Portuguese writers enumerate minutely the productions of the group, and dwell on the brisk exchange carried on there for silver, rice, salt and earthenware which the Islanders needed.§ The native-made cloth of silk and gold—an industry, if not quite extinct, long since reduced to a minimum—was in special request.

Máldive coir had the chief attraction for the Portuguese ; nor were they slow to force the then powerful "Moor" Mamale into an annual payment of coir rope for the privilege of an exclusive monopoly of Máldive trade as against all other natives of India. A conflicting contract with the Máldive Sovereign followed‖ ; and both alike were soon shamelessly violated through the malversation of Portuguese agents *(feitors)*, and favourites of the Viceroys at Goa permitted to harry the Islanders by private descents, made nominally on behalf of the King of Portugal.¶

Finally, later in the same century, the terms of the treaty of peace at the conclusion of the protracted war, (based on the lines of those with every native Prince once overpowered), gave the Portuguese, besides an annual tribute, the exclusive right of trade with the Máldives, and the consequent control over the price of their produce and manufactures.**

As Portuguese influence waned, the foreign traffic of the Islands expanded with increased vigour—the result of reaction—developing into no mean proportions.

---

* *V. s.*, p. 24.

† Gray, quoting *Voyages d' Ibn Bat.*, Tome IV., 120.

‡ Barbosa (*Collecçuo* &c., Tom. II., 352) ; Barros, Dec. III., Lib. III., Cap. vii. As late as A.D. 1589 the Christian ex-King of the Máldives complained to the Portuguese Sovereign that the "Moors" of Cannanore were absolute masters of the Islands, and appropriated the produce *(se queixa que os Mouros de Cananor são sinhores absolutos da quellas Ilhas, e as defructam de tudo o que elles dão)*—Archivo Portuguez Oriental, Fasc. III. Pt. I., 211, (King to D. Duarte de Meneses, Viceroy, dated 22nd February, 1589), Goa, 1861.

§ Correa, *Lendas*, Tom., I. 341—2 ; Barros, Barbosa, *loc cit.*

‖ *V. s.*, p. 27.

¶ Correa, *Lendas*, Tom , II., 132. The converted Máldive Sultan, Don Manuel, seems himself to have issued at Cochin "Letters Patent" to various Portuguese adventurers for one or more voyages to the Islands.—See Archivo Portuguez Oriental, Fasc. V., Pt. I., 455–6, for the record of such a privilege granted to Manoel Silveira d' Arauja, as *Capitão mor*, in A.D. 1560.

** *V. s.*, p. 29 ; See Pyrard, Pt. II., p. 131.

THE MÁLDIVES.

TRADE AND COMMERCE.

17th century. Pyrard's description.

The 17th century was, so to speak, the heyday of Máldive trade. Pyrard saw it at its height, and more than a hundred years later, during the reign of the prudent Sultan Ibráhím Iskandar, it showed but faint signs of decay.

"Commerce at the Máldives," wrote Pyrard in A.D. 1611, "is extensive, and they are much frequented for purposes of trade. From all quarters may be seen there merchants—from Malabar, Barcelor, Onor, Bacalor, Cananor, Calecut, Tananor, Cochin, Coilam, Caël, Guzerat, Cambaye, Surat, and from Chaul; Arabs, Persians, natives of Bengal, St. Thomé, Masulipatam, Ceylon and Sumatra, who bring the commodities which are valued and in demand there, and take away those products in which the Máldives are so rich. First of all, the cocoanut tree, which grows wild, from which are derived many articles held in request by foreigners; to wit, the cordage with which all the vessels of the Indies are rigged; then the cocoanut, which is exported in such quantity to Arabia, the Malabar coast, and all parts of India, that every year more than 100 vessels are loaded with it, as well as with the oil and the honey [jaggery] of the same tree, and its platted leaves [cadjan] of which they make sails. But the greatest traffic is in [coir] rope."*

"They vend also little shells, that contain a creature in them of the bigness of the end of one's little finger, white, very smooth and glittering. * * * * These go only to Bengal, the inhabitants of which esteem them so much that I have seen thirty or forty ships laden without any other commodity bound thither; though in Bengal they have [gold and silver and] enough of other metals, yet these shells pass there as money, and the King and noblemen hoard up prodigious quantities of them, accounting them their treasure. They give twenty measures *(coquetées)* of rice for a fardel [*kotta*] of shells, each fardel containing 12,000.

"They have besides these a sort of tortoise-shell called *cambe* [*kahabu*] which is black and smooth and has many natural figures. It is found nowhere but there and in the Philippines, and goes off best in Cambaye. Here they also make fine reed-mats and cloths of cotton and silk. In exchange the merchants export some cotton and silk cloths, a sort of [toilet] oil, [arecanut, for chewing with betel leaves], iron, steel, pieces of porcelain, and in short, all the necessaries of life; yet everything is cheap, because of the number and frequency of ships. They import all their gold and silver, which they never send out again, but lay it up among their wives' jewels as their chief treasure."†

17th and 18th centuries.

During the 17th and 18th centuries a considerable trade in dried-fish, cocoanuts, cowries and coir continued to be carried on, both with the foreign vessels that visited Málé, and by the Islanders themselves in the course of annual voyages to Indian and Ceylon ports in their native craft.

The Dutch, with but a precarious hold on Ceylon and still engaged in the struggle with the Portuguese for supremacy in the East, yet assayed even in A.D. 1640 the unknown Máldive trade, mindful as ever of their commercial interests.‡

Hitherto, and until the demand for cowries induced by the Dutch rendered the export of these shells to Ceylon profitable, Máldive boats visiting the Islands loaded up mainly with dried-fish and cocoanuts. Captain Hamilton§ and Abbé Raynal‖ assert that Achin (Sumatra) vessels purchased this "*comelamash*" fish largely for gold dust and benzoin, the latter being exchanged by the Islanders for coffee at Mocha. The price in the former's time was as high as £8 per thousand.

By the Dutch the general products of the Máldives were held beneath notice, nor were restrictions placed on their free sale¶; but they were not slow to gauge the advantage of a complete control over the traffic in cowries. This monopoly they attempted, with fair success, to establish throughout the latter part of the 17th and much of last century.

---

* Pyrard, p. 165.

† Pyrard, quoted in Harris Vol. I., p. 715.

‡ *V. s.*, p. 30.

§ Pinkerton, Vol. 85, p. 389.

‖ History of the Settlements and Trade of the Europeans in the East and West Indies (Justamond's Translation, Vol. 2, p. 83).

¶ Cf. Dutch Records, Miscellaneous (Diary, October 25th, 1663).

THE MÁLDIVES.

TRADE AND COMMERCE.

Some details of the course of this trade during the Dutch period of rule in Ceylon may be supplied.

Governor Ryckloff Van Goens, in his Memoir* of A.D. 1663, commends to his successor as remunerative the business to be done in Máldive cowries "and sometimes large quantities of ambergris."

Trade in cowries with the Dutch. A.D. 1669. A.D. 1688.

The annual supply of cowries brought over by native vessels being at times insufficient to meet the home requirements, the Dutch not unfrequently sent over their own vessels to Málé to negotiate. As early as 1669 the "Cocatoe" was despatched, and brought back 1,149 *koṭṭas* (27,576 lbs.). The price then ruling was $1\frac{1}{8}$ rds. the *koṭṭa*. In 1688 it was $6\frac{1}{4}$ larins, and the Dutch were anxious to establish an exclusive contract with the Sultan. Governor Laurens Van Pyl wrote :—"The Company is very glad the Sultan has always entertained friendly feelings towards them ; as regards the commercial relation, however, between the Company and the Sultan there is room for an agreement to be entered into."†

Fortunately for the Islanders no such contract seems to have been ever concluded.

Upon each successive Governor was constantly impressed from Batavia the duty of inciting the Máldivians to larger supplies of cowries *(den Maldiver in den aanbreng van cauris meer en meer te animeeren)*, whilst the purchase price was stringently fixed at much below the fair market value.

As a kind of set off, however, against the low rate at which cowries were taken over, and also with the object of inducing larger importations year by year, the Máldivians were permitted to purchase a certain quantity of arecanuts upon favourable terms, as compared with other vendees, though much above cost price. Thus in 1687 the Máldive Ambassador was allowed 15 *amuṇams* of arecanuts at $6\frac{1}{3}$ rds. the *amuṇam ;* in 1704 the price was reduced to $5\frac{1}{3}$ rds. ; and by 1740 to 5 rds.

A.D. 1697.

The state of the trade with the Islands at the close of the 17th century is described by Governor Thomas Van Rhee :—"For some years Máldive vessels have arrived here (Colombo) and at Galle with dried-fish (*comblemass*) and now and then with cowries. These small shells we have purchased from them, in settlement of the home demand, for $1\frac{1}{2}$ rds. the *koṭṭa* of 12,000, or 24 lbs. In exchange they take arecanuts and spices of small value, paying for Colombo and Galle arecanuts $6\frac{1}{3}$ rds., and for those of Calpentyn (Kalpiṭiya) 5 rds. the *amuṇam* of 24,000. To encourage them to bring over larger quantities we are earnestly recommended to court their good will *(Haer Edelen Achtbear tot Batavia ons ook seer ernstig recommandeeren de Maldives vaerdaers in alles te carresseeren)*"‡

18th century. A.D. 1700-1720.

The price of cowries, which had been raised from $1\frac{7}{8}$ rds. to 2 rds. the *koṭṭa*, or 5 stuivers per lb. (1703), remained the same till 1718, but was insufficient to induce the Máldivians to face the risks of the sea in transporting them to Ceylon ; for in 1721 Governor Rumpf remonstrated with the Sultan that in spite of the higher price offered by the Dutch in Ceylon, French ships brought away large quantities of cowries from the Islands purchased at $1\frac{1}{2}$ rds. the *koṭṭa*. At this time the Netherlands demand was 20,000 *koṭṭas*, or 480,000 lbs.

The period between 1720 and 1750§ was, perhaps, marked by the briskest trade between the Dutch and the Islands. To prevent the cowry trade falling into the hands of other nations, special vessels laden with spices and grain were despatched to Málé, sometimes annually.

---

* *Memorie voor den E. Heere Jacob Hustaert, Raad Ext. van India, &c.*, dated Colombo, December 26th, 1663.—Valentyn, *Oud en Nieuw Oost Indien*, 1724-6., p. 183.

† Letter to S. Muhammad, dated December 4th, 1688.

‡ Memoir for his successor, Gerrit de Heere, dated Colombo, February 25th, 1697.

§ "The Island of Male, according to the latest accounts we have, is in a better condition than ever, and the Dutch carry on there a very considerable commerce, the natives themselves also trading in their own vessels to Ceylon, where they are well used by the Dutch, and make a very great profit of those little shells which are called *cauris, coris,* and by our seamen *cowries*."—Harris, "Collection of Voyages," 1744, Vol. I., p. 715. Other European nations usually procured them from the Dutch to be employed in slave traffic on the Guinea coast.

THE MÁLDIVES.

TRADE AND COMMERCE.

A.D. 1720-1750.
A.D. 1723.

In 1723 the vessels 'Adam' and 'Africa' visited Málé, freighted with 70 lasts (1312 maunds) of rice, besides spices, under instructions to bring back from 8,000 to 10,000 *koṭṭas* of cowries. Vessels were despatched again in 1727, 1728, 1732 and 1734.

"The wholesome dread" of the Dutch would seem to have made a ready market for their goods at any cost. The Sultan's letter of 1723 (in Portuguese) states that owing to the sickness of the crew the captain transacted no business, but that the Sultan had exempted the Dutch vessels from the payment of the usual port dues, and ordered his people to take the goods at the price demanded, viz.:—

1 *amuṇam* arecanuts, for 3½ *koṭṭas* cowries.

1 candy rice { 8 Bengal maunds / 4 parras = 1 maund } for 4½ *koṭṭas*.

2 lbs. cloves for 2 *koṭṭas*.

2 lbs. nutmeg for 2 *koṭṭas*.

36½ lbs. sugar for 1 *koṭṭa*.

A.D. 1734.

Again in 1734 the Sultan writes:—"As for the merchandize, I have taken it to the best of my power, and the captain has taken back the rest. The pepper I bought from the company I have sold to the captain of an English brig at a loss of 8 *koṭṭas* of cowries on each candy. Ships from Bellapor and Bengal arriving with supplies wait till August or September: if they cannot sell they take back their goods, or sell on credit till the ensuing year; but I have paid in full for all the goods brought by the Dutch ships, and, as there were no cowries to be had from the Islands (owing to the late inundation), was forced to borrow the requisite quantity from various merchants.*"

These ventures were not altogether successful. Thus from one trip of the 'Colombo' the Batavia Government complained that no more than *f* 2,970 (about £14) profit resulted, and that on the 10 lasts of rice shipped no gain was made owing to foreign competition.†

Renewed efforts—apparently fruitless—were made to inveigle the Sultan into a firm contract for exclusive trade with the Dutch Company *(een vast contract om met dien Sultan handel te dryven met seclusive van alle ander natien)*.

It is probable that the Dutch continued to send over their own vessels to the Islands occasionally during the latter half of this century, but not to the extent they had done in the reign of Sultan Ibráhím, who displayed much tact in simulating peculiar attachment to the Dutch while steadily encouraging trade with other nations.

A.D. 1740.

"The Máldive boats," Governor Van Imhoff writes in 1740, "import cowries, which also form an article of our trade. It is not a profitable business, but also not expensive; and, therefore, even as ballast, cowries are worth sending home. I have fixed the price this year at 2½ rds. the *koṭṭa* of 24 lbs. All that the Máldive Sultan asks in return is to have 50 *amuṇams* of arecanuts at 5 rds. per *amuṇam* without paying export duties. This I have granted; and he has shown his gratitude by sending us a larger quantity of cowries this year than the last. The annual demand from home is 400,000 lbs. weight, and we must therefore encourage the Máldive merchants to give us exclusively all they can find. This quantity would sell for *f* 100,000 (£8,300), but yet if we can send home Madura cloths the vessels need not be filled up with casks of these shells, which yield so disproportionate a profit."‡

---

* Sultan's letter in Portuguese, dated May 9th, 1734.

† Possibly defeated by the very outrageousness of the fixed profit required on the several commodities offered for sale at the Islands. The following is the outward manifest of the 'Elisabeth' in 1727:—

	Purchase price.			Sale price.		
100 lbs. mace, per lb.	*f* 0	11	3 ...	*f* 8	0	0
100 „ nutmeg „	0	1	8 ...	3	12	0
100 „ cloves „	0	6	11 ...	5	0	0
6,000 „ cast-lead „	0	2	6 ...	0	4	3
6,000 „ peper, per *bhar* (480 lbs.)	48	0	0 ...	121	10	0
200 *amuṇams*, Colombo arecanuts, per *amuṇam* ...	8	6	2 ...	17	5	0
10 lasts (750 *parras*) rice, per *parra*	1	0	6 ...	1	10	9
and Rds. 2,000, cash.						

‡ Memoir, left for the in-coming Governor, W. M. Bruininck, dated March 12, 1740.—Lee's "Ribeyro," Appen., p. 175.

A.D. 1752–53.

In 1752 each return vessel to the Netherlands was expected to take 500,000 lbs. (2,000 *kottas*.)*

The following year permission was received from Batavia to purchase cowries at 1½ rds. instead of 1 rd. the *kotta*, to which price they had gradually fallen.†

A.D. 1764–73.

The annual home demand slackened (1764–66) to 150,000, 200,000, or 300,000 lbs. (6,000 to 12,000 *kottas*), if needed to fill the lower tier of vessels as ballast. In 1773 it remained the same. Meanwhile the price was raised (1767) from *f* 3·12 (72 st. = 6*s.* 6*d.*) to *f* 4·5 (85 st. = 7*s.* 7*d.*) or even *f* 4·10 (90 st. = 8*s.* 2*d.*) the *kotta*.

In 1769, Governor Falck refused to accede to the Sultan's request to raise the price to 2 rds. per *kotta* on the ground that the Company did not make so much profit on the trade as formerly.‡

A few years later the Dutch were effectually 'hoist with their own petard.'

A.D. 1777–8.

The Sultan apologised in 1777 for his inability to supply cowries as usual, because the Ceylon price remained so low, whereas English and French vessels purchased them at the Máldives for Rs. 4 the *kotta*.§ In spite of the counter assertion by the Governor that the Batavia and Netherlands Government had made it a fast rule that no change should be endured except in the last necessity (which did not exist), the Dutch thought it desirable the next year (1778) to make a reluctant concession of 5 stuivers (*i.e.*, from 85 to 90) on the *kotta*,—and this when 12,000 *kottas* (900,000 lbs.) were selling at Amsterdam for 7½ stuivers the lb., or more than 100 per cent. over cost price !‖

A.D. 1795.

How rapidly the price advanced, now that foreigners had regularly entered the market, is proved by the fact that in 1795 the Sultan sent over to Ceylon a vessel laden with cowries to be paid for at the stipulated price of Rs. 3 a *kotta*.¶

Suicidal policy of the Dutch.

The above sketch will suffice to show that the Dutch, with everything originally in their favour, from the illiberality which characterized their commercial policy, saw a trade that, judiciously fostered, would have continued to yield them ample profits, gradually slip through their hands to the enrichment of other nations.

MODERN TRADE, A.D. 1830–80.

The whole of the export and import trade of the Islands is conducted at Málé, whither the produce of each Atol is brought to be exchanged for that of other groups.

Customs regulations and dues at Málé.

The port charges and duties are moderate, and levied in a very simple manner. A port due [M. *hagu-langa*] of Rs. 40 is payable by every trading vessel, without reference to the period of her stay. The only customs duty is a 10 per-cent. charge on rice. Certain presents (M. *hadiyá*), however—sometimes amounting to Rs. 200 in value—are required to be made to the Sultan and officers of Government.

Christopher has specified the port regulations and charges in force in 1835, and there is reason to believe these have varied but slightly since. "From a large ship one candy weight of merchandize is exacted in addition to what is demanded for a small brig. The traders do not, however, take advantage of this custom, because they say a large ship would not be able to barter her cargo within the season, and that consequently her profits would scarcely cover the expenses of such delay.

"The *hadiya* is distributed as follows:—To the Sultan, one candy and one hundred and thirty-three bamboos of rice (equal to five bags and a-half), and seven red handkerchiefs, which are carried to his house at seven different periods. After the handkerchiefs

* First reckoned by the lb. in 1744, upon instructions from Batavia. The *kotta* was also made to equal 25 lbs. about this time.

† Cauris de Maldivo; tegens ander half rd 't cotty, en niet hoger, t' accepteeren.—(D. R. Misc.)

‡ Reply, dated January 26th, 1769, to Sultan's letter of October 27th, 1768. Note (1).

§ Sultan's letter, dated October 15th, 1777. Colombo letters, February 9th, 1778, and December 19th, 1778. Abbé Raynal states that foreign vessels annually took away cargoes of cowries, valued at 7,000 or 8.000 *livres*, purchased at 6 *sous* and sold from 12 to 18 *sous* per lb. in their several capitals, and 35 *livres* in Guinea.

‖ Wilcocke's Stavorinus, Vol. I., p. 352, note.

¶ Sultan's letter, dated July 13, 1795.

THE MÁLDIVES.

TRADE AND COMMERCE.

are thus delivered one is returned to the lascars who carried them, to which is added a quantity of betel. To the officers of Government, the Sultan's relatives, &c., according to a list which is provided by the Hindeggeree, eleven candies and fifty-three bamboos, making a total of fifty bags of rice.

"The above presents may be made either in rice, salt, cummin-seed, chillies, coriander seed, which are taken by measure; or in dates, catechu, turmeric, and onions, which are taken by weight; six gull [*gau*], or one and a-half pound, of the latter being considered equal to six bamboos, or twelve seers, of the former.

"The Emir-el-Bahr is the officer whose duty it is to superintend the division and distribution of the presents: for his trouble he is entitled to a sixth part of everything given, which constitutes the principal emolument of his office.

"The presents are sent in small quantities on wooden platters carried by the lascars, who are required to sing as they go to the different houses. The traders can so arrange as to select for presents the articles in least demand in the market. This privilege, and the inferior quality of the articles, render the duties very light. Besides the presents abovementioned, forty cotton handkerchiefs are required to be given when they are delivered, the cheapest of any color being taken without objection. There is a small present of Rs. 5 in a handkerchief required to be sent to the Sultan, after the other presents are delivered, to obtain permission to barter.

"There is another exaction of a different nature to which traders are subject according to the established custom of the place. They are liable on a requisition to supply the public stores with a certain quantity of rice, at a price fixed by the Hindeggeree, which is about half the market value. The trader is always paid for such rice in *kotas* of cowries, a *kota* consisting of 12,000, and valued at Rs. 2 each, though they can be purchased in the bazaar for Rs. 1; but this is made up by the charges for godown rent and anchorage being received by the Hindeggeree in *kotas* at his own valuation. If this be not attended to and the charges be paid in cash by the trader, he sustains considerable loss.

"On the arrival of a vessel from the eastward near any of the Attols a boat immediately puts off to her. The pilot receives a fixed and handsome remuneration from the Hindeggeree, as does also the headman of the Attol to which the pilot-boat belongs. On a vessel anchoring off the town of Malé, the Emir-el-Bahr approaches her in a boat, and hailing the pilot inquires whether there is any sickness on board. Should there be none, he goes on board, when he is generally presented with a piece of chintz or a shawl, and he then takes the master of the vessel on shore. If there be small-pox on board the vessel is put under the strictest quarantine for forty days after the recovery of the person last effected. In case the disease was prevalent at the place from which the vessel has come, though there be no sickness, quarantine is nevertheless enforced, but the period under such circumstances is regulated as the Sultan may see fit to order."*

Boutiqnes and godowns—generally outside the Fort wall—are rented to the traders (mostly "Moormen," with, of late years, a few Parsís) who barter their goods in them. The rent charged is from Rs. 20 to Rs. 50 a month. "Should all the public buildings be occupied, temporary thatched huts are put up as required."†

External trade.

The external trade from Málé consists of two branches, one carried on by foreign traders, either themselves resorting to that place from Chittagong, Ceylon, and the Malabar Coast, or by means of resident agents on the Island, and the other by the natives in their own vessels.

The foreign traders call regularly, generally arriving about March and leaving with the South-West monsoon in July or August. "The part of the external trade which is conducted by the natives themselves is carried on chiefly with Calcutta, [Madras and Ceylon,] in boats of from 100 to 200 tons burthen, which leave for the coast late in August or early in September, annually, having the South-West monsoon in their favour, and return in December and January with the North-East monsoon." The boats which visit Ceylon rarely exceed 50 to 60 tons.

---

* Trans. Bom. Geo. Soc., 1836-8, p. 85.

† Note (2).

"Unfaltering in their adherence to their ancestral pursuits, the commodities which the Islanders produce at the present day consist of precisely the same articles which they exported a thousand years ago."* These exports are fish (dried and salted), fish-blood, cocoanuts, coir-yarn, cowries, tortoise-shell, and sometimes a few mats and sweetmeats. In return they take back grain (chiefly rice,) arecanuts, curry-stuffs, spices, earthenware, provisions, sugar, tobacco, cotton and silk (raw and manufactured,) some timber, and a variety of sundries.

Progress of trade.

The progress of the commerce of the Máldive Islands since 1841 is indicated in the annexed tables (A., B., C.,)† and is the more satisfactory as completely refuting the prevalent notion that it has for years been in a state of decline.

The following table exhibits the average annual value for quinquennial periods of the trade with British India and Ceylon :—

TRADE.

Years.	British India.			Ceylon.			British India & Ceylon.		
	Imports.	Exports.	Total Trade.	Imports.	Exports.	Total Trade.	Imports.	Exports.	Total Trade.
	£	£	£	£	£	£	£	£	£
1836 to 1840 ...	21,157	9,469	30,626	—	—	—	—	—	—
1841—1845 ...	18,509	—	—	—	—	—	—	—	—
1846—1850 ...	19,644	—	—	—	—	—	—	—	—
1851—1855 ...	17,928	11,597	29,525	—	—	—	—	—	—
1856—1860 ...	15,776	13,953	29,729	26,118	4,854	30.972	41,894	18,807	60,701
1861—1865 ...	23,504	22,805	46,309	33,648	7,273	40,921	57,152	30,078	87,230
1866—1870 ...	39,146	35,034	74,180	32,974	6,078	39,052	72,120	41,112	113,232
1871—1875 ...	47,580	33,328	80,908	38,750	17,940	56,690	86,330	51,268	137,598
1876—1880 ...	23,187	34,302	57,488	35,160	30,493	65,652	58,347	64,794	123,121

British India.

Whilst between 1830 and 1840 the annual trade with British India averaged £30,626, it had more than doubled in the corresponding period thirty years later (1866-1870), and amounted to £74,180. In the following period of five years it had further increased to £80,908 ; but has sunk considerably since.

Ceylon.

With Ceylon the trade has advanced with faster strides. Between 1856-1860 the combined import and export trade averaged £30,972 yearly, or less than half of the annual amount reached between 1876 and 1880, viz., £65,652.

Total trade.

The total imports into, and exports from, British India and Ceylon rose from £60,701 (1856-1860) to £137,598 (1871-1875), or two and-a-quarter fold, though they fell to £123,121 in the next five years.

The united commerce with British India and Ceylon for 1880 amounted to an aggregate of £123,562, of which £57,300 were imports and £66,262 exports.

The course of the external trade of the Islands is clearly shown in the accompanying **Diagram**. The progressive improvement during decennial periods has been steady in spite of curious fluctuations difficult to explain.

Of the whole trade with British India and Ceylon, the latter is able to claim as much as 44 per cent.—a larger proportion than might fairly be expected.

Bengal absorbs three-fourths of the Indian trade, the whole of which may be said to lie between that and the Madras Presidency, as Máldive boats of late years have rarely visited Burmese ports or Bombay.

In order to further illustrate the description of Máldive external trade, statements (B., C.,) are appended showing the value of the chief articles imported into, and exported from, British India and Ceylon since 1853.

---

* Tennent, Ceylon, Vol. II., p. 175.

† The review of Máldive trade extends to 1880 only. Figures for 1881 have been added to the tables subsequently.

THE MÁLDIVES.

TRADE AND COMMERCE.

IMPORTS.*

Cocoanuts.

Cocoanuts (M. *kárhi.*) The high estimate set on Máldive cocoanuts renders their sale very profitable. In 1853 the value of nuts imported into British India was £8,668, which had trebled by 1864 (£24,691), and in 1872 amounted to £46,241. The annual average value during the six years 1870-75 equalled as much as £30,403, but only reached £17,041 for the last five (1876-80).

Ceylon, with her home supply, naturally takes but a small quantity. The average for the past twenty years (1861-1880) has been only £103. The largest importation—valued at £651—was in 1871.

The wholesale price of cocoanuts at Málé is about 3,000 for one candy (4 bags) rice, or 1,000 for Rs. 7 to Rs. 8. In Ceylon these nuts sell at Rs. 8 to Rs. 10 per 1,000.

A small quantity of Máldive *copperah* is in some years imported into Ceylon.

Coir.

Coir (M. *rónu.*) Máldive and Lakkadive coir has always borne a higher market value than that of the Continent or Ceylon owing to its being not only stronger but of finer quality and better colour. That of Tiladummatí is estimated at 30 per cent. above the coir of other Atols.

In Ibn Batúta's time, and during the Portuguese period, as stated above, coir formed the chief article of export, and throughout last century large quantities continued to be annually brought over to Ceylon to be exchanged for arecanuts.†

The average yearly value imported into India was £7,812 between 1870-1875, but only £3,130 for 1876-80.

The importation into Ceylon shows an extraordinary increase. In 1859 the value was £544 ; in ten years it had about doubled (£1,027), and in 1879 amounted to £3,997, so that in twenty years the trade has increased more than seven-fold. The average value for the last five years (1876-1880) has been £3,091.

Fifty years ago coir yarn of the first quality exchanged at the Máldives at the rate of 20 lbs. for 12 lbs. rice, or against dates weight for weight, equivalent to Rs. 3 per maund (82 lbs.) Purchased in cash at Rs. 18 per candy, it sold at Calcutta from Rs. 25 to Rs. 30. The present price in Ceylon varies from Rs. 5 to Rs. 15 per cwt.

Cowries.

Cowries (M. *boli.*) The trade in these small shells has steadily declined since last century, and is almost certain to dwindle year by year as civilization advances.

The ultimate destination of the large shipments of the money cowry (*Cypraea moneta*) was, and to some extent is still, the Guinea coast of Africa. They were formerly much used in the slave trade, though even a century and a half ago a cargo of slaves could not be purchased for less than 12 to 14 tons of cowries.‡

In 1820 nearly 6,000 cowries could be purchased for Rs. 1 § ; twelve years later the price in England was £20 per ton, and £50 to £60 on the coast of Guinea‖; in 1835 at Málé it was Rs. 2 the *koṭṭa* (12,000)¶ ; at the present day it has fallen to Rs. 1·50, or Rs. 5 the cwt. About 1843 in India the exchange was 64 for one pice—which will now purchase 200 to 400—or about 5,000 for Rs. 1.** Some twenty years ago a temporary rise in price is said to have occurred owing to a sudden home demand, and vessels visiting Málé paid as high as Rs. 6 the *koṭṭa*††.

---

* Note (3).

† Abbé Raynal, *loc. cit.*, Vol. II., p. 83. The Dutch exported yearly 800,000 lbs. Ceylon-made coir-rope to Batavia and the Cape, besides 400,000 lbs. in yarn to Batavia, paying the natives a fixed sum—3½ fanams per bundle of 24 lbs.—and levying a heavy export duty. (Bertolacci, Ceylon, p. 178.) In 1816-17 Máldive coir sold in Ceylon from Rs. 11 to Rs. 14 per maund; Island-made at Rs. 6½ to Rs. 8. (Asiatic Annual Register).

‡ Harris, Voyages, Vol. I., p. 716.

§ Princep's Indian Antiquities (Thomas' edn.).

‖ Journ. R. Geo. Soc., 1832, p. 83.

¶ Trans. Bom. Geo. Soc., 1836-8, p. 85.

** Bennett, Ceylon, &c., p. 351.

†† The present dulness of the market is borne out by the following recent Produce Market Report (Brookes and Faith's, London, Nov. 19th, 1880) :—" Cowries, Maldive, small, 15*s.* to 18*s.* per ton ; medium, 10*s.* to 12*s.* ; large, 6*s.* Very dull. Bombay large common Maldive, 8*s.* to 10*s.* per cwt. ; medium Calcutta, 20*s.*" The trade in the *Cassis rufa* for cameos (Tennent, Ceylon, Vol. II., p. 175) has equally declined.

The chief trade is with British India direct: the Ceylon supply is merely warehoused temporarily to be reshipped to Bengal.

If the returns are reliable as showing the actual value of cowries annually imported (which may reasonably be doubted), the rise and fall is remarkable. The annual value absorbed by British India between 1853 and 1855 averaged only £568, but rose in 1856 to £2,008.

The same year Ceylon is credited with £15,905 worth; but in ten years the value imported had fallen as low as £59. Between 1870 and 1875 the trade appears to have been brisker, the importation into British India reaching £6,774 in 1870 and averaging for the five years 1871–75 £3,590, as compared with £2,049 during the same period into Ceylon.

Dried-fish.

Dried-fish (M. *kaḷu-bili-mas*) forms by far the largest article of export, amounting during the last twenty years to more than 73 per cent. of the total value of imports into Ceylon from the Máldives. It is noticeable that of the whole supply of fish required by Ceylon nearly one-third is drawn from these Islands.

About forty or fifty years ago the quantity shipped from the Máldives rose in some years to 75 lacs (1824), though in others it fell as low as 10 lacs. At Galle and Sumatra the demand was greatest. Chittagong traders exchanged most of their fish for pepper, which they carried to Bengal, generally making a profit of 300 to 400 per cent. on the speculation. A lac of fish, which cost something less than Rs. 2,000 at Málé, sold at Sumatra for 2,000 Spanish dollars.*

The wholesale barter rate for dried fish at the Máldives is at the present day 1 candy rice for 2¼ cwt. A few years back, before the system of modern weights was introduced, the same quantity of rice exchanged for 400 fish (*i.e.*, 1,600 pieces.) In Ceylon the price runs from Rs. 12 to Rs. 20 the cwt., according to the several sorts.†

From the returns it will be seen that the value of fish imported into Ceylon exceeded £20,000 by 1862, and attained its maximum in 1876 (£35,548.) The annual average since 1856 has amounted to £23,337 and has remained very steady during periods of five years:—

			£
Between	1856–60	it equalled	12,684
	1861–65	,,	22,075
	1866–70	,,	23.819
	1871–75	,,	29,932
	1876–80	,,	28,223

Fish-blood.

For the value of *fish-blood* (M. *rhi-hakuru*, 'fish-sugar'), as distinct from dried fish imported into Ceylon, the returns give figures only from 1856-1869, showing an average of nearly £100 annually.

Tortoise shell.

Tortoise-shell (M. *kahabu.*) In Pyrard's day the trade was chiefly with Cambaye: a *gau* (¼lb.) could be purchased for one *larin*. Máldive tortoise-shell is considered of first-class quality. Ceylon and Bengal are the markets for it.

Five maunds (lbs. 420) were exported from Málé in one season (1835). The Ceylon returns show that the trade is steady. In 1856 the value imported was £1,157, fell to £630 in 1862, rose to £1,510 in 1865, but fell again in the next two years to £992, after which it progressively improved till 1875, when it amounted to £2,184. The last five years, however, show an average of only £1,146. The annual average since 1856 has been £1,296.

Tortoise-shell purchased at Málé for Rs. 16 to Rs. 25 per cwt. realizes in Ceylon as much as Rs. 5 to Rs. 10 per lb. It is in great demand at Colombo and Galle for the manufacture of native combs and ornaments.

---

* Trans. Bom. Geo. Soc., 1836-8, pp. 83, 106.

† Dried fish per cwt.: *goḍá-mas*, Rs. 20; *gaḍu-mas*, Rs. 20; *Himiti-mas*, Rs. 19; *medu-mas*, Rs. 18; *kirá-mas*, Rs. 12 to Rs. 15: fish-blood, Rs. 12 to Rs. 20 per lb.; salt-fish, Rs. 20 to Rs. 25 per 100.

THE MÁLDIVES.

TRADE AND COMMERCE.

Mats.

Jaggery.

The only other exports worth particular mention are *mats, jaggery, confectionery* and *grain.*

Mats seldom make good the price expected, and are frequently taken back in hope of a better market another season. The large mats of best quality are valued at Rs. 5 or Rs. 6 each at Málé, and can rarely be procured under Rs. 8 to 10 in Ceylon. The value imported since 1856 has only averaged £74, whilst that of *jaggery* has been less.

Confectionery.

The figures under the head *confectionery and provisions* are so large as to leave no doubt of their being exports from India and Ceylon returned, as in the case of *grain*, for want of a market. Máldive confectionery is limited to *boṇḍialuva* (M. *boḍi*), *koliappam*, and a few other sweetmeats mostly consumed on the Atols. Taking the figures as they stand, whilst £1,258 worth of confectionery was imported into British India in 1853, the value amounted to £2,304 in 1872, and averaged £1,912 annually between 1871 and 1875, but fell off (1876-80) to £531 only. A much smaller quantity is taken by Ceylon, the average for the last 20 years (1861-80) being only £533.

Grain.

The large quantity of *grain* returned from the Máldives every year—the whole of which must have been shipped thither from India and Ceylon—is so far satisfactory as going to prove that the Máldivians are never threatened by impending famine, which on occasions afflicts the more Northern Islanders, the Lakkadivians, calling for special Government aid.

The import of superfluous grain has necessarily fluctuated with the requirements of the market at the Máldives. In 1859 grain to the value of £15,135 was imported, but the next year it fell to £34. The re-importation in 1867 amounted to £16,939. Less grain has been returned of late years. The average for the last five years (1876-1880) was £906, whereas that for the five years previous (1871-1875) equalled £2,112. The annual average since 1856 has been £3,997.

Sundries.

Among *miscellaneous articles* occasionally brought over from the Máldives it is not surprising to find *wreck goods.* Besides £30 wreckage, £57 worth of *wine* and *spirits* appear among the imports in 1859 ; two years later (1861) wreck goods to the value of £137 were sent over; in 1863 £116, and the following year £53 worth. *Brass* and *copper*—chiefly old cooking utensils—may also be found almost annually among the minor sundry imports to Ceylon.

EXPORTS.

Arecanuts.

Arecanuts form an annual and large proportion of the exports to the Máldives. As but few areca trees grow on the Islands, a very high value is set on these nuts for masticatory purposes, either raw or in the preparation known as *cutch.* The special indulgence as regards the purchase of arecanuts granted to Máldivians by the Dutch has been mentioned (*V.s.*, p. 99.) Nearly the whole quantity required by the Islanders is supplied by Ceylon. The value of arecanuts exported from this Island has averaged £1,323 since 1856, exceeding £2,000 in 1856, 1872, 1876, 1879 and 1880, but falling to £842 in 1869.

The wholesale price of best arecanuts in Ceylon is Rs. 30 per *amuṇam* of 24,000, weighing about 2½ cwt. At the Máldives 1 cwt. exchanges for ¾ cwt. of dried fish : a few years back 1 *amuṇam* was valued at 500 fish (*i.e.*, 2,000 pieces).

Cotton and Silk goods.

Cotton manufactures.—The value in 1853 of Indian cotton goods exported was only £895 ; rose three-and-half fold in 1855 (£2,921) ; fell to £1,085 in 1862, but suddenly rose again the following year to £3,517—a considerably higher value than the annual average attained between 1870 and 1875 (£1,809), though close to that of 1876-80 (£3,087).

Cotton goods exported from Ceylon have shown a steady annual value since 1871, viz., £4,299, as against £2,362 for the ten years previous (1861-70.) In three years only (1857, 1859 and 1869) has the value fallen short of £1,000.

Whereas the total value of cotton manufactures exported from British India and Ceylon in 1856 was £3,462, in 1863 it had increased to £5,203, and by 1876 to £10,359.

If the purchasing of cotton goods be taken as a test of the prosperity of a people, it may safely be said that the Máldive Islanders are considerably better off now than they were twenty years ago.

Some *silk goods* are also yearly purchased from British India, averaging between 1870 and 1875 £565 worth.

Grain.

Grain.—The returns furnish interesting facts regarding this, the staple export to the Islands. With increasing population, the amount required for consumption has rapidly advanced. This is made clear by the following statement. The value of grain annually exported from British India direct averaged—

Bewteen	1834–1841	(8 years)	£ 7,124
	*1853–1862	(do.)	9,401
	1870–1874	(5 years)	21,245
	1875–1879	(do.)	20,614

so that in 40 years it has nearly trebled. No doubt quantities, if obtainable, would be a fairer test, as the market price of grain has doubled during the last quarter of this century.

The average value shipped from Ceylon annually during successive quinquennial periods exhibits extraordinary increase :—

1856–1860	...	£ 1,186
1861–1865	...	1,690
1866–1870	...	1,327
1871–1875	...	9,794
1876–1880	...	20,479

or a growth of over 17-fold in the last twenty-five years.

The expansion of the grain trade has probably in the main been due to the enterprize of the few Parsí merchants, who have, during the last ten years, established regular commercial relations with the Islands.

Practically, the whole supply of grain is drawn from Bengal. Rice purchased at False-Point (Calcutta) for Rs. 4 to Rs. 5 per bag (2 maunds) is either shipped to the Máldives direct or brought to Ceylon and retained undor bond for profitable reshipment.

It is believed (not without reason) that between 40,000 and 50,000 bags of rice are now carried over to the Islands yearly.

Curry stuffs, spices, earthenware

The exports of *curry stuffs* and *spices*, as well as *earthenware*, from Ceylon, though comparatively small, have been progressively improving during the last twenty years, the annual average of the former between 1861 and 1870 being £172, as against £278 for 1871–1880, (from British India £258), and of the latter £309, against £626.

Merchandize.

Merchandize exported amounted in 1874 to £1,337, and in 1879 to £1,893. Under this vague term are included a large variety of sundry articles of insufficient value to be classed under their respective heads.

Provisions, and Sugar.

Provisions and oilmanstores.—The average value exported from India between 1871 and 1880 was £2,246, and from Ceylon £234.

Sugar.—The exportation from India for the same ten years averaged £1,784 (£3,072 in 1872), or more than five-fold that from Ceylon, viz., £322.

Tobacco.

Tobacco, snuff, &c., exported from India between 1871 and 1880 is valued at £1,352 annually, as compared with £338 from Ceylon. The yearly value taken from Ceylon has fluctuated considerably. It rose from £87 worth in 1856 to £822 in 1861, had fallen to £15 in 1866, rose the following year to £323, dropped to £1 in 1870, sprang as high as £1,015 in 1874, but has sunk somewhat since.

Among other articles shipped to the Islands the chief are *haberdashery* (£634 worth from India, 1879) *gunnies* (£1,000 from India, 1861), *furniture, timber, mats, medicines, oils*, and *terrajaponica*, or *cutch*. Of these the only two calling for remark are *furniture*

* Returns for 1842-1852, 1857, 1860, not available.

THE MÁLDIVES.

TRADE AND COMMERCE.

and *timber* (annually shipped) as proving the dearth of serviceable wood on the Islands already noticed (*V. s.*, p. 84).

Sundries.

Miscellaneous exports.—In addition to the above a variety of sundries are exported every year. Among the commonest are *ghee*, *glassware*, *grind-stones*, *perfumery* and *soap*, with *bricks* (40,000—£57 value—in 1867), *carts and carriages*—probably hand-carts —(12—value £12—in 1879), *gunpowder* (never exceeding £5 value), and even such luxuries as *sodawater*, *lemonade*, and *biscuits*. The taste for the last item is evidently growing, for £12 worth were purchased in 1876, £46 in 1877, and £40 in 1879.

As intelligent navigators, Máldivians appreciate *scientific instruments*, *charts*, *&c.*; and that their children are not forgotten, *crackers* (£19, in 1874, and in 1878) and *toys* will testify.

Live-stock.

Live stock is little needed.* Two *horses*, valued at £50, were shipped from Ceylon in 1862 (of which one was returned four years later†) and two head of *cattle*, valued at £12, in 1871.

Specie and precious stones.

Where barter still rules in business transactions it is to be expected that *specie* would be rarely imported. In two years only, viz., 1862 (£2,000) and 1868 (£400) does it figure in the Ceylon returns. *Precious stones*, too, seem to have little attraction for these Islanders, as £1,506 worth have sufficed them during the last 24 years (£1,306 value, 1860; £200, 1878).

SHIPPING.†

Shipping.

It is curious that the growth of the external commerce of the Máldives has not necessitated the employment of an increased amount of shipping. This will be seen from the following return of average annual tonnage. Apparently the limit has been reached—for native vessels at least; and any increase in tonnage under the lifeless administration which has been suffered to exist for centuries must depend upon the larger use of foreign vessels in the trade.

TONNAGE.

YEAR.	British India.			Ceylon.			British India and Ceylon.		
	Inwards.	Outwards.	Total.	Inwards.	Outwards.	Total.	Inwards.	Outwards.	Total.
1801—1810 ...	4,535	3,932	8,467	...	...	...	...	...	...
1811—1820 ...	4,762	4,729	9,491	...	...	...	...	...	...
1821—1830 ...	3,311	3,611	6,922	...	...	...	...	...	...
1831—1840 ...	...	...	...	...	...	...	...	...	...
1841—1850 ...	3,806	5,404	9,210	...	...	...	...	...	...
1851—1860 ...	2,707‡	3,685‡	6,572‡	4,145	3,819§	7,964§	...	...	...
1861—1870 ...	3,944‡	4,504‡	8,448‡	5,377	4,035	9,412	9,321‡	8,539‡	17,860‡
1871—1880 ...	3,391	4,718	8,109	6,377	4,376	10,753	9,768	9,094	18,862

In 1841 87 vessels, of a total capacity of 5,259 tons, entered inwards and cleared outwards at British India ports, and 70 vessels, carrying 7,349 tons, in 1880, so that there has been virtually no advance during 40 years. If the figures are correct, some very exceptional cause must have brought about the extraordinary abnormal rise for one year (1845) to 345 vessels from an average of 104 since 1841, and, on the tonnage, 1½-fold the aggregate tonnage for the four previous years. Between 1868 and 1874 the British India returns are swelled by the addition of Lakkadive (including Minakaï) vessels.

---

* *V. s.*, p. 84. ‖

† See tabular statements, D., E.

‡ For 9 years only: no returns for 1853 and 1867.

§ For 6 years only, viz., 1855–1860.

The shipping to and from Ceylon Ports shows some improvement since 1855. One hundred and eleven vessels, of 8,529 total tonnage capacity, entered and cleared out in 1856, against 131 vessels, amounting to 12,928 registered tonnage, during last year (1880).

On a rough average, the number of Máldivian craft which annually visit Ceylon is about 22, of 1,380 total tons burthen, manned by 440 sailors, or 20 men to each vessel of 63 tons.

Of the total shipping inwards and outwards (classed in the Ceylon returns as "British" and "Foreign"), Máldive vessels claim a percentage of 45, though the proportion of tonnage is but 15 per cent. The largest number of Máldivian vessels entered Ceylon ports in 1875 (31, tons 3415) and 1876 (40, tons 3167) ; the fewest in the two following years, viz., in 1877 (6, tons 534) and 1878 (1, tons 65).

The generally slight fluctuations in the annual tonnage of the shipping may best be seen by reference to the Diagram.

NOTES.

Notes.

(1)

The following letter from Sultan M. 'Izz-ud-dín—in French so villainous that a copy had to be made—with reference to the visit of the Dutch vessel "Triton," Capt. Blume, in 1769, affords an instance of the high-handed action of European nations at that period in their commercial dealings with native Princes :—

Seal of Sultan M. 'Izz-ud-dín.

Au gouvemeur de Coulombe
Pour le roi des Maldives

" J'ay Recu avec plaisir La lettre que vous mavée ecrit par le Senault* Captne Blüme J'ay fait tous seque Jay pũ pour satisfaire le Dit Capitne etant anoncée de votre [part] ayant pris les Marchandise au pris quil me L'est a fait : Je compte Envoyer quelqu'uns de mes Bateaux J'esperre que vous les Receverez comme le tems passée. Vous scavez que nous Commercions depuis longtems et esperé que vous me constinurée votre amitiée Le Capitne n'a pas paiyée Les usages nous avons Laissée sa à sa Disposition : s'il Rien† Lan prochain nous esperrons qu'il nous sastisfera Le Roy vous fait toute sorte D'amitiée.

"le 3me Juin 1769.

" Raportée vous en á seque le Captne Blüme vous Dira. Seque Je n'est que par Complesance.'

Translation.

Seal of Sultan M. 'Izz-ud-dín.

" To the Governor of Colombo.

For the King of the Máldives."

" I HAVE had the pleasure of receiving the letter which You wrote to me by Captain Blume. I have done all that I could to satisfy the said Captain, accredited as he was from You, having bought the merchandise at the price at which he set them to Me. I intend to send some of My ships, (and) I hope that You will receive them as in time past. You know that We (have) traded together for a long time, and (I) hope that You will continue Your friendliness to Me. The Captain has not paid the dues : We have left that to his settlement. If he comes back next year, We hope that he will satisfy Us. The King sends You every kind of friendship.

" The 3rd June, 1769.'

---

* *Senault* = ? *Senhor.* † *Rien* for *revient.*

THE MÁLDIVES.

TRADE AND COMMERCE.

Notes.

"Satisfy yourself as to that which Captain Blume will tell you. What I (? have done) is merely out of good will."

It seems that not content with driving a hard bargain, Captain Blume further forgot to pay the Customs duties!

(2)

The following is a list of approximate retail prices ruling at Málé a few years back for the chief bazár articles*:—

Arecanuts ...	...	12 for 1 cocoanut.
Cocoanuts ...	...	90 for Rs. 1.
Coir ...	...	1 *boḍi* for 8 fanams, or 6 *náli* rice, or 600 arecanuts.
Corriander-seed	...	1 *láhi* (¼ *náliya*) for 1 dried-fish (4 pieces).
Chillies ...	...	1 *gau* (½ lb.) for 1 fish.
Eggs ...	...	24 for 1 *náliya* rice.
Fish (fresh, large)	...	1 for 8 *kuḍa lári*.
Do. (salt) ...	...	1 *adubá* for 8 fish.
Flour ...	...	1 *gau* for 4 fish.
Ghee ...	...	1 *náliya* for 30 fish.
Jaggery ...	...	1 *adubá* for 8 fish.
Oil (cocoanut)	...	1 *náliya* for 24 fish.
Pepper ...	...	1 *láhi* for 4 fish.
Plantains ...	...	2 for 1 fish.
Potatoes ...	...	1 *gau* for 1 fish.
Do. (sweet)	...	do. for half a fish (2 pieces).
Rice ...	...	1 *náliya* for 3 fish or 8 *kuḍa lári*.
Saffron ...	...	1 *gau* for 1 fish.
Salt ...	...	1 *náliya* for 1½ fish (6 pieces).
Sugar ...	...	1 *gau* for 1 fish, or 1 *kuḍa lári*.
Do.-candy ...	...	do. for 1½ fish.
Tea ...	...	do. for 8 fish.
Tobacco ...	...	do. for 2 fish, or 8 *kuḍa lári*.
Tortoise-shell	...	do. for 12 *náliya* rice.
Vinegar ...	...	1 *adubá* for 3 fish.
Chatties (M. *boḍu fufé*), S. *muṭṭiya*)		1 for 8 fish.
Do. (M. *etiri*, S. *ẹtiliya*) ...		1 for 2 fish.
Cloth (white) ...	...	4 *riya* (2 *gazu*, 'yards') for 8 fish.
Do. (*mundu*)	...	1 for 24 fish.
Do. (*rumá*)	...	do.
Do. (*féliya*)...	...	do.
Do. (*libás*) ...	...	1 for 32 fish.

(3)

A comparative table of duties levied in India and Ceylon upon the chief articles exported to, and imported from, the Máldive Islands is given below.

It is astonishing how insignificant a proportion of the Customs revenue of this Island is drawn from the Máldives. The total value of the duty derived from the goods imported into Ceylon reached Rs. 5,624,401 between 1856 and 1879, of which the Máldive Islands contributed only Rs. 36,318, or a yearly average of Rs. 1,513 against Rs. 234,350. Again, whereas the total Customs collection of export duty between 1858 and 1869 amounted to Rs. 576,741, or Rs. 48,062 annually, that recovered upon goods exported to the Máldives was but Rs. 389, or an average of Rs. 32 for each year!

In port dues, between 1855 and 1879 Máldive vessels yielded an aggregate of Rs. 5,558, or Rs. 2,815 for vessels entered inwards, and Rs. 2,743 for those which cleared outwards.

---

* In Pyrard's time necessaries of life were far cheaper: for a *larin*, or 8 *sous*, could be purchased 400 cocoanuts, 500 plantains, a dozen fowls, 100 large fish, or 300 cwt. of roots.—Pyrard, p. 88.

THE MÁLDIVES

TRADE AND COMMERCE.

Notes.

COMPARATIVE STATEMENT of CUSTOMS TARIFF.

Articles.	British India.				Ceylon.			
	Imports.		Exports.		Imports.		Exports.	
	Value on which duty is assessed.	Rate of duty.	Value on which duty is assessed.	Rate of duty.	Value on which duty is assessed.	Rate of duty.	Value on which duty is assessed.	Value of duty.
Arecanuts ...	Free.	Nil.	Free.	Nil.	Free.	Nil.	Free.	Nil.
Do. in husk ...	do.	do.	do.	do.	do.	do.	do.	do.
Cocoanuts ...	do.	do.	do.	do.	do.	do.	do.	do.
Coir ...	do.	do.	do.	do.	do.	do.	do.	do.
Confectionery ...	Rated and *Ad val.*	5 o/o	do.	do.	Declared.	5 o/o	do.	do.
Copperah ...	Free	Nil.	do.	do.	Free.	Nil.	do.	do.
Cotton goods ...	Rated and *Ad val.*	5 o/o	do.	do.	Rated	5 o/o	do.	do.
Cowries (Máldive)...	Rs. 7·8 ⅌ cwt.	do.	do.	do.	Free.	Nil.	do.	do.
Earthenware ...	*Ad val.*	do.	do.	do.	Declared.	5 o/o	do.	do.
Fish, salted ...	Free*	Nil.	do.	do.	Rated.	cts. 50 ⅌ cwt.	do.	do.
,, other sorts ...	do.	do.	do.	do.	do.	do.	do.	do.
Grain, Paddy ...	do.	do.	do.	3 annas ⅌ maund of 3200 tolas	do.	cts. 13 ⅌ bushel	do.	do.
,, rice ...	do.	do.	do.	Nil.	do.	cts. 29 ⅌ bushel	do.	do.
Mats (rush) ...	do.	do.	do.	do.	Free.	Nil.	do.	do.
Metal ...	Rated and *Ad val.*	5 o/o	do.	do.	Rated.	Various.	do.	do.
Oil (cocoanut) ...	Free	Nil.	do.	do.	Free.	Nil.	do.	do.
Provisions ...	Rated and *Ad val.*	5 o/o	do.	do.	*Ad. val.*	5 o/o	do.	do.
Silk ...	do.	do.	do.	do.	do.	do.	do.	do.
Spices ...	do.	do.	do.	do.	do.	do.	do.	do.
Sugar, candy, (China)	Rs. 22 ⅌ cwt.	do.	do.	do.	Rated.	Rs. 2·50 ⅌ cwt.	do.	do.
,, ,, loaf ...	Rs. 26 do.	do.	do.	do.	do.	do.	do.	do.
,, ,, soft ...	Rs. 16·8 do.	do.	do.	do.	do.	Rs. 1·25 ⅌ cwt.	do.	do.
,, other sorts of sacharine produce	*Ad val.*	do.	do.	do.	do.	cts. 50 ⅌ cwt.	do.	do.
Tea, black ...	10 annas ⅌ lb	do.	do.	do.	do.	cts. 25 ⅌ lb.	do.	do.
,, green ...	Rs. 1·2 ⅌ lb.	do.	do.	do.	do.	do.	do.	do.
Tobacco, manufactured	*Ad val.*	do.	do.	do.	do.	cts. 17 ⅌ lb.	do.	do.
,, unmanufactured	*Ad val.*	do.	do.	do.	do.	cts. 9 ⅌ lb.	do.	do.
Tortoise Shell ..	Rs. 6 ⅌ lb	do.	do.	do.	*Ad. val.*	5 o/o	do.	do.

(4)

It is unlikely that slave vessels from Muskat now venture to the Máldives. Even fifty years ago their visits were rare. Christopher mentions that about five years before the time he wrote a vessel had arrived at Málé (*circa*, 1830) and sold about 25 lads at an average price of Rs. 80 each.†

By Treaties of August and September, 1822, and May 31st, 1839, the Imauns of Muskat bound themselves to use every effort for the suppression of the slave trade within their dominions, and by the Further Agreement of October 2nd, 1845, it was stipulated that this trade should definitely cease after 1st January, 1847.

* Except into the Bombay Presidency, where 12 annas per cwt. is charged.

† Trans. Bom. Geo. Soc., 1836-8, p. 82.

THE MÁLDIVES.

TRADE AND COMMERCE.

(5)

In 1843, when the obnoxious Navigation Laws (finally abolished by 12 & 13 Vict. c. 29) still remained in force, a question regarding the right of Máldive and Lakkadive vessels to land goods at Ceylon in their passage to and from the continent of India led to the boats of these Islands being placed on the same footing as British vessels.

By Order in Council dated 21st January, 1823, and subsequently by Act of 3 & 4 Wm. IV. c. 54, trade with Ceylon could only be conducted in British vessels or vessels of friendly foreign States exercising reciprocal indulgence.

Upon it being pointed out to the Board of Customs in England that the privilege of free trade had hitherto been allowed these Islanders, that their situation was peculiar, and that they were under the protection of the Indian and Ceylon Governments, it was not deemed expedient to disturb the practice which had always prevailed.

A.

THE MÁLDIVE ISLANDS.

VALUE of IMPORTS into, and EXPORTS from BRITISH INDIA and CEYLON.

(Converted into sterling at 2s. the rupee.)

Year.	Bengal.		Madras.		Total of British India.		Ceylon.		British India and Ceylon.		Combined Import and Export trade with British India.	Combined Import and Export trade with Ceylon.	Combined Import and Export trade with British India and Ceylon.
	Imports.	Exports.	Imports.	Exports.	Imports.	Exports.	Imports.	Exports.	Total Imports.	Total Exports.			
£	£	£	£	£	£	£	£	£	£	£	£	£	£
1841	13,433	11,731	6,549	...	20,082	...	...	...	...	...	...	...	...
1942	15,716	4,368	10.170	...	15,886	...	...	...	...	...	...	...	...
1843	10,279	3,848	6,921	...	17,218	...	...	...	...	...	...	...	...
1844	16,344	3,458	7,498	...	13,842	...	...	...	...	...	...	...	...
1845	18,190	8,937	7,325	...	25,515	...	...	...	...	...	...	...	...
1846	17,413	9,562	6,728	...	14,141	...	...	...	...	...	...	...	...
1847	19,062	7,655	6,247	...	25,329	...	...	...	...	...	...	...	...
1848	20,573	14,403	4,632	2,620	25,205	17,023	...	...	...	...	42,228	...	...
1849	15,178	8.843	6,286	5,896	21,464	14,739	...	...	...	...	36,203	...	...
1850	16,453	10,845	5,630	3,352	12,083	14,207	...	...	...	...	26,290	...	...
1851	15,748	7,945	4,956	3,301	20,704	11,246	...	...	...	...	31,950	...	...
1852	13,629	6,063	3,339	2,051	16,968	8,114	...	...	...	...	25,082	...	...
1853	8,339	6,119	5,582	1,769	13,921	7,888	...	...	...	...	21,809	...	...
1854	11,633	6,035	5,174	1,538	16,807	7,573	...	...	...	...	24,380	...	...
1855	20,752	22,666	487	496	21,239	23,162	...	...	...	...	44,401	...	...
1856*	12,877	12,678	2,205	756	15,082	13,434	31.934	5,072	47,016	18,506	28,516	37,006	65,522
1857	13,972	13,585	610	427	14,582	14,012	28,531	4,032	43,113	18,044	28,594	32,563	61,157
1858	16,305	11,575	3,276	601	19,581	12,176	24,508	4,314	44,089	16,490	31,757	28,822	60,579
1859	10,156	9,567	882	424	11,038	9,991	25,479	5,749	36.517	15,740	21,029	31,228	52,257
1860	17,761	19,767	838	387	18,599	20,154	20,136	5,101	38,735	25,255	38,753	25,327	63,990
1861	21,765	26,003	365	214	22,130	26,217	26,649	6,740	48,779	32,957	48,347	33,389	81,736
1862	20,313	17,165	823	399	21,136	17,564	35,604	9,385	56,740	26,949	38,700	44,989	83,689
1863	17,669	18,890	1,653	617	19,322	19,507	32,978	7,418	52,300	26,925	38,829	40,396	79,225
1864	29,893	27,272	1,440	414	31,333	27,686	41,881	6,741	73,214	34,427	59,019	48,622	107,641
1865	21,313	22,374	2,288	677	23,601	23,051	31,129	6,079	54,730	29,130	46,652	37,208	83,860
1866	28,077	25,587	1,419	816	29,496	26,568	29,789	4,255	59,285	30,823	56,064	34,044	90,108
1867†	...	...	...	...	19.353	38,864	44,531	9,074	63,884	47,938	58,217	53,605	111,822
1868	17,294	26,848	17,795	3,906	35,089	31,399	26,914	6,579	62,003	37,978	66,488	33,493	99,981
1869	33,571	31,351	25,190	5,605	‡ 59,030	39,014 ‡	30,104	4,774	89,134	43,788	98,044	34,878	132,922
1870	31,117	31,643	21,561	7,048	52,760	39,324	33,536	5,709	86,296	45,033	92,084	39,245	131,329
1871§	...	...	...	...	48,614 ‖	‖ 38,907	39,683	10,413	88,297	49,320	87,521	50,096	137,617
1872	...	...	...	...	68,222	38,849	40,427	12,776	108,649	51,625	107,071	53,203	160,274
1873	...	...	...	...	50,711	31,567	10,666	15,819	91,377	47,386	82,278	56,485	138,763
1874	...	...	...	...	40,790	27,487	37,744	25,584	78,534	53,070	68,277	63,328	131,605
1875	...	...	...	...	29,562	29,829	35,231	25,109	64,793	64,938	59,391	60,340	119,731
1876	...	...	...	...	26,026	34,758	39,955	34,554	65,981	69,312	60,784	74,509	135,293
1877	...	...	...	...	21,954	32,635	35,395	21,105	57,349	53,740	54,589	56,500	111,089
1878	...	...	...	...	20,562	34,485	26,964	25,091	47,526	59,576	55,047	52,055	107,102
1879	...	...	...	...	29,297	42,110	34,273	32,970	63,570	75,080	71,407	67,243	138,650
1880	...	...	...	...	18,085	27,519	39,215	38.743	57,300	66,262	45,604	77,958	123,562
1881	...	...	...	...	24,276	38,997	37,150	35,293	61,426	74,290	63,273	72,443	135,716

* Prior to 1856 the Máldives were included under the head "Other Countries" in the Ceylon Blue Books.

† Prior to 1867 the Indian financial year closed on April 30th ; since then it has ended on March 31st. The returns for 1867 are for 11 months only.

‡ Another return gives the figures for 1868-70 as :—

	British India.		Combined trade with British India.	Combined trade with British India and Ceylon.
	Imports.	Exports.		
1868...	34,020	30,882	64,902	98,495
1869...	63,782	38,414	102,196	137,074
1870...	49,608	38,584	88,192	127,537

§ Since 1870 the Máldives appear to have been included under the head "Other Countries" in the Bengal and Madras returns.

‖ Including the Lakkadives and Minakal, classed since 1875 among British India Ports.

B.

THE MALDIVE ISLANDS.

IMPORTS.

COMPARATIVE STATEMENT of the VALUES of the PRINCIPAL ARTICLES Imported into BRITISH INDIA* and CEYLON† from the Máldive Islands.

(Converted into sterling at 2s. the rupee.)

Year.	Cocoanuts.		Coir.		Confectionery, and Provisions.		Copperah.		Cowries, and Shells.		Fish, dried and salted.		Fish-blood.		Mats.		Sugar, jaggery, &c.		Tortoise-shell.		Grain.	
	British India.	Ceylon.	British India.	Ceylon.	British India.	Ceylon.	British India.	Ceylon.	British India.	Ceylon.	British India.	Ceylon.	British India.	Ceylon.	British India.	Ceylon.	British India.	Ceylon.	British India.	Ceylon.	British India.	Ceylon.
	£	£	£	£	£	£	£	£	£	£	£	£	£	£	£	£	£	£	£	£	£	£
1853 ...	8,668	—	2,716	—	1,258	—	—	—	379	—	34	—	—	—	—	—	293	—	314	—	12	—
1854 ...	11,500	—	—	—	833	—	—	—	445	—	—	—	—	—	1	—	371	—	184	—	190	—
1855 ...	16,654	—	—	—	461	—	—	—	881	—	—	—	—	—	—	—	1	—	220	—	—	—
1856 ...	10,748	—	—	13	671	163	—	39	2,008	15,905	—	14,262	—	—	10	14	—	—	94	1,157	—	21
1857 ...	10,003	72	—	4	—	206	—	2	—	13,865	—	10,948	—	78	—	20	—	—	—	1,657	—	1,573
1858 ...	10,094	100	—	76	—	118	—	1	—	10,317	—	9,771	—	70	—	6	—	—	—	1,042	—	10,003
1859 ...	—	126	—	544	—	153	—	—	—	6,632	—	15,092	—	185	—	19	—	—	—	867	—	15,135
1860 ...	9,593	40	—	540	—	254	—	3	—	4,143	—	13,098	—	94	—	—	—	22	—	1,778	—	34
1861 ...	16,197	—	—	500	—	490	—	—	—	4,825	—	15,616	—	107	—	61	—	4	—	743	—	3,773
1862 ...	14,123	174	—	590	—	382	—	10	—	4,321	—	23,477	—	128	—	23	—	4	—	630	—	5,704
1863 ...	13,942	220	—	851	—	622	—	70	—	5,161	—	21,998	—	81	—	92	—	3	—	1,118	—	2,529
1864 ...	24,691	36	—	496	953	592	—	6	—	2,501	—	25,790	—	132	—	174	—	12	—	1,519	—	10,367
1865 ...	16,942	44	—	158	—	498	—	17	—	990	—	23,495	—	78	—	146	—	5	—	1,510	—	4,053
1866 ...	17,450	87	—	108	—	576	—	—	—	89	—	24,109	—	154	—	173	—	8	—	996	—	3,279
1867 ...	—	44	—	1,451	—	728	—	—	—	1,113	—	22,516	—	51	—	33	—	30	—	993	—	16,939
1868 ...	—	28	—	462	—	729	—	—	—	481	—	21,232	—	61	—	59	—	10	—	1,377	—	2,380
1869 ...	—	—	—	1,027	—	—	—	25	—	574	—	25,543	—	68	—	189	—	8	—	1,072	—	892
1870 ...	28,432	—	7,940	738	1,692	453	—	—	6,774	1,884	—	25,696	—	—	—	93	2,976	8	—	1,476	—	3,142
1871 ..	24,933	651	9,736	960	2,150	730	—	50	5,631	2,222	—	27,436	—	—	—	123	3,929	21	—	1,462	—	5,938
1872 ..	46,241	3	9,702	879	2,304	406	—	19	3,981	2,750	—	31,291	—	—	—	63	3,744	4	—	1,651	—	3,149
1873 ...	35,780	83	9,051	2,352	1,563	879	—	6	1,879	2,283	—	32,763	—	—	—	90	1,845	49	—	1,664	—	282
1874 ...	26,701	22	7,143	1,584	1,520	472	—	62	2,573	1,632	—	30,222	—	—	—	49	2,502	203	—	1,778	200	1,141
1875 ...	20,330	16	3,301	2,629	2,022	525	—	31	3,886	1,358	—	27,949	—	—	—	136	—	10	—	2,184	—	51
1876 ...	17,537	28	3,684	1,589	1,209	490	—	20	2,792	224	—	35,548	—	—	—	47	—	23	—	1,267	—	556
1877 ...	15,169	165	4,288	2,645	350	672	—	35	1,914	212	—	28,055	—	—	—	150	—	22	—	1,528	—	1,669
1878 ...	15,256	—	2,381	4,331	221	539	—	2	2,629	993	—	18,527	—	—	—	38	—	15	—	999	—	1,109
1879 ...	23,937	444	2,931	3,997	440	458	—	6	1,853	1,137	—	26,065	—	—	—	36	—	31	—	1,046	—	778
1880 ..	13,812	—	2,364	2,895	414	430	—	24	1,333	959	—	32,919	—	—	—	22	—	40	—	892	—	421
1881 ...	—	—	—	3,560	—	579	—	19	—	948	—	29,508	—	—	—	23	—	—	—	2,063	—	10

* The figures for British India are very incomplete owing to want of details in the Annual Returns.

† Ceylon returns commence from 1856.

C.

THE MÁLDIVE ISLANDS.

EXPORTS.

COMPARATIVE STATEMENT of the VALUES of the PRINCIPAL ARTICLES Exported from BRITISH INDIA* and CEYLON † to the Máldive Islands.

(Converted into sterling at 2s. the rupee.)

	Arecanuts.		Cotton Manufactures, Twist, and Wool.		Curry Stuffs, and spices.		Earthenware and Porcelain.		Furniture.		Grain and Pulse.		Gunnies and Twine (Jute.)		Haberdashery and Millinery.		Mats, Bags, and Baskets.		Medicines.		Merchandise (Sundries.)		Metals: Cutlery and Hardware.		Oils.		Provisions, Oilmanstores, Confectionery.		Seeds.		Silk goods.		Sugar, and other Sacharine matter.		Terra-japonica (Catch.)		Timber, and Woods of sorts.		Tobacco, Cigars, and Snuff.	
	British India.	Ceylon.	British India.	Ceylon.	British India.	Ceylon.	British India.	Ceylon.	British India.	Ceylon.	British India.	Ceylon.	British India.	Ceylon.	British India.	Ceylon.	British India.	Ceylon.	British India.	Ceylon.	British India.	Ceylon.	British India.	Ceylon.	British India.	Ceylon.	British India.	Ceylon.	British India.	Ceylon.	British India.	Ceylon.	British India.	Ceylon.	British India.	Ceylon.	British India.	Ceylon.	British India.	Ceylon.	British India.	Ceylon.
	£	£	£	£	£	£	£	£	£	£	£	£	£	£	£	£	£	£	£	£	£	£	£	£	£	£	£	£	£	£	£	£	£	£	£	£	£	£	£	£	£	£
1853 ...	—	—	895	—	48	—	57	—	—	—	4,646	—	—	—	—	—	—	—	—	—	—	—	41	—	20	—	11	—	2	—	653	—	470	—	—	—	37	—	56	—
1854 ...	—	—	435	—	10	—	60	—	—	—	5,936	—	—	—	—	—	2	—	—	—	—	—	10	—	27	—	75	—	2	—	15	—	132	—	—	—	66	—	65	—
1855 ...	—	—	2,921	—	282	—	45	—	—	—	10,384	—	15	—	—	—	180	—	79	—	—	—	527	—	6	—	83	—	100	—	4,560	—	1,106	—	—	—	25	—	890	—
1856 ...	—	2,103	2,286	1,176	116	84	102	282	—	100	7,505	624	5	—	—	21	68	1	45	30	—	40	150	92	6	42	88	199	47	—	18	—	503	33	—	9	16	61	737	87
1857 ...	—	1,012	—	662	—	42	—	157	—	44	—	1,258	—	2	—	6	—	21	—	—	—	—	—	392	—	26	—	43	—	—	—	—	—	32	—	1	—	12	—	24
1858 ...	—	1,047	—	2,191	—	115	—	209	—	7	8,684	285	—	3	—	19	—	4	—	17	—	2	—	42	—	219	—	145	—	7	—	—	—	23	—	—	—	41	—	40
1859 ...	—	1,081	—	953	—	164	—	198	—	3	8,033	2,901	—	13	—	41	—	1	—	3	—	—	—	64	—	9	—	26	—	12	—	—	—	56	—	23	—	35	—	126
1860 ...	—	1,197	—	1,020	—	107	—	745	—	6	—	860	—	5	—	4	—	8	—	1	—	—	—	1	—	—	—	42	—	5	—	—	—	124	—	2	—	11	—	262
1861 ...	—	1,126	—	2,576	—	188	—	330	—	10	17,261	1,167	1,000	3	—	—	—	16	—	4	—	—	—	34	—	6	—	139	—	—	—	—	—	122	—	47	—	81	—	822
1862 ...	—	996	1,085	1,820	—	229	—	268	—	38	12,761	2,069	—	6	—	36	—	11	—	19	—	31	—	40	—	3	—	214	—	2	—	—	—	63	—	17	—	15	—	508
1863 ...	—	1,906	3,517	1,686	—	313	—	435	—	4	—	2,710	—	22	—	28	—	3	—	6	—	31	—	96	—	—	—	83	—	—	—	—	—	227	—	47	—	8	—	73
1864 ...	—	1,513	—	2,660	—	192	—	387	—	22	—	1,422	—	7	—	25	—	3	—	5	—	40	—	19	—	9	—	23	—	—	—	3	1,113	69	—	30	—	91	—	96
1865 ...	—	1,082	—	2,467	—	162	—	432	—	22	—	1,082	—	36	—	10	—	5	—	15	—	—	—	85	—	6	—	212	—	—	—	—	—	4	—	1	—	72	—	356
1866 ...	—	852	—	2,379	—	110	—	165	—	52	—	486	—	28	—	33	—	1	—	2	—	—	—	28	—	—	—	41	—	—	—	—	—	3	—	56	—	30	—	15
1867 ...	—	1,332	—	4,331	—	214	—	176	—	22	—	2,050	—	—	—	100	—	1	—	4	—	33	—	76	—	75	—	163	—	—	—	—	—	18	—	5	—	32	—	323
1868 ...	—	1,301	—	2,520	—	127	—	324	—	19	—	1,261	—	19	—	65	—	1	—	20	—	92	—	4	—	33	—	78	—	—	—	—	—	220	—	—	—	54	—	—
1869 ...	—	842	—	834	—	77	—	301	—	15	—	1,632	—	27	—	37	—	—	—	10	—	7	—	40	—	1	—	368	—	—	—	—	—	31	—	—	—	249	—	—
1870 ...	—	1,128	1,972	2,351	—	112	—	271	—	63	27,290	1,207	—	42	—	75	—	5	—	37	—	—	538	62	—	17	1,200	157	26	—	577	—	1,253	38	—	15	—	5	1,501	1
1871 ...	—	1,750	1,499	5,730	501	166	—	489	—	61	21,166	1,370	—	19	—	99	—	—	—	1	—	14	288	46	181	23	1,787	215	6,938	—	549	—	1,600	93	—	28	318	8	1,214	86
1872 ...	—	2,040	2,120	3,764	489	195	—	667	—	32	22,771	5,324	—	6	—	40	253	—	—	—	—	—	729	—	167	4	2,207	292	195	—	483	20	3,072	253	—	—	351	4	1,406	36
1873 ...	—	1,803	1,957	2,840	334	125	—	405	—	15	17,915	8,986	167	4	—	133	207	—	—	11	—	379	415	52	111	111	1,671	182	203	—	449	—	1,698	195	—	2	127	24	1,407	168
1874 ...	—	1,126	1,375	4,482	307	283	—	362	—	68	17,081	14,780	—	139	—	120	153	16	—	39	—	1,337	462	134	214	55	1,333	616	15	—	708	130	1,310	400	—	43	168	26	988	1,015
1875 ...	—	915	1,930	2,897	268	312	—	370	—	18	17,338	18,509	164	8	—	79	152	18	—	19	—	131	577	245	—	62	1,625	385	327	—	622	2	1,667	438	—	18	219	35	1,304	570
1876 ...	165	2,669	4,619	5,740	114	444	101	1,175	—	32	19,614	21,762	—	8	—	53	316	74	—	12	—	765	626	303	102	—	2,647	206	—	—	317	—	2,262	166	—	23	102	261	1,435	362
1877 ...	—	1,143	2,890	3,509	128	297	208	596	201	10	19,064	14,686	—	15	164	10	446	1	—	1	—	155	1,161	67	155	98	2,541	136	—	—	278	—	1,769	98	—	44	373	—	1,494	166
1878 ...	—	947	3,616	3,256	145	322	142	230	167	10	19,722	18,752	—	12	383	85	285	1	—	11	—	120	855	43	—	37	2,996	199	121	—	—	—	2,192	328	—	6	164	23	1,582	128
1879 ...	172	2,167	2,824	5,417	242	314	—	945	161	66	27,334	20,039	—	3	634	—	294	—	104	40	—	1,893	1,170	110	—	86	3,797	—	124	—	139	—	1,852	754	—	6	—	36	1,573	435
1880 ...	334	2,296	1,490	5,354	51	322	—	1,021	144	64	18,603	27,158	—	—	223	35	192	3	—	28	—	411	549	325	—	20	1,853	108	112	—	—	120	1,417	495	—	—	—	226	1,118	417
1881 ...	—	2,086	—	6,036	—	414	—	329	—	68	—	23,112	—	13	—	105	—	33	—	41	—	575	—	290	—	11	—	194	—	—	—	—	—	579	—	191	—	78	—	794

* The figures for British India are very incomplete owing to want of details in the annual returns.

† Ceylon return commences from 1856.

D.

THE MÁLDIVE ISLANDS.

NUMBER and TONNAGE of Vessels entered and cleared (with Cargoes or in Ballast) at Ports of BRITISH INDIA and CEYLON from and to the Máldive Islands.

YEAR.	BENGAL.				MADRAS.				TOTAL OF BRITISH INDIA.				TOTAL SHIPPING (Inwards and Outwards).					
	Entered.		Cleared.		Entered.		Cleared.		Entered.		Cleared.		British India.		Ceylon.		British India and Ceylon.	
	Vessels.	Tons.	Vessels.	Tons.	Vessels.	Tons.	Vessels.	Tons.	Vessels.	Tons.	Vessels.	Tons.	Vessels.	Tons.	Vessels.	Tons.	Vessels.	Tons.
1841	—	—	—	—	—	—	—	—	45	2,581	42	2,678	87	5,259	—	—	—	—
1842	—	—	—	—	—	—	—	—	55	3,161	52	3,390	107	6,551	—	—	—	—
1843	—	—	—	—	—	—	—	—	60	3,084	54	2,924	114	6,008	—	—	—	—
1844	—	—	—	—	—	—	—	—	59	2,502	48	3,185	107	5,687	—	—	—	—
1845	—	—	—	—	—	—	—	—	153	13,861	192	26,045	345	39,906	—	—	—	—
1846	—	—	—	—	—	—	—	—	38	2,568	49	3,334	87	5,902	—	—	—	—
1847	—	—	—	—	—	—	—	—	33	1,584	30	1,728	63	3,312	—	—	—	—
1848	—	—	—	—	—	—	—	—	38	2,606	44	3,219	82	5,825	—	—	—	—
1849	—	—	—	—	—	—	—	—	83	3,021	54	3,914	137	6,935	—	—	—	—
1850	—	—	—	—	—	—	—	—	42	3,095	43	3,627	85	6,722	—	—	—	—
1851	18	1,340	18	1,340	16	1,071	17	1,276	34	2,411	35	2,616	69	5,027	—	—	—	—
1852	27	3,315	26	2,585	17	965	26	1,741	44	4,280	48	4,326	92	8,606	—	—	—	—
1853*	—	—	—	—	60	1,444	30	1,182	—	—	—	—	—	—	—	—	—	—
1854	13	1,070	14	1,209	26	1,277	19	847	39	2,347	33	2,056	72	4,403	—	—	—	—
1855	20	1,916	22	2,048	8	175	10	354	28	2,091	32	2,402	60	4,493	65	6,472	125	10,965
1856	13	1,330	28	3,409	13	543	11	404	26	1,873	39	3,813	65	5,686	111	8,529	166	14,215
1857	26	2,674	42	4,907	8	254	8	243	34	2,928	50	5,150	84	8,078	93	9,896	177	17,974
1858	22	2,376	40	5,799	15	1,013	9	716	37	3,389	49	6,515	86	9,904	73	7,745	159	17,649
1859	22	2,124	30	3,507	13	376	10	224	35	2,500	40	3,731	75	6,231	84	8,198	159	14,429
1860	21	2,084	31	3,738	15	462	15	443	36	2,546	46	4,181	82	6,727	80	6,945	162	13,672
1861	36	3,455	37	3,885	4	85	4	85	40	3,540	41	3,970	81	7,510	97	9,274	178	16,784
1862	28	3,001	28	3,329	5	117	9	419	33	3,118	37	3,748	70	6,866	96	11,488	166	18,354
1863	17	2,067	32	3,897	11	367	8	278	28	2,434	40	4,175	68	6,609	83	9,135	151	15,744
1864	41	4,815	45	5,028	7	200	9	383	48	5,015	54	5,411	102	10,426	94	10,279	196	20,705
1865	43	5,246	31	3,753	9	300	8	226	52	5,546	39	3,979	91	9,525	89	8,422	180	17,947
1866	29	4,058	35	4,310	5	385	6	466	34	4,443	42	4,888	76	9,331	84	10,740	160	20,071
1867*	—	—	—	—	—	—	—	—	—	—	—	—	—	—	82	9,427	—	—
1868	16	2,009	24	3,775	113	1,897	50	1,533	129	3,816	74	5,608	203	9,424	70	7,067	273	16,591
1869	14	2,325	11	2,143	120	2,765	35	2,268	134	5,030	46	4,411	180	9,441	85	7,896	165	17,337
1870	4	666	16	2,961	103	1,839	46	1,391	107	2,555	62	4,352	169	6,907	90	10,400	259	17,307
1871	8	1,256	7	1,509	124	2,220	38	953	† 132	3,476	45	2,462	177	5,938 †	88	10,022	† 165	15,960 †
1872	8	1,508	14	2,408	163	2,714	54	1,487	172	4,297	81	5,202	253	9,499	100	9,608	353	19,107
1873	20	2,425	31	4,370	117	2,386	66	2,934	119	2,743	79	5,029	198	7,772	74	9,226	272	16,998
1874	1	118	17	2,270	115	2,865	60	2,415	116	2,983	71	3,946	187	6,929	87	9,201	274	16,130
1875	27	2,844	41	4,470	—	—	—	—	35	2,923	54	6,879	89	9,802	93	10,453	182	20,255
1876	30	3,130	36	3,545	2	213	—	—	41	3,585	58	5,809	99	9,394	124	12,518	223	21,912
1877	21	2,185	26	2,773	2	247	2	867	38	3,918	48	4,838	86	8,756	83	9,164	169	17,920
1878	25	2,867	33	3,835	2	182	1	116	34	3,411	40	3,950	74	7,361	78	7,635	152	15,196
1879	—	—	—	—	—	—	—	—	35	3,393	47	4,889	82	8,282	135	16,566	217	24,848
1880	—	—	—	—	—	—	—	—	30	3,177	40	4,172	70	7,349	131	12,928	201	20,277
1881	—	—	—	—	—	—	—	—	41	4,087	57	6,023	98	10,110	128	13,651	226	23,761

* British India returns for 1853 and 1867 not forthcoming.

† Including the Lakkadives and Minakai, classed among British India ports since 1875.

E.

THE MÁLDIVE ISLANDS.

NUMBER, TONNAGE and CREWS of BRITISH, FOREIGN, and MÁLDIVIAN Vessels entered from, and cleared to, the Máldive Islands (with Cargoes or in Ballast), at Ports of CEYLON.

YEAR.	British.						Foreign.						Total. (British and Foreign.)						Máldivian.					
	Entered.			Cleared.			Entered.			Cleared.			Entered.			Cleared.			Entered.			Cleared.		
	Vessels.	Tons.	Crews.	Vessels.	Tons.	Crews.	Vessels.	Tons.	Crews.	Vessels.	Tons.	Crews.	Vessels.	Tons.	Crews.	Vessels.	Tons.	Crews.	Vessels.	Tons.	Crews.	Vessels.	Tons.	Crews.
1855 ...	—	—	—	—	—	—	—	—	—	—	—	—	34	3,433	638	31	3,039	671	22	1,556	482	20	1,413	458
1856 ...	29	3,839	690	19	2,697	382	28	1,111	558	25	882	473	57	4,950	1,248	44	3,579	855	28	1,089	540	27	1,089	526
1857 ...	25	3,793	597	29	4,642	666	20	743	398	19	718	364	45	4,536	995	48	5,360	1,030	21	843	429	23	1,122	481
1858 ...	21	2,991	499	23	3,345	492	20	755	391	19	654	357	41	3,746	890	42	3,999	849	22	922	435	24	1,105	515
1859 ...	30	3,929	647	23	2,964	506	16	696	336	15	609	312	46	4,625	983	38	3,573	818	17	797	370	17	803	378
1860 ...	21	2,506	427	19	2,565	399	21	1,073	457	19	801	392	42	3,579	884	38	3,366	791	28	1,575	627	25	1,326	552
1861 ...	27	3,674	590	23	3,314	513	25	1,225	459	22	1,061	455	52	4,899	1,049	45	4,375	968	29	1,690	590	28	1,471	593
1862 ...	32	4,918	765	20	2,962	482	22	1,781	462	22	1,827	470	54	6,699	1,227	42	4,789	952	26	1,265	573	23	1,161	514
1863 ...	26	3,899	668	24	3,684	533	18	702	346	15	850	268	44	4,601	1,014	39	4,534	801	18	702	346	18	702	346
1864 ...	31	4,644	649	22	3,679	420	21	1,111	411	20	845	401	52	5,755	1,060	42	4,524	821	17	638	349	21	946	434
1865 ...	24	3,914	592	17	2,623	337	25	1,115	448	23	770	392	49	5,029	1,040	40	3,393	730	26	1,147	463	23	770	393
1866 ...	24	3,669	614	21	4,908	479	20	1,146	374	19	1,117	361	44	4,715	988	40	6,025	840	29	1,146	374	19	1,117	361
1867* ...	32	5,538	796	16	2,478	312	18	724	378	16	687	338	50	6,262	1,174	32	3,165	650	23	1,228	472	23	1,285	463
1868 ...	22	3,449	518	10	2,068	227	19	775	395	19	775	395	41	4,224	913	29	2,843	622	19	775	395	19	775	395
1869 ...	19	3,914	503	8	1,698	172	32	1,325	579	26	959	479	51	5,239	1,082	34	2,657	651	32	1,325	579	27	989	494
1870 ...	30	5,481	751	17	2,927	372	22	873	418	21	1,119	448	52	6,354	1,169	38	4,046	820	22	873	418	20	947	418
1871 ...	29	4,752	653	17	2,908	331	21	1,181	445	21	1,181	445	50	5,933	1,098	38	4,089	776	21	1,181	445	21	1,181	445
1872 ...	34	4,462	602	20	2,742	363	20	736	383	26	1,668	516	54	5,198	985	46	4,410	879	28	2,297	569	35	3,118	719
1873 ...	28	3,871	532	15	1,961	289	19	2,254	331	12	1,140	259	47	6,125	863	27	3,101	548	21	2,725	391	14	1,882	309
1874 ...	21	3,352	401	14	1,710	205	24	1,825	384	28	2,314	445	45	5,177	785	42	4,024	650	29	2,835	515	30	2,748	495
1875 ...	24	2,892	470	19	3,021	348	29	2,967	450	21	1,573	348	53	5,859	920	40	4,594	696	32	3,427	545	26	3,220	497
1876 ...	30	4,042	524	15	2,042	305	39	3,167	515	40	3,267	533	69	7,209	1,039	55	5,309	838	40	3,267	547	40	3,267	533
1877 ...	48	5,463	814	29	3,263	361	3	254	67	3	184	69	51	5,717	881	32	3,447	430	6	534	153	6	534	152
1878 ...	45	4,768	741	30	2,975	426	2	65	37	1	30	18	47	4,833	778	31	3,005	414	2	65	37	1	30	18
1879 ...	63	9,799	1,039	35	5,554	597	18	589	343	19	624	362	81	10,388	1,382	54	6,178	959	18	539	343	19	624	362
1880 ...	57	6,756	908	44	5,058	597	15	574	307	15	540	313	72	7,330	1,215	59	5,598	910	15	574	307	16	623	338
1881 ...	65	8,073	1,039	40	4,570	577	12	447	230	11	561	198	77	8,520	1,269	51	5,131	775	13	664	271	12	644	232

* The Returns are probably for 11 months only, as the financial year, which prior to 1867 closed on April 30th, ended in that year, and has ended since annually, on March 31st.

VIII.—MONEY, WEIGHTS, AND MEASURES.

TRADE at the Máldives has always been conducted for the most part by barter.

At the same time, the advantages of a circulating medium could not fail to be recognised, if but partially, at an early period.

Cowries.

Cowries, still employed on occasions, sufficiently served the purpose for centuries.

Not to go back to the 9th century—when, as Suleimán the Persian traveller certifies, the Queen's treasury was stocked with cowries, in which lay the Islander's wealth,* Ibn Batúta, writing 500 years later, found them passing as money on the group (A. D. 1344.) " A hundred of these shells is called *syâh*, and 700 *fâl*, 12,000 are called *cotta*, and 100,000 *bostoû*. Bargains are struck through the medium of these cowries at the rate of 4 *bostoû* to a *dînâr* of gold. Often they are of less value, such as 12 *bostoû* to a *dînâr*. The Islanders sell them to the people of Bengal for rice, for they, too, use them for money. They are sold in the same way to the people of Yemen, who use them for ballast in their ships in place of sand. These cowries serve also as a medium of exchange with the negroes in their native country. I have seen them sold at Mâly and at Djoudjou [Soudán] at the rate of 1,150 to a *dînâr* of gold."†

A machinery so cumbrous for the adjustment of an extensive external commerce naturally yielded before the more portable metal currency of intrinsic value introduced by strangers.

The Persians and Arabs—the first to develope the trade of the Máldives—would soon familiarize the Islanders to the use of their money in commercial transactions.

Silver 'fish-hook *larin*

It is interesting, therefore, to learn from Pyrard, that in his time (A.D. 1602–7), with the exception of foreign coins of gold and silver alone, which were accepted at their value by weight, the sole Máldivian coin was a silver "*larin*," evidently copied from the Persian coin of that name then current throughout the East.‡ "The money of the Realm is only of silver. The (coins) are pieces of silver, which they call *larins*, worth as much as eight sous (*sols*) or thereabout of our (French) money, as I have already said ; long as the finger, but doubled back. The King has them struck in his Island and his name stamped on them in Arabic characters * * * They make no other coins of less value there, so that for the purposes of their traffic they cut the silver, and hand over a weight of the same value as the goods bought : this, however, cannot be done without some loss, because by cutting the *larin* one loses one twelfth of it * * * * Instead of copper coin (*billon*) they make use of cowries (*coquilles*); 12,000 are worth a *larin*."§

To obviate the inconvenience of cutting up the "*larin*" for small payments, this awkward 'fish-hook money' had given way a century later to the circular coins of the same name (M. *lári*), but of baser metal, still in currency.

---

* V. s., p. 24. † Gray, quoting *Voyages d' Ibn Batoutah*, Tome IV.

‡ " Le *Larin* est une ancienne monnoye de Balsare et d' Arabie, et qui a cours jusqa' à l'isle de Ceylan, ou l'on ne parle que de *Larins*. Cette monnoye est un fil d'argent plié en deux, de la grosseur d'un tuyan de plume ordinaire, et long de deux travers de doigt ou euviron. Sur ce fil d' argent ainsi plié on voit le nom du Prince dans les pays duquel cette monnoye a esté fabriquée. Le huit *Larins* font un *or*, et les quatre-vint *Larins* un *toman*."—Tavernier, " Travels," 1625-1664, (A' la Haye, Vol. I., pp. 135–6.) See, too, Rhys Davids in the "International Numismata Orientalia," Vol. I., 1877, 'Ancient coins and measures of Ceylon, pp. 33–5, and the authorities there quoted.

§ Pyrard, pp. 163–4. With considerable difficulty the writer obtained (too late for insertion) a single specimen of this unique coin. It weighs 71½ grains, and is apparently of the purest silver : age doubtful.

THE MÁLDIVES.

MONEY, WEIGHTS AND MEASURES.

Circular *lári.*

These coins are of two sizes and values, called by the Islanders *boḍu* ('large') *lári* and *kuḍa* ('small') *lári.* They are still struck at the Málé mint, of mixed metal,* and bear on one side the reigning Sultan's name, and on the reverse his title and the date *Anno Hijrae.*

COINS.

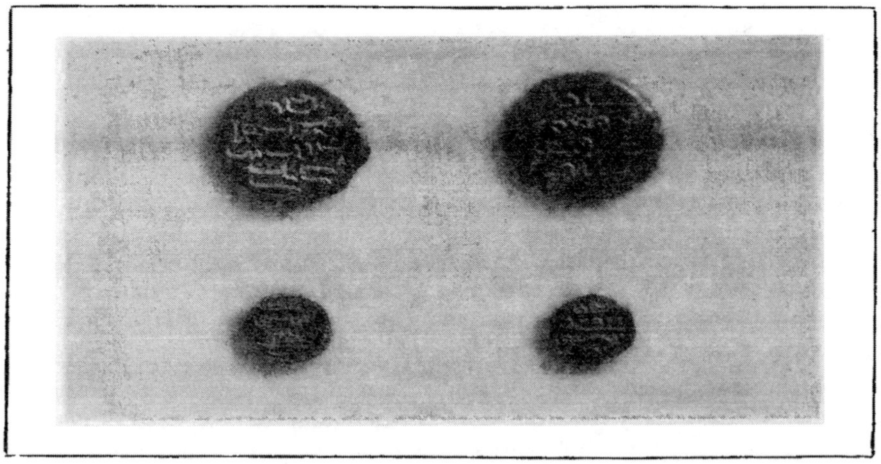

The average weight of the modern *boḍu lári* is about 135 grains, and of the *kuḍa lári*—valued roughly at one-fourth (1-4th) the other—about 20 grains.†

At the present day these coins have a nominal exchange value respectively of 25 and 100 to the Bengal rupee; but not being made legal tender at that rate, nor too plentiful, their actual value fluctuates considerably. It is generally about 20 per cent. above their nominal value; a rupee will rarely exchange for more than 20 *boḍu* or 80 *kuḍa lári.*

The *Bengal rupee* is received everywhere for large payments; but money of any kind is scarce, and all gold and silver coins are in request more or less for the melting pot according to their purity.

Kuḍa lári.
4 = *Boḍu lári*
100 = 25 = *Rufiya*

Weights.

WEIGHTS.

The principal are:—

1 *gau* (M. *eg-gau*) or *galė* (M. *eggalė*) = ¼ lb.‡
4 *gau* (M. *hatara-gau*) = 1 *rátalu* = 1 lb.
8 *gau* (M. *ag-gau*) = 1 *boḍi.*
12 *boḍi* (M. *bára-boḍi*) = *tuḷu.*
1 *tuḷu* (M. *et-tuḷu*) = 24 lbs.
1 *man* (M. *em-manu*) = 84 lbs.

Coir is occasionally weighed and sold by the *boḍi*; but of late years, since the arrival of Parsí and "Moor" traders at Málé, the use of the *cwt.* has been gradually superseding all other weights for bulky goods, such as fish, coir, and cowries.

Gau.
4 = *Rátalu*
8 = 2 = *Boḍi*
96 = 24 = 12 = *Tuḷu*
336 = 84 = 42 = 3½ = *Manu*

---

* An analysis of fourteen of these coins of various dates, made by Mr. A. C. Dixon, B. Sc., shows them to contain 83·54 per cent. copper, 2·61 tin, 13·78 zinc, and a trace of iron. In modern coins the proportion of copper is as high as 95 to 97 per cent.

† Note (1).

‡ A *Cypraea mauritiana* shell bearing the Sultan's seal in wax is the regular 'Imperial *gau*' weight in the Southern Atols.

Dry Measures.

For grain the following are in use :—

½ *láhi* (M. *baya láhi)*.
1 *láhi* or *láse* = 1 *hunḍuwa* (S.)
4 *láhi* = 1 *náliya* = 1 *séruwa* (S.)
4 *náli* = 1 *kotuwa*.
12 *náli* = 1 *fá* or *fara* ('bushel.')
12 *kotu* = 1 *muḷiya*.
300 *náli* = 1 *kaḍiya*.

Fractions and multiples of the above are also sometimes adopted :—

½ *náliya* (M. *baya-náli*) = 2 *láhi (*M. *delahi)*.
1½ *náli* (M. *tin-baya-náli*) = 6 *láhi*.
½ *fara* of 10 *náli* (M. *diha-náli-fá*).
2 *muḷi* (M. *dem-muḷi*) = 100 *náli*.
3 *muḷi* (M. *tin-muḷi*) } = 150 *náli*.
½ *kaḍi* (M. *baya-kaḍi*) } = 150 *náli*.
4 *muḷi* (M. *hatara-muḷi*) = 200 *náli*.
5 *muḷi* (M. *fas-muḷi*) = 250 *náli*.

Cowries are now usually sold in the Islands by the *hiya* = 100, the *falé* = 800 to 1,000, and the *koṭṭé* = 12,000 *(bára-fá)*.

The Dutch in purchasing cowries reckoned the *koṭṭa* rather by weight than by tale, and latterly insisted on its being made equal to 25 lbs., at which it still remains approximately.

Láhi.
4 = *Náliya*.
16 = 4 = *Kotuwa*.
48 = 12 = 3 = *Fara*.
192 = 48 = 12 = 4 = *Muḷiya*.
1,200 = 300 = 75 = 25 = 6¼ = *Kaḍiya*.

Liquid Measures.

The two commonly used are :—

Náliya—for oil, ghee, and salt.
Adubá = 5 *láhi*—for jaggery, fish-blood, and vinegar.

Lineal Measures.

Inch = *en-igili*.
Foot = *ef-fúṭú*.
Span = *baya-murhé* or *hávayi*.
Cubit = *murhé* or *kuru riya*.
Length of the arm = *boḍu riya*.
Yard = *gazu* = 2 *kuru riya* or 2 *murhé*.
Fathom = *eb-bammé* = 2 *gazu*.
Half mile = *baya-kos*.
Mile = *ek-kos*.

Land is measured by *bammé* (fathoms).

Division of Time.

Minute = *sahadé*.
Hour = *eg-gadi* = 1 *pẹya* (S.) = 24 minutes = ∴ 2½ *gadi* = 1 English hour.
Three hours = 1 watch = *ed-dama* (S. *yámaya)*.
Day = *duvahu*.
Week = *had-duvas* ('7 days').
Fortnight = *foya duvas*.
Month = *mahaku*.
Year = *aharu*.

Long distances are generally computed by time. For instance :—

Ed-dam hisábu = the distance traversible (sailing) in one watch of 3 hours (*lit.* 'one-watch account').
Ed-duvas hisábu = (the distance of) a day's sail.
Bá-tiris dam hisábu = the distance to Colombo, *i.e.*, 32 watches, or 4 days' sail.

THE MÁLDIVES.

MONEY, WEIGHTS AND MEASURES.

The old A'ryan system of chronology (common to the Sinhalese) rules concurrently with the purely lunar year of the *Hijra* era, adopted since the conversion to Muhammadanism. Sanskrit terms, in Máldive dress, are retained both for the days of the week and the astronomical divisions of the firmament into *rási* and 'lunar mansions' *(nekat)*.

Days of the Week.

English.	Máldive.	Sinhalese.
Sunday ...	... *A'dita*	... *Iri-dá.*
Monday ...	... *Hóma*	... *Sandu-dá.*
Tuesday ...	... *Angára*	... *Angaharuvá-dá.*
Wednesday ...	... *Buda*	... *Badá-dá.*
Thursday ...	... *Burasfati*	... *Brahaspatin-dá.*
Friday ...	... *Hukuru*	... *Sikurá-dá.*
Saturday ...	... *Honihiru*	... *Senasurá-dá.*

NAUTICAL INSTRUMENTS.

Nautical Instruments.

The Máldivians, following 'the sexagesimal system', divide the circle into 360 degrees.

They make use of the modern mariners' compass *(M. samugá)*, and copy the Arab navigators in the notation of its 32 points* :—

N = *gavvu* or *gahá.*

N by W. = *farugadi*	*astamán*	N. by E. = *farugadi*	*irán.*
N. N. W. = *nási*	do.	N. N. E. = *nási*	do.
N. W. by N. = *nágá*	do.	N. E. by N. = *nágá*	do.
N. W. = *a'yúgu*	do.	N. E. = *a'yúgu*	do.
N. W. by W. = *gásilu* or *gasal*	do.	N. E. by E. = *gásilu* or *gasal*	do.
W. N. W. = *simágu*	do.	E. N. E. = *simágu*	do.
W. by N. = *tura'yánu*	do.	E. by N. = *tura'yánu*	do.
W. = *murigu*	do.	E. = *murigu*	do.
W. by S. = *jauza*	do.	E. by S. = *jauza*	do.
W. S.W. = *tíru*	do.	E. S. E. = *tíru*	do.
S. W. by S. = *agurabu*	do.	S. E. by E. = *agurabu*	do.
S. W. = *galbu*	do.	S. E. = *galbu*	do.
S.W. by S. = *himáriyan*	do.	S. E. by S. = *himáriyan*	do.
S. S. W. = *silli*	do.	S. S. E. = *silli*	do.
S. by W. = *sillaváru* or *sullaváru*	do.	S. by E. = *sillaváru* or *sullaváru*	do.

S. = *suhailu* or *dakunu.*

"These names would seem to point to a time anterior to the invention of the magnetic compass, when, indeed, the only way of ascertaining the relative position of a ship at night in the broad ocean was by observing the points of the horizon where prominent stars rose and set. The system could only have been adapted to intertropical navigation, wherein no very great variation occurs in these azimuths, and it is necessarily but an approximation to truth, as hardly any of the prominent stars selected rise or set at the precise azimuth named from them.†"

Their *quadrant* or T shaped cross-bow for taking bearings (M. *digu-fila)* is a rudely-designed but ingenious instrument. It is merely a square wooden rod, with a cross piece at one end, on which the divisions are laid off, and a sliding radius, but capable of giving very accurate results.

"To avoid looking at the sun the eye is directed to the opposite point of the horizon, [through a tiny hole in a slightly-projecting metal plate at] the lower end of the cross-bar, while it brings the solar shadow of the upper end of the same to meet the horizon by

* The names are transcribed from a list obtained from a Máldive *Mu'allim*. Subsequently the writer met with Prinsep's careful "Note on the Nautical Instruments of the Arabs" (Jour. Bengal A. S., Vol. V., 1836, pp. 784–94), in which is given a very similar list in Máldivian–Arabic character. The whole article will repay perusal.

† Prinsep, (*loc. cit.* p. 788), who proceeds to identify the majority of the stars upon which the Máldivians sail in accordance with the old Arab treatises on navigation

adjusting the slider to or fro on the divided arm."* The *bilistry*, or astrolabe, (M. *ré-fila*) is of yet simpler construction.

The Islanders are, besides, well acquainted with the European sextant, which they call *góduran*.

NUMERATION.

Numeration.

The inconvenient duodecimal mode of numeration was formerly exclusively used by the Máldivians—the numerals from 1 to 12 being almost identical with the Sinhalese; but though still in vogue here and there, is gradually dying out, and rarely employed in business calculations. Beyond 10 a modified form of the Hindústání decimal numeration is that in common use. Some confusion, however, arises from the co-existence of the two systems; thus, *fanas* or *fansás* may be either 48 or 50; *hiya* or *satéka*, 96 or 100.

NOTES.

Notes.

COINS. The specimens given are of nearly the last issue from the Málé mint, prior to the death of the late Sultan. The present Sultan, Ibráhím Núr-ud-dín, has not yet uttered a coinage.†

Obverse.

i.e.,

"Sultan Muhammad 'Imád-ud-dín Iskandar."

Reverse.

i.e.,

"Sultan of land and sea. A. H. 1294" [A.D. 1877].‡

---

* Prinsep, *loc. cit.* p. 787. A comparison of the actual divisions on the *digu-fila* with a scale of co-tangents showed that the Máldive instrument was constructed on correct principles.

† As it is doubtful whether a single specimen of these coins is to be found in any Museum, a detailed description of the collection in the writer's own cabinet, dating from A. H. 1129 [A. D. 1716-17] to A. H. 1298 [A. D. 1880] will shortly be communicated to the Royal Asiatic, or Numismatic, Society.

‡ Date of *kuḍa lári* specimen, A. H. 1292, *i.e.*, A. D. 1875.

APPENDIX A.

POLITICAL STATUS OF THE SULTAN.

It may not be disadvantageous to attempt to set at rest the question of the exact political status of the Máldive Sultan as regards the English Government in Ceylon.

The Sultans have been past the records of their country Sovereigns of the Máldive group, and have ever, as far as is known, exercised supreme rule in the internal affairs of the Islands uncontrolled by other nations, except on the rare and temporary occasions of forcible foreign interposition, such as that of the Portuguese in the 16th century.

Their external sovereignty, or "independence in respect to all other political societies," originally complete, has suffered modification, varying in degree, certainly since the Portuguese conquest (*circa* 1552), if not from the period of Muhammadan supremacy some centuries earlier.

Portuguese period

At the commencement of the 16th century the Máldive Sultans appear to have been mere vassals of the "Moor" merchants of Cannanore,* and later of the Portuguese at Goa, indirectly paying them tribute, and having ceased, in the strict sense, to be independent sovereigns.†

The terms of the treaty of peace obtained by the Islanders at the conclusion of a subsequent protracted struggle with the Portuguese in the same century are given in detail by Pyrard. The compact guaranteed a restricted sovereignty to the Sultans, but as virtual tributaries of Portugal. (*V. supra*, p. 29).

The benefits resulting from alliance with the chief European power in the East could not but be recognised. Upon the ascendancy, therefore, of the Dutch in Ceylon, the Sultans wisely courted their friendship and protection by tacitly transferring the allegiance hitherto accorded to the Portuguese. (*V. s.*, p. 30.)

Dutch period.

The alliance begun with the Dutch upon the principle of mutual advantage has been cementing during a series of more than two centuries by the exchange of good offices, so that at this time it has ripened into something approaching a sincere attachment.

Our influence in the Máldive Islands, as that of the Dutch before us, is founded on the free will and consent of the Sultans. From their confidence in our attachment and our power they made themselves the feudatories, first of Holland, and subsequently of Great Britain, by placing themselves, of their own accord, under the protection of the successive Governments in Ceylon.

English period.

It is a matter of surprise that a connection of nearly two hundred and fifty years' standing should have subsisted without any specific treaty or agreement,—unless, indeed, the annual letters are held to have the force of a treaty renewed year by year. Possibly it may be owing to this circumstance that the friendship has continued so long. "Where express stipulations are established as the ground of an alliance, the parties are so much upon their guard, and so watchful of the conduct of each other, that jealousy and distrust too often assume the place of confidence and good will. By maintaining a connection upon the mutual exchange of good offices without expressly defining the views and wishes of either party, such a latitude is given as cannot fail of producing confidence and friendship."‡

In the absence of any express treaty, ample evidence of the status of the Sultans may, however, be deduced from the official correspondence with the Ceylon Governors, taken in connection with the fact of the annual embassy.

The Portuguese enforced an actual tribute of coir and cowries. The Dutch confined their demand to the latter commodity under the pretence of trade, but in reality rendered the burden heavy by constantly insisting on larger supplies, purchasable at fixed rates much below market value. It was left for the English to be content with the annual "presents," the tender of which by the Sultan's Ambassador, though reciprocated by return presents of a similar description, if of

* Barbosa (Collecçao de Noticias para a Historia e Geographia das Naçoes Ultramarinas, Tom. II. p. 352).

† The earliest treaty was concluded with the renowned Alboquerque in A. D. 1512 :—Legatus praeterea quidam a rege omnium, qui Maldiuenses insulas imperio tenebant, amplissimo, ad illum venit ; & ab eo nomine regis sui postulauit, vtillum in fidem et clientelam reciperet. Illum namq, velle regis Emmanuelis imperio subdi, & tributum constitutum summa fide persoluere. Hujus promissi foedus statim fuit rite percussum, et Saracenus quidam, Mamelles nomine, qui aliquot illius insulas occuparat, ex illis excedere jussus. Quod sine vlla recusatione confectum repente fuit."—(Osorius, *De Rebus Emmanvelis Regis Lusitaniae inuictissimi, virtute et auspicio, &c., gestis.* Lib. VIII., 229, 1597).

‡ Sir T. Rumbold, "Considerations upon the present political state of the Company in India," Madras, 1780, (Sixth Report, Committee of Secrecy, p. 970).

greater value, is no less tantamount to the payment of tribute than the yearly delivery of an elephant to the Madras Govenment by the Rájá of the petty Púdúkottái State.

As regards the wording of the annual letters from the Sultans, a few extracts will suffice to show that the feudal relation with the dominant European power in Ceylon has continued undissolved to the present day.

Under the Dutch, as early as 1718, Sultan M. 'Imád-ud-dín Muzaffar writes to Governor Rumpf:—"Beneath the protection of Your Excellency, as under the shade of a spreading tree, I am continuing in health and prosperity, and shall henceforth always look for Your Excellency's powerful favour towards me, being assured of Your Excellency's remembrance of me here; for in case of attack from (foreign) enemies or other ill-meaning parties, I, an insignificant person, have no other to rely on for help save Your Excellency." 'Protection from enemies' is the keynote taken up by his son, Sultan Ibráhím Iskandar,* and constantly restruck throughout the Sultans' letters to the Dutch Governors during this century. On their part the Dutch, always cautiously avoiding specific promises of armed assistance and protection, were profuse in assurances of a negative nature.†

Coming to the English period of rule in Ceylon. In 1805 Sultan M. M'nín-ud-dín expressed himself:—"I humbly beg Your Excellency will be so kind as to treat Me and My people like the other Governors of Colombo used to do; and should any hostilities be committed by any nation against Maldive Island, I request Your Excellency will be so kind as to protect Us." To which Sir Thomas Maitland replied:—"I shall do everything in My power to promote the good understanding which subsists between us"—stereotyped phraseology annually repeated to the present time, which, in the connection, can mean nothing less than an implied acknowledgment and acceptance of the *rôle* of protector.

Again in 1817 the Sultan writes:—"In conformity to the relations of amity subsisting between Your Excellency and Me, which will ever continue advancing, I beg Your Excellency, if any one should declare himself My enemy, to defend Me on such occasions by making war with such person."‡ And in 1822:—"I beg Your Excellency will have mercy on Me and protect Me by making war with My enemies."§

Ahmad Dídí, the late Sultan's uncle and Prime Minister, in a letter to Governor Campbell in 1841, says:—"Your Excellency's Government being a great protection to Our islands, I entreat for a continuation of Our friendship."

In 1849 Sultan Muhammad 'Imád-ud-dín writes:—"We have been faithful to friendship and We have the honour of Your alliance and protection against Our enemies, to whom, if Your Excellency knows them to be so, Your Excellency will not extend Your auspices."‖

The following year:—"We highly appreciate the influence which We have the honour to possess in the alliance and protection We have from You against Our enemies."¶

The expression is varied slightly in 1855:—"As Kings are gracious and live in kindly fellowship with each other, so We hope that You will deal with Us in a friendly manner and treat Our enemies as Your own."

Should it, however, be held that a defensive alliance, if existing at all, has been created merely on the Sultan's own part, and is not warranted by the cautious negative language adopted generally in the replies of the Ceylon Government, this cannot be urged of the Governor's letters of 1828-29 and 1832. To the appeal for aid against the Lakkadivians in 1828, Sir E. Barnes (prepared to act on the sound principle which should govern these compacts, viz., 'clearly menaced injustice may be prevented by an ally') answered:—"If any attack is made upon Your Highness by the Laccadivians, or any other native power, without any connection with, or countenance from, the East India Company, I shall feel disposed to render Your Highness every assistance which the justice of Your case, when more fully explained, may appear to deserve."**

In 1829 again:—"The protection and assistance of the British Government of Ceylon will continue to be readily extended to the vessels and natives of the Máldive Islands, and a reciprocal amity and good understanding is expected from the Sultan's people to the British interests.††

---

* *E. g.*, Sultan's letters of 1722 and 1735.

† *E. g.*, Dutch Governor's replies of 1722 and 1727.

‡ Sultan's letter, A.H. 1232. (Translation dated September 29th, 1817.) See also letters of 1819, 182., 1831, 1832, 1835, 1837, 1838, 1839, 1841, and 1844.

§ Sultan's letter, A.H. 1239.

‖ Sultan's letter, A.H. 1265.

¶ See also letters of 1853, 1854, and from 1858 to the present day.

** Governor's reply, dated December 8th, 1828.

†† Reply, dated December 9th, 1829.

"Your Ambassador," wrote Sir R. Wilmot Horton in 1832, "had the opportunity of seeing the Admiral Commanding the Fleets of the King, my master, in those seas, who promised to afford all protection to Your ships, and received an assurance of similar assistance on Your part."*

To sum up. It appears from the above :—

(i.)—That the Máldive Sultans have voluntarily courted defensive alliance with the dominant European power in Ceylon by placing themselves of their own accord under its protection, and by the tender of actual or virtual tribute.

(ii.)—That in the absence of any express treaty or agreement, the *rôle* of suzerain has been accepted by each power in turn, by inference clearly deducible from official correspondence.

(iii.)—That the present political status of the Máldives is that of a semi-sovereign State, under the exclusive protectorate of the English Government in Ceylon—a relation very similar to that of the King of the Isle of Man with John of England, established by Treaty of A. D. 1212.

The following remarks of Sir T. Rumbold, when Governor of Madras in 1780, explaining the position of the Nawáb of the Carnatic with regard to the East India Company, apply *mutatis mutandis* with equal force to the connection, of a century later, between the Ceylon Government and the Máldive Sultan.

"It must be confessed that the want of some precise line for the guidance of this Government in its intercourse with the *Sultans*, such as is clearly laid down in the engagements between the Indian Government and the Protected States (*e.g.*, of Rájput, Burdela, Málwá, &c.) may be productive of some embarrassment. The *Sultan* has always been considered and treated by the English as an independent Prince; but it has not yet been settled by express stipulation, how far the *Sultan*, in virtue of his independence, or the *Ceylon Government* in the character of his friends and protectors, should direct and superintend the external interests of the *Máldive Islands*. If this right belongs solely to the *Sultan*—as in the eye of international law it undoubtedly does until it has passed, not by inference, but *per expressum*—this Government may be without, and even against their consent drawn into measures affecting their own interests and possessions. On the other hand, if the *Ceylon Government*, in virtue of their character as protectors of the *Sultan's* dominions, claim the right of directing the interests of the *Máldive Islands*, then they infringe the acknowledged independency of the *Sultan*, and become, in fact, the rulers, instead of the defenders of his country. It seems reasonable, indeed, that the Government who have taken upon themselves the office of protector should be allowed the lead in all political transactions that affect the *Máldives*, and this the *Sultans* have admitted *suâ sponte* by appealing to the *Ceylon Government* whenever likely to be involved in difficulties with foreign powers. But should the *Sultan* claim the privilege of acting for himself, the *Ceylon Government*, if determined to follow the strict law of nations, may find themselves perplexed until it be absolutely settled how far they or the *Sultan* are to yield upon any difference of opinion.

"It is easy to imagine that in certain eventualities no small advantage would be derived from an exclusive influence in the *Sultan's* dominions sufficient to establish a decided superiority and to exclude all competitors. A sense of interest suggests both the importance of so useful an attachment, and also how embarrassing might be our situation if that attachment should ever be dissolved or transferred to another European nation. Fortunately, the benefits resulting from this connection are reciprocal; and the *Sultans*, having received at least as much advantage from our alliance and support as we have derived from their friendship, are equally bound upon principles of gratitude and interest to remain steadfast in their attachment to the English."†

Another question arising from the present undefined relationship with the Máldive Sultan (which, though of minor importance, has already cropped up more than once, and is likely to recur at any moment) is to what extent, if at all, should the Ceylon Government hold themselves responsible for disbursements made directly or indirectly by other Governments on account of the Sultan's subjects.

It seems to have been accepted of late years that this Government is bound, according to received and long-standing custom, to pay all charges for the relief of Máldive sailors in actual distress, in return for the assistance and hospitality expected of the Sultan towards persons shipwrecked on his coasts.

---

* Governor's reply, dated December 14th, 1832.

† Sir T. Rumbold, *loc. cit.* (quoted in Parliamentary Papers, 1861, East India, 'Náwaubs of the Carnatic').

Opinions will hardly be divided as regards the justice and sound policy of the liberal line of action which the Government have apparently determined to adopt for the future; but it is a misapprehension to suppose that it is altogether warranted by former precedent, or necessarily required of this Government from the nature of the connection which has always existed with the Sultans.

The Sultans most certainly understand, and have always understood, that the protection and favour of the Government in Ceylon is dependent on the succour they afford to shipwrecked European subjects. Always forward to admit that the obligation is entirely on their side, they have eagerly embraced every opportunity of proving the sincerity of their attachment and gratitude. It is true that reciprocal aid to British and Máldive subjects has been stipulated for since the commencement of English rule in Ceylon, but it is equally true that the Sultans, up to thirty years ago, at least, offered, and were expected to recoup this Government for any sums spent on behalf of Máldivians detained in Ceylon ports by stress of weather or other cause.

In 1798 an account amounting to Rs. 500 was tendered to the Sultan for repairs to his vessel and allowance to the crew. The Sultan's letter of 1804 contains a distinct request that the Governor would allow subsistence to the Máldive vessels on his account.* But not to go back further than 1850, the late Sultan specially desired the Governor to notify to his Ambassador the sum spent the previous year for the maintenance of the Ambassador and crew, and for repairs to his vessel, that it might be refunded. "It is desirable that We should be acquainted with what amount was advanced, and We beg Your Excellency will let Us know the same."† The sum was £40. It is the more strange, therefore, that within a few years Government authorized (1856), without query or comment, a special grant, in Colombo alone, of £20 to Máldivians alleged to be sick and destitute, and that similar allowances were conceded in succeeding years, viz., £50 in 1857, a smaller sum in 1858, £50 in 1859, £10 in 1862, and £30 in 1866. These grants were in some instances fondly made—not to luckless Máldivians cast adrift in Ceylon by shipwreck or other accident beyond their control, but to Islanders who had deliberately left their country *more suo* without a copper chally, and provisions barely sufficient for the voyage, trusting to the charity of the Government or of their co-religionists in Ceylon for maintenance until the change of the monsoon allowed of their departure—to men who actually refused work on the preposterous plea that they were the Sultan's subjects!

A recent claim by the Indian Government (1879) for Rs. 3,679 in reimbursement of expenses incurred for the maintenance and despatch to their country of a crew of Máldivians picked up from a sinking vessel in the Bay of Bengal brought the question prominently forward. By the Secretary of State's Despatch, No. 59, dated 26th March, 1872, the Indian Government is liable to bear the expenses incurred in relieving distressed seamen who are subjects of that Government, *i. e.*, natives of British India. As the seamen in question were held to be neither subjects of the Indian Government, nor were serving in a British ship at the time of their rescue, the Indian authorities considered it advisable to prefer a claim against the Government of Ceylon, under the evident impression that the incidence of the charge, resting immediately upon this Government, would probably be transferred ultimately to the Máldive Sultan. The claim was paid and accepted—though not without some hesitation—as a legitimate liability of the Colony; but it was hinted that, had the relations of this Government with the Sultan been of less vague a character, some pressure might have been brought to bear in respect of the refund of the money.

---

* Sultan's letter, dated November 2nd, 1804.

† Sultan's letter, A. H. 1266.

APPENDIX B.

TREATMENT OF WRECKS.

Treatment of wrecks.

GRAVE doubts were formerly—and, perhaps, by superficial inquirers are still,—entertained regarding the humane conduct displayed by the Máldive Islanders towards persons shipwrecked on their Atols. These doubts have had their origin in the vague rumours ever and anon wafted across from this *Ultima Thule*, caught up, and naturally exaggerated by a confiding public, ever ready to be deceived, whilst indisposed to sift out the truth.

Lieutenants Christopher and Young were perhaps the first to combat the popular notion, and to show that the too prevalent suspicion was generally unfounded. It is curious, however, that they should have contented themselves with deciding that the credibility of the evidence regarding the treatment of a wreck which had occurred more than forty years previously was in favour of the Islanders, instead of citing more recent cases, of which they must have been fully cognizant, *e.g.*, the "Hayston" (1819), "Adonis" (1835), and "Vicissitude" (1836), in confirmation of the opinion they had formed.

Testimony of Lieuts. Christopher and Young.

"During the early part of our residence we did indeed hear of certain transactions which, if true, would have stamped with deceit and treachery the character of these Islanders; but subsequent observations induced us to attach little credit to the reports in question. We allude to certain reports of the crews of wrecked vessels alleged to have suffered inhumane treatment at the hands of the natives; but the statements of those individuals who were said to have witnessed the facts, when questioned by us, marked as they were with consistency and with every appearance of truth, greatly strengthened our suspicions of the incorrectness of the accounts which had reached us............It is not at all improbable that traders visiting Malé, hearing some accounts of shipwrecks, or seeing in the possession of the natives articles which, not being usually imported, could only have been acquired from vessels driven amongst the Islands; observing also the backwardness of the natives to answer inquiries respecting those matters, and attributing this to a desire to conceal the facts, though they are equally incommunicative on every subject relating to the affairs of the Islands,—it is, we think, not unlikely that under such circumstances the traders would, out of such questionable materials, conjure up tales of murder and bloodshed which had no foundation in fact.

"We ourselves were at first inclined to credit some of the reports of this nature which we heard, and Lieutenant Young considered it his duty to address the Superintendent of the Indian Navy to make known to him what we had heard respecting one particular case, in which a vessel driven on shore on Malé was stated to have been plundered by the natives, who, it was alleged, murdered the crew, and found much treasure on board. We were led to doubt the truth of the statement from a conversation we had with a native of Chittagong who had been 35 years an exile in the Suadiva Attol, whither he had been banished for having purchased stolen goods. On the accession of the present Sultan [M. 'Imád-ud-dín], he, with many others, was released from the operation of his sentence and permitted to return. When the abovementioned wreck occurred he was resident trader at Malé, and some of the particulars relating to it he had from the native portion of the crew............As our informant, who stood a close cross-examination, was consistent in his account, and had apparently no motive for deceiving us or concealing the truth, his statement appears more entitled to credit than the other version of the story, resting, as it does, merely on vague reports."*

The experience of a further half century, though in the main of a negative character, has done much to strengthen public confidence in the character of the Máldivians. That it is not fully assured can only be due to ignorance of the circumstances attending the many wrecks among the Atols.

Wrecks.

Appended is a rough list of wrecks which have occured on the Máldives between 1797 and 1880.

In three cases only—the "Tranquebar" (1797), the "St. Clair" (1851), and the S.S. "Sea Gull" (1879)—have charges of misconduct been made against the Máldivians.

As regards the "Tranquebar," from the account given in the correspondence with the Madras Government by Mr. Fisher, one of the owners of the vessel, there are, unfortunately, good grounds for believing that in this instance the Islanders cannot be acquitted of nefarious action.

* Transactions, Bombay Geographical Society, 1836-8 (Reprint 1844), pp. 64–5.

THE MÁLDIVES.

APPENDIX B.

"Tranquebar," 1797.

The "Tranquebar," freighted with piece goods for Colombo by her owners, Captain Overend and Mr. Fisher, was driven by stress of weather to the Máldives in January, 1797. On the 29th they fell in with one of the lesser islands. "At 10 o'clock a boat from the shore came alongside the vessel, and the crew were desired to shew good and safe anchorage, which they promised to do; but, after a great deal of evasion, having got the vessel into a critical situation, they suddenly left her and returned to the shore." Capt. Overend had to come to anchor in 60 fathoms, and proceeded on shore to procure assistance from the Chief of the Island, "who readily promised his aid, but delayed the fulfilment so long that the vessel stranded, and three or four boats were instantly perceived going off to her." The Master and part of the crew then swam on board to prevent pillage, and to save the cargo, "which could easily have been effected, as the vessel lay in five feet water." .... "The Master had scarcely got up the side when he was knocked overboard by the Islanders, who declared that he should not meddle with anything, and that they would save the cargo, and would make a report to their King, and if it pleased him to restore the property they should have it." The Islanders proceeded to remove the cargo as well as the lead of the vessel, and helped themselves to several pieces from the bales. The crew were sent to another Island "that they might not see how much of the cargo was saved," and subsequently to Sultan's Island (Málé). Frequent demands made to "the Second of the Island" for the restitution of property were met by the evasive reply that very little was saved; but upon a threat of complaint to the Madras Government the Chief became more friendly, and promised to have all the cargo that was saved brought to Málé. "Fifteen days elapsed, but no cargo appeared," and the Master, being struck down with violent fever, was then taken off by an English ship. Captain Overend died at the Máldives.*

Sir F. North forwarded a translation of the whole correspondence to the reigning Sultan (M. M'uín-ud-dín), remarking:—"Had Your Highness at that time commenced Your auspicious reign, an act of such outrageous and unwarrantable violence would not have happened; and I am confident that Your justice will induce You to make ample reparation for an event so contrary to the hospitality which a friendly nation has a right to find in Your dominions, and so incompatible with those sentiments of friendship and goodwill which Your Highness possesses towards the ships and subjects of Great Britain."†

It has already been stated (*V. s.*, p. 35) that the Sultan's reply was considered satisfactory; but as the complaint was not instituted for more than three years, and in the interval a new Sultan had succeeded to the throne, it could not have been difficult to fabricate some plausible explanation. The only reparation Mr. Fisher obtained was by the sale of a very small portion of the wrecked goods which had found their way to Ceylon.

For the conduct of the Islanders, outrageous as it was, it is still possible to find some extenuation so far as regards the claim asserted to the vessel after she became a wreck. By Máldive law or long-standing custom, all wrecks are strictly held to be the property of the Sultan—a custom mentioned by Pyrard‡, and formerly ruling in other sea-board States of India, *e.g.*, Kálastri Sáwantwári, &c. By different Treaties with the East India Company, these Indian Princes consented to waive their right to wrecks; but it should be remembered that no such agreement has ever been contracted with the Máldive Sultans. Indeed, it is rather a matter for wonder that, thus untrammelled, the Sultans have never preferred claim to salvage for the recovery of the cargoes from the wrecks which have occurred in their dominions.

From the mention of "the Second of the Island," it is not unlikely that the Sultan (Hasan Núr-ud-dín) was at the time absent on the pilgrimage to Mekka which terminated his life, and that the knowledge of this fact induced his subjects to be less scrupulous than usual about appropriating property chance had offered.

"St. Clair" 1851.

The "St. Clair" is the second doubtful case. The Indian Government received on the 16th April, 1851, a letter from the Máldive Sultan to this effect:—"On the 10th February, 1851, Captain Tierney and twenty-seven men of the "St. Clair," which was destroyed by fire in longitude 74° and latitude 7° 48′, came to My Island of *Mahal* in four boats. When I saw the condition to which they had been reduced I bad them landed and showed them great kindness—that is, I gave them a house to live in and supplied them with provisions. They lived with Us for a few days, and I intended to send them in My boats which annually go to Your ports. Meanwhile, they made arrangements with a Gooncha (vessel) by name 'Pudarut', belonging to Ibrahimjee, and asked Me for permission to embark. As the vessel was to sail before any other, I gave them permission, and

* Attested statement made at Colombo by J. H. Thuring, Commander of the "Tranquebar."

† Governor's letter, dated December 8th, 1800. ‡ Pyrard, pp. 163, 211.

the Captain and thirteen of his men embarked on board the 'Pudarut.' The remaining fourteen men embarked on board the Goducha 'Lukmepursad,' Nakhooda Kara, and took with them such of the articles as were saved from the wreck. They have all left this place. The Captain was satisfied with Me, and I with him. If it pleases God they will arrive safe at Your port."*

A reference through the Chamber of Commerce at Bombay to the Captain of the "St. Clair" regarding the nature of the treatment received by himself and the crew during their stay at the Máldives drew from the Captain the following complaint :—

"I beg leave to inform you that I did not receive at the Máldives the kindness the Sultan mentions in his letter. I was not supplied with any provisions except the following, viz., one bag of rice, a few cocoanuts, 20 lbs. sugar, and 4 ounces tea.......... We got a house to live in. It is my firm belief they would have treated us harshly if it were not for the dread of the British Government in India. The Sultan did not offer to provide the crew and me a passage to India, nor did I express my satisfaction at the treatment we received. .... I complied with all their rules and regulations, and was in every way submissive to the authorities as became an Englishman and a gentleman. I had a good crew, and the best of order and regularity was preserved among them. I acquainted the Ibondagaree [Hadégiri], Collector of Customs, who is the principal man under the Sultan, by letter that the men would require a little fresh provisions, they having been so long living on salt, but my letter was taken no notice of. I wrote then to the Sultan, but it met with the same treatment. I had to provide provisions in the best manner I could, by exchanging one of the boats to a Chittagong trader for some rice, tea, and sugar.

"I made the authorities to understand that in our Sailing (Horsburgh's) Directory, Captain Moresby spoke of their hospitality to strangers, and the British Government were of that opinion. I must say that the Islanders of the other Atolls—viz., Tilla Dou Medowmatta [Tiladummatí], Milla Dou Madow [Miladummaḍuḷu], Phaideepholo [Fádiffoḷu]—that I passed through were more civil, they were very courteous, and I found them honest.

"The Sultan detained the pattimars 3 days after they were ready for sailing, by not giving the sailing orders or allowing a pilot, and for what reason I could never learn."†

Upon the correspondence being referred to the Ceylon Government, a strong letter was addressed to the Sultan by Sir Charles McCarthy, detailing the subjects of complaint, and concluding as follows :—"All nations in community act with great consideration and kindness to shipwrecked mariners. I therefore trust You will also order Your people that this kindness may never fail on such occasions, by which friendship will be maintained between Your Highness and the British nation to the great advantage of all concerned."‡

The Sultan replied the ensuing year :—"The letter which was sent Us by Your Excellency has been received and perused by Us ; and as We learn from the contents thereof that certain shipwrecked mariners, unknown to Us, had preferred a complaint, We beg to acquaint Your Excellency that some seamen from a wrecked ship came to Us, and We furnished them with lodgings and supplies of such articles of food as We have here."

"It has been usual with Us to find passage for persons in that situation to take them to some British territory where they could conveniently be sent to, provided the weather is favourable ; but on the particular occasion alluded to it was not practicable for Us to do so, as the weather was contrary, and Our Dhonies (which are small, and tackled with slender ropes) could not venture to sea.........If under such circumstances they will have no patience, it is not right.........Permission was granted by Us when applied for by the traders, &c., to proceed on their journey."§

The explanation was forwarded to the Indian Government, and the matter ended.

No one acquainted with the ordinary supplies obtainable at the Máldives would feel surprized at strangers imagining themselves somewhat stinted with the provisions dealt out to them; but, on the contrary, would learn with considerable astonishment that they had been indulged with such rare and expensive luxuries as tea and sugar. Perhaps the true explanation of the curtailed supply of provisions may be found in the Captain's own admission that he possessed the means of purchasing them.

Regarding the detention of the "pattimars," delay in issuing sailing orders is an established, though doubtless unpleasant, custom, still in force at Málé, owing to tedious preliminary formalities to which Europeans and natives alike have to submit.

---

* Substance of Sultan's letter to the Governor of Bombay, received April, 1851.

† Letter to Chamber of Commerce, Bombay. ‡ Governor's letter, dated 30th July, 1851.

§ Sultan's reply, A. H. 1268.

THE MÁLDIVES.

APPENDIX B.

S.S. "Sea-Gull," 1879.

After all, the asserted "misconduct" was rather an omission on the sole part of the authorities at Málé, for the Captain had no fault to find with the Islanders generally.

It is not necessary to do more than just refer to the recent charge of alleged assault and petty larceny by the inhabitants of Gáfaru Island (North Málé Atol) in connection with operations for the recovery of the cargo from the wreck of the S.S. "Sea-Gull" (1879), as the complaint, though referred to the Sultan at the time, was considered too trivial to be pressed.*

The first two cases have been dwelt on in some detail designedly, in order not to hide in any degree the full extent of the alleged misdoings of the Máldivians.

Turning now to the evidence in favour of the Islanders, it is satisfactory to find that there is 'enough and to spare' to convince every impartial inquirer that their professed humanity is "not a myth, but a sober and pleasing reality."

Several cases of substantial aid rendered to vessels wrecked on the Atols in the 17th and 18th centuries have been briefly noted in glancing at Máldive history (*V. s.* pp. 31, 35, 37.)† It will suffice to confine investigation to the present century.

"Europa," 1812.

Referring to the wreck of the "Europa" (*V. s.* pp. 35. 36, 47, 48) Sir R. Brownrigg wrote in January, 1815:—"The wreck of a vessel off the coast of this Island in the month of October last, belonging to some subjects of Your Highness, gave me an opportunity of again testifying my sense of the kindness afforded by Your Highness to the crew of the British ship 'Europa,' wrecked on the Maldive Islands in the year 1812.‡" Again in 1817 the Sultan was presented with nineteen bales of cinnamon, the cargo of a Galle dhoney which had been wrecked on the Islands, in acknowledgment of his "humanity and care".§ In 1819 the Governor writes, with reference to the wreck of the "Hayston":—"I have had with great satisfaction the letter which Your Highness's messenger, who lately arrived at Galle, brought to the Collector of that District, containing the particulars of the loss of an English ship off the Maldive Islands, and of the humane treatment the officer, passengers, and crew who were so fortunate as to survive the wreck, received from Your Highness during the period of their detention within Your dominions. The vessel in which they were despatched to Ceylon arrived in safety.........I am most happy to learn that the conduct of the unfortunate sufferers gave Your Highness so much satisfaction while they remained under Your protection, and thereby rendered themselves worthy of the kind and benevolent care Your Highness was pleased to take of them"‖

1817.

"Hayston," 1819.

"Adonis," "Vicissitude," 1835, 1836.

For "the humane and liberal conduct" of the Máldivians towards the Commander, officers and crew of the "Adonis" (1835) and "Vicissitude" (1836), the Sultan received the thanks of the Government of India. Presents were accepted as a mark of friendship, but all payment was declined, though liberally offered.

Returning to Ceylon. The Right Honourable J. A. Stewart Mackenzie writes, in 1839:—"I cannot lose this opportunity of expressing to Your Highness my thanks for the kind treatment You have afforded to the Captain and the crew of the British ship 'Mac Imroy,' lately wrecked on one of the isles of Your dominions, and for the aid You have bestowed for their safe conveyance to Ceylon by lending one of Your Highness's vessels for that purpose.¶

"Mac Imroy," 1839.

1842.

Three years later (1842) a native vessel belonging to a "Pakeer Tamby" struck on one of the Máldive reefs and "was completely wrecked." The Sultan "caused every needful assistance to be rendered to the crew," and finally sent them back to Colombo in a hired vessel, "paying their passage money." This good service was duly acknowledged by Governor Campbell.**

"Prazer e Allegria," 1844.

The Sultan's kindly treatment, in 1844, of the passengers and crew of the Portuguese transport, "Prazer e Allegria," has already been referred to (*V. s.* 37.)

"Paramatta," 1855.

In 1855 the Sultan sent over to Ceylon the shipwrecked crew of the "Paramatta," which was "wrecked and foundered opposite the shores of Attumatty Island" [? Haddumatí Atol.] "They

* *V. s*, p. 38. † See, too, Stephen's Faria-y-Sousa, Vol. III., Pt. IV., chap. XI., p. 397, of the shipwreck of D. George de Almeyda on the Máldives in A.D. 1631:—"The King of the Islands wrote to D. George condoling his misfortune and sending him a parcel of rice."

‡ In the Asiatic Annual Register, 1801, is reported the wreck on the Máldives of a thirty-five ton vessel, with between 20 and 30 Europeans on board, when bound to Colombo:—"Capt. Meik expresses himself in the highest terms of the attention shown to him, his officers and crew by the inhabitants during their stay."

§ Governor's letter, dated November 8th, 1817.

‖ Sultan's letter (translation dated August 26th, 1819):—"So good a man as this Captain did never come to Our country." Governor's reply, dated September 6th, 1819. ¶ Governor's letter, dated December 19th, 1839.

** Sultan's letter, datad Muharram, A.H. 1259. Governor's reply, dated December 7th, 1842.

were in all eleven persons," writes the Sultan, "of whom five have since died. They were accommodated with lodging and victuals, and the Captain and Pilot treated with special honors by Us. We offered to embark them in Our own vessel; but the Captain declined it, and desired that We should order a vessel belonging to some of Our subjects, and We complied with his desire. We afterwards provided them with their travelling expenses, and have also sent Our own pilot to accompany them as Our Agent with instructions to see those people safely conveyed to where Your Excellency is. May God grant his favour."* In acknowledging the Sultan's letter and returning "cordial thanks" for the assistance he had rendered, Sir C. J. McCarthy added:—"It has afforded me much pleasure to learn from the master of the vessel that he had met with such kind and hospitable treatment in Your Highness's dominions, and I shall be happy to reciprocate Your good offices whenever it lies in my power."†

"Spirit," 1856.

The following year the "Spirit" was wrecked on Suvádiva Atol. The Captain and crew were treated with similar kindness by the Sultan:—"We felt it Our duty to render them every assistance by procuring for them lodgings and maintenance, and to show every mark of respect due to such persons. We subsequently despatched the Captain and three of his men, Nagoda Ali and the rest by another vessel of Our own."‡ "In returning My sincere thanks for these good offices on the part of Your Highness," writes Sir Henry Ward, "I feel it right to acknowledge with equal thankfulness the kindly and liberal spirit in which the duties of good neighbourhood have always been discharged by You."‡

1873.

The year 1873 witnessed four wrecks on the Máldives, of which two were French vessels—the "François" and the "L'Ecureuil." The crews were hospitably entertained and provided with free passages to Ceylon. As the Sultan had twice acted so well towards French subjects, it was almost decided to communicate an account of his good deeds to the French Government. Sir William Gregory did not fail to express to the Sultan his deep sense of these satisfactory marks of good feeling and friendship.§

There is no need to adduce additional evidence in support of what—to those who cared to acquaint themselves with the facts—must almost from the outset have been a foregone conclusion.

The Máldivians may lay claim to the proud distinction of being probably the only race similarly situated on the face of the globe who have not required to be taught by special contract, or legal enactment, the duty they owe their fellow men who have fallen into "troubles by shipwreck" on their "tempest-haunted" Atols.

Homines ad deos nullâ re proprius accedunt quam salutem hominibus dando.

Nothing is more certain, however, than that, had the Máldives come within the influence of the English East India Company, the Sultans would have been bound down long ago to a Treaty clearly defining the action expected from them in cases of wrecks. Hardly a compact entered into with any Oriental Potentate, whose dominions bordered the sea, but contained an express clause stipulating for aid to wrecks—coupled, in most cases, with a provision for the relinquishment of any claim thereto.

These covenants were of two main descriptions:—

1. Agreements binding one party only, providing for assistance to wrecks and their abandonment to the claimants.
   - (*a*) Unconditionally, *e. g.*, Turkey (1661-2), Kálastri (1760), Persia (1763), Muskat (1798), Joasmí (1806), Aramra and Bét (1807), Diagi (1807), Pusitra (1807), Junágarh (1808), Purbandar (1808), Kolhápur (1812), Kachch (1816), Muskat (with America, 1846).
   - (*b*) Conditional, on payment of reasonable expenses, *e.g.*, Kartinad (1761), Bushire (1763), Peshwá (1775), Broach (1785).
2. Reciprocal agreements, requiring aid and the restoration of wrecks.
   - (*a*) Unconditionally, *e. g.*, Sáwantwári (1730), Jafarábád (1761), Muskat (with England, 1839; with France, 1846).
   - (*b*) Conditional,
     - (i) On payment of reasonable expenses, *e.g.*, Sáwantwári (1765, 1766), Peshwá (1776), Portugal (salvage, &c., 1842).
     - (ii) On equal division of cargo, *e. g.*, Peshwá (1839).

---

* Sultan's letter, dated A.H. 1271. † Governor's reply, dated March 29th, 1855.

‡ Sultan's letter, dated October, A.H. 1273. Governor's reply, dated November 27th, 1856.

§ Governor's letters, dated August 5th and December 9th, 1873.

THE MÁLDIVES.

APPENDIX B.

That these Treaties have had a wholesome effect will hardly be disputed; and, fairly as the tacit understanding with the Sultans has proved to have worked, it may reasonably be doubted whether the time has not arrived for a closer and more defined compact drawn on the lines of some of the above agreements.

Nothing could be clearer or better meet the case than the reciprocal provisions of Article XIV., paragraph 3, of the "Treaty of Commerce and Navigation" between Great Britain and Portugal dated 3rd July, 1842 :—

"If any ships of war, or merchant vessels, should be wrecked on the coasts of either of the high contracting parties, such ships or vessels, or any parts thereof, and all furniture and appurtenances belonging thereunto, and all goods and merchandise which shall be saved therefrom, or the produce thereof, if sold, shall be faithfully restored to the proprietors upon being duly claimed by them, or by their Agents duly authorized ; or if there are no such proprietors or Agents on the spot, by the respective Consuls of the nations to which the properties of the said ships, vessels, or goods may belong, and in whose districts such wrecks may have taken place, provided such claim be preferred within a year and a day from the time of such wreck; and such Consul, proprietor, or Agent shall pay only the expenses incurred in the preservation of the property, together with the rate of salvage which would have been payable in the like case of a wreck of a national vessel; and the goods and merchandise saved from the wreck shall not be subject to duties unless cleared for local consumption."

Considering that the Máldives lie in the direct track of vessels bound to the East—the number of which has enormously increased of late years, and is certain to grow with the spread of civilisation and trade in the many new fields now opening out to European enterprize—and the weighty interests involved in the assurance of safety to life and property in the event of disaster on these treacherous Atols, it becames the bounden duty of this Government to use all means in its power in order to induce a more general feeling of security.

Since 1867 alone (when the Board of Trade first commenced a systematic registry of these casualties) 13 wrecks have occurred on the Máldive group, or an average of one every year.

It is still thought by the Máldivians that after the occurrence of a wreck the Captain has lost all right to his goods and cargo. "When the 'Liffey' was wrecked on Nilandu Atoll in August last year [1877], the people would in no way assist the master to recover any of the cargo. They could not do so without express leave of the Sultan, though they provided boats, pilots, and provisions for the conveyance of the crew to Male."* "This," as Mr. Gray truly remarks, "is hardly a satisfactory state of things," and, it must be confessed, is in great part due to the indifference with which everything connected with the Máldives has hitherto been regarded.

Of the Lakkadive Islanders, Mr. Allen Hume writes, in 1876 :—"They have been accused of plundering wrecks, but I believe the worst that can be said of them is, when they have found abandoned wrecks on the reefs, and useful articles lying about handy, they have very sensibly helped themselves. Considering that no salvage had ever been offered to them, or any inducement held out to them to act otherwise, I think that no great blame attaches to them. They have never been inhospitable or unfriendly to shipwrecked mariners, and now that salvage has been duly offered to them, and the law on this subject explained to them, I do not believe that anything more than petty pilfering, such as goes on to this day on our own English coasts, will be heard of."†

It is useless to wait until the Sultan—meekest of Rulers—puts forward claim for salvage. A demand so presumptuous to Máldive minds will never be made from their powerful and dreaded protectors. It would be both more generous, and in public interests the wiser course, for the offer to emanate from the Ceylon Government.

The Board of Trade has long had in contemplation the erection of a light-house on Minakaĭ, but year by year 'dies and makes no sign' of its commencement.‡

There are other and more dangerous passages than the "Eight-Degree-Channel"—such as the Karadiva Channel—regularly traversed at certain seasons, which must sooner or later engage attention.

Whilst Kánkésanturai and the Paumben Channel remains without even a fourth-class light, it is hardly to be expected that this Colony will consider the wants of her Dependency. But something might possibly be done towards minimising—by day at least—the difficulties of navigation through the intricacies of the Máldive Atols by urging upon the Sultan the desirability of causing obelisks, or towers, to be erected as land marks at the entrance of the more frequented passages.

---

* J. R. A. S., Vol. X., n.s., 1878, p. 208. † Stray Feathers, 1876, Vol. IV., p. 441.

‡ This work has since been commenced by the Imperial Government.

LIST of WRECKS on the MÁLDIVE ISLANDS between 1797 and 1880.*

Year.	Month and Day.	Name of Vessel.	Port of Registry.	Description of Vessel, and whether iron, composite, or wood.	Tons.	Crew.	Port sailed from.	Port bound to.	Description of Cargo and Number of Passengers (if any.)	Wind.	No. of lives lost.	Place of Casualty.	Total or partial loss of Vessel
1797	January 29	*Tranquebar*	—	—	—	—	—	Colombo	Cloth	—	—	Near Málé	—
1800	—	Native vessel	—	—	35	—	—	Colombo	—	—	13	—	Total
1802	—	*Surat*	—	Ship, wood	—	—	—	—	—	—	—	SE. by S. Máfurhi Island, Suvádiva Atol.	—
1806	—	French vessel	—	—	—	—	—	—	—	—	—	—	—
1812	May 23	*Europa*	—	—	—	29	—	—	Arms and cloth	—	—	Southern Atols	—
1819	—	*Hayston*	—	—	—	—	—	—	Metals, wine, glass, and spices.	—	—	Málé Atol	—
1835	July —	*Adonis*	—	—	—	—	—	—	—	—	—	Veligadu Island, Kolumadulu Atol.	Total
1836	—	*Vicissitude*	—	—	—	—	Mauritius	Ceylon	—	—	—	Ihavandu-fulu Atol	Total
1837	—	*James McInroy*	—	—	—	—	—	—	—	—	—	—	—
1842	—	Native vessel	Ceylon	—	—	—	—	—	—	—	—	—	Total
1844	March 16	*Prazere Alegria.*	Lisbon	—	—	—	Lisbon	Goa	Passengers and Convicts, 104.	—	11	Málaveli Island, Mulaku Atol.	—
1851	February 15	*St. Clair*	—	—	—	29	—	—	—	—	—	—	—
1855	—	*Paramatta*	—	—	—	11	—	—	—	—	—	Haddummati Atol	—
1856	September —	*Spirit*	—	—	—	9	—	—	—	—	—	Suvádiva Atol	—
1862	November —	*Colombo*	—	S. S., iron	—	—	London	Point-de-Galle	—	—	—	Minakai Island	—
1868	May 29	*Reindeer*	Liverpool	Ship, composite	965	26	Mauritius	Point-de-Galle	Ballast	WSW., 7	—	SW. point of Kurumati Island.	Total
,,	August 9	*Royal Family*	Liverpool	Ship, wood	1750	34	Aden	Callao	Ballast	NW., 6	—	Rufurhi Reef, NW of Máldive Islands.	Total
1869†	April 17	*Sarah Sands*	Liverpool	Barque, iron	1150	26	Liverpool	Bombay	Coal	—	—	Kálpeni Reef, N. of Máldive Islands.	Total
1872	September 25	*George Reid*	Bridgewater	S. S., iron	115	19	London	Galle	Ballast	— 6	—	SW. barrier reef of Miladummadulu Atol.	Total
1873	May 4	*Ægean*	Leith	S. S., iron	836	26	Sourabaya	Amsterdam	Cotton, tobacco, sugar.	SW., light	—	Suvádiva Atol	Partial
,,	June 3	*François*	Bordeaux	Barque	—	22	Bourbon	Calcutta	—	—	—	Haddummati Atol	—
,,	August 12	*Aracan*	Glasgow	S. S., iron	1174	41	Rangoon	London	General; Passengers, 9.	W., moderate	—	Gáfaru Island reef, S. of Karadiva Channel.	Total
,,	,, 23	*L'Ecureuil*	Bayonne	Brig, wood	204	10	Buenos Ayres	Singapore	Ballast	WNW., 8	—	Coral reefs of One and a Half Degree Channel.	Total
1874	November 8	*Adeline*	Port Louis	Schooner, iron, 3-masted.	145	11	Mauritius	Colombo	Sugar and empty casks; Passengers, 2.	WSW., strong.	—	Suvádiva Atol	Total
1877	August 3	*Liffey*	London	Ship, iron	1339	35	Mauritius	Calcutta	Ballast; Passengers, 3.	Slight	—	Entrance of Kuda-Huvadú channel.	Total
1879	,, 21	*Sea Gull*	Leith	S. S., iron	1012	32	Calcutta	London	General; Passengers, 3.	—	—	Gáfaru Island reef	Total
,,	October —	*Clan Alpine*	Leith	Barque, wood	363	—	Mauritius	Bombay	Sugar	—	—	Gáfaru Island	Total
1880	May 7	*Consett*	Newcastle	S. S., iron	1105	28	Bassein	Port Said	—	—	—	N. E. edge Suvádiva Atol.	Total

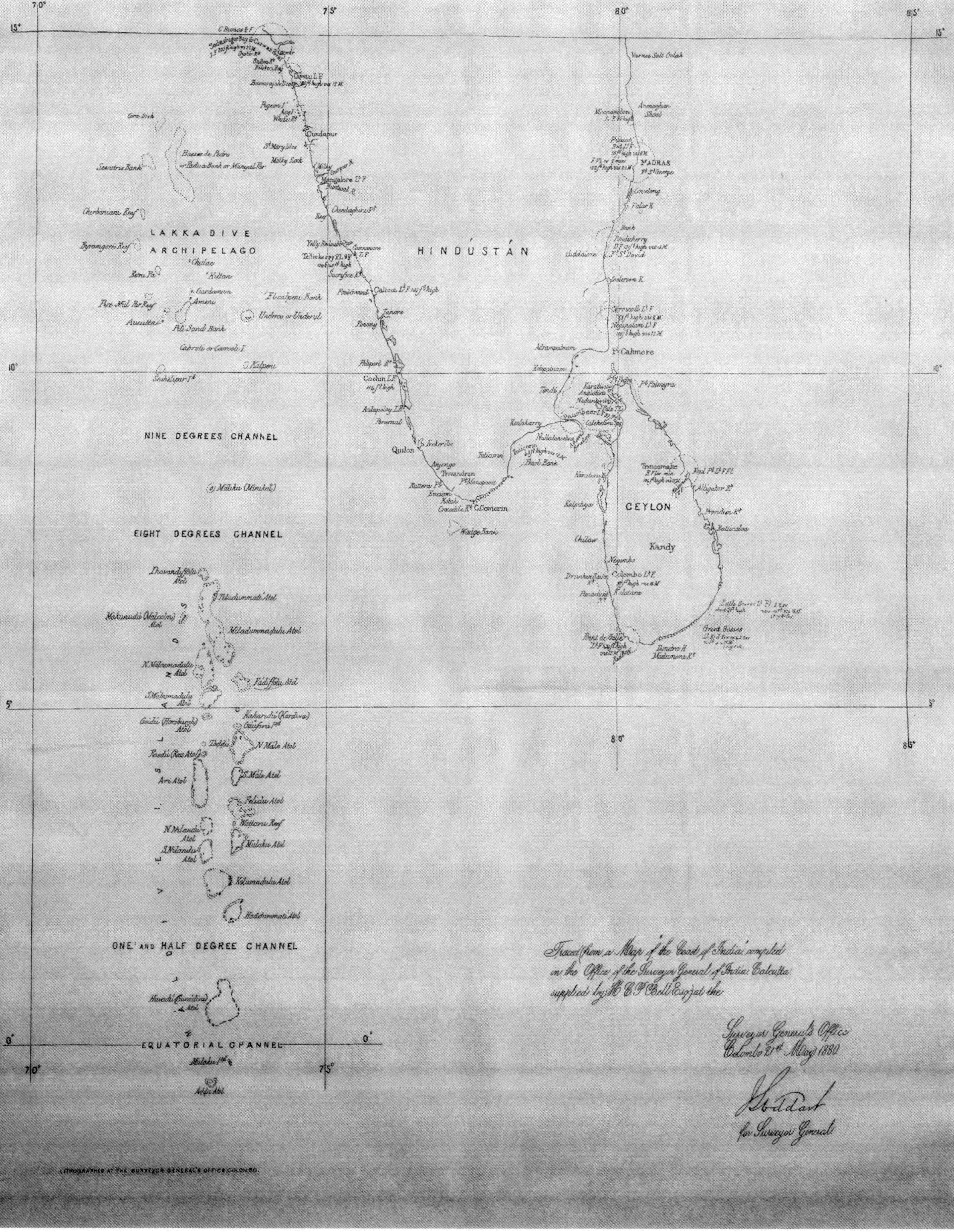

Traced from a Map of the Coast of India compiled in the Office of the Surveyor General of India Calcutta supplied by H. C. P. Bell Esq. at the

Surveyor General's Office
Colombo 21st May 1880

[signature]
for Surveyor General

LITHOGRAPHED AT THE SURVEYOR GENERAL'S OFFICE COLOMBO.

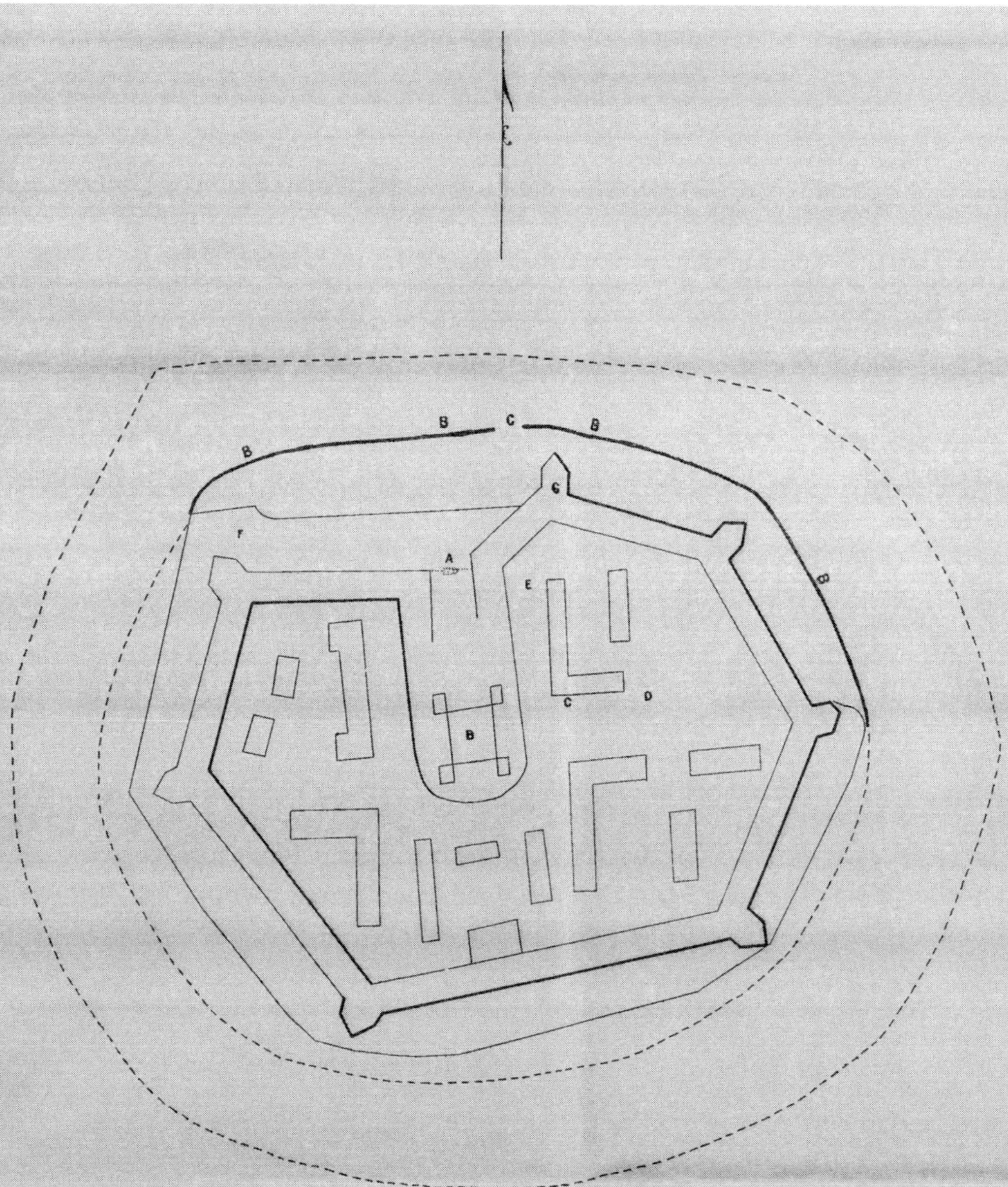

A Main gateway.
B Sultan's Palace & grounds.
C Approximate position of Chief Mosque.
D. — Do. — Sports arena.
E. — Do — building set apart for shipwrecked Europeans.
F Site of Parsee & Moormen traders' boutiques (outside the wall)
G. Main bastion of the Fort, with flagstaff
BB Artificial breakwater.
C Entrance thro' — do. —

SKETCH

0 — MILE.

Scale of (about) 7 Inches to One Geographical Mile.

OF

MÁLÉ.

(Sultan's Island)

Furnished at the request of H.C.P. Bell, Esqre.

Surveyor General's Office
Colombo 13th January 1880.

(Signed) J. Stoddart
for Surveyor General.

LITHOGRAPHED AT THE SURVEYOR GENERAL'S OFFICE, COLOMBO.

THE MÁLDIVE ISLANDS

DIAGRAM

shewing the Shipping, Exports, Imports, and Combined Import and Export Trade with

BRITISH INDIA & CEYLON

FROM 1841 TO 1879.

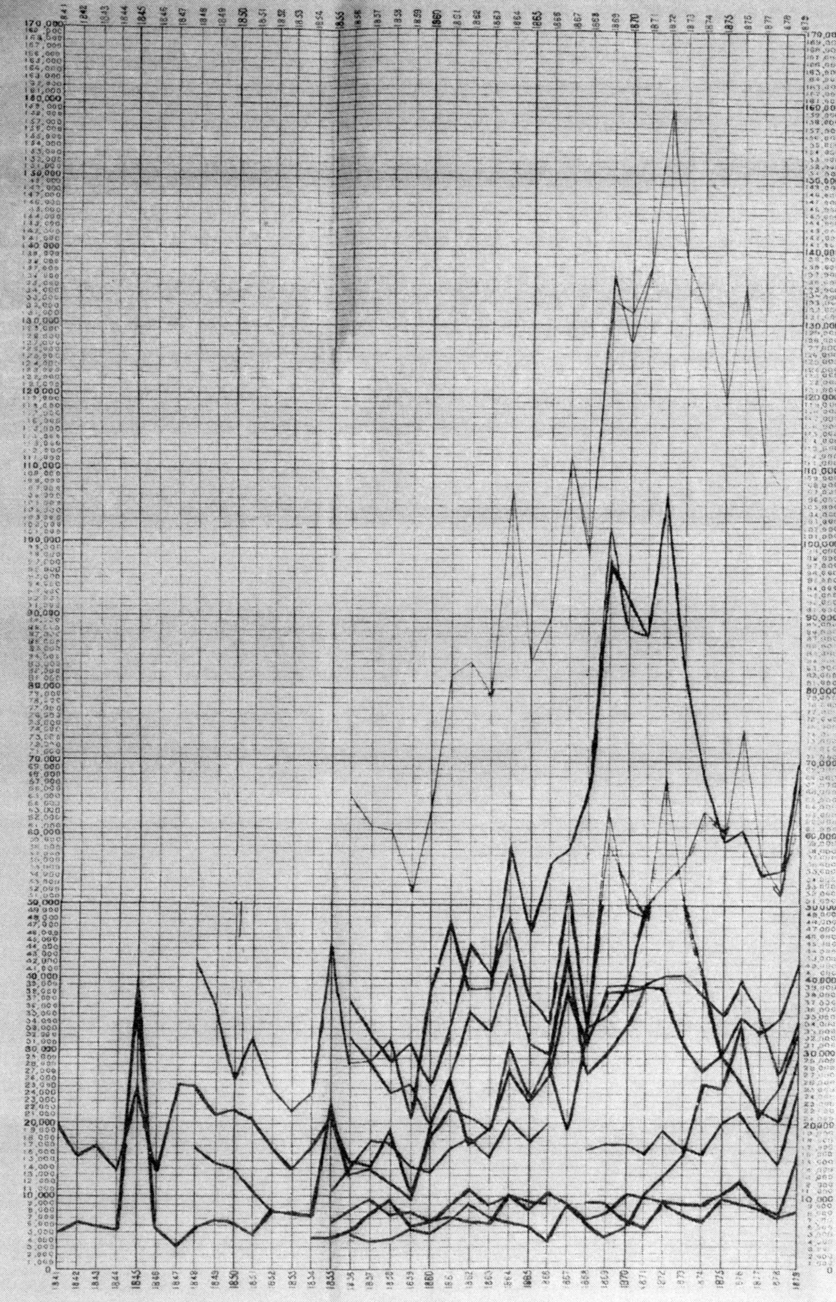

Shipping [Tons] to and from British India from 1841 to 1879 [Light Green]	Imports [£] into British India from 1844 to 1879 [Purple]	Imports [£] into Ceylon from 1856 to 1879 [Yellow]
Shipping [Tons] to and from Ceylon from 1855 to 1879 [Neutral tint]	Exports [£] from British India from 1848 to 1879 [Lake]	Exports [£] from Ceylon from 1856 to 1879 [Burnt Sienna]
Total Shipping [Tons] to and from British India and Ceylon from 1855 to 1879 [Brown]	Combined Import and Export Trade [£] with British India from 1848 to 1879 [Vermilion]	Combined Import and Export Trade [£] with Ceylon from 1856 to 1879 [Dark Green]
		Combined Import and Export Trade [£] with British India and Ceylon from 1856 to 1878 [Blue]

Prepared from a diagram drawn by H. C. P. Bell Esq[re]

The thick and thin lines thus N *represent two different returns.*

Surveyor General's Office
Colombo 23rd July 1880.

A. B. Fyers Colonel R.E.
Surveyor General

LITHOGRAPHED AT THE SURVEYOR GENERAL'S OFFICE COLOMBO